GORDON FALLOWS OF SHEFFIELD

Gordon Fallows of Sheffield

by

John S Peart-Binns

The Memoir Club

© John S. Peart-Binns 2007

First published in 2007 by
The Memoir Club
Stanhope Old Hall
Stanhope
Weardale
County Durham
DL13 2PF

British Library Cataloguing in
Publication Data.
A catalogue record for this book
is available from the
British Library

ISBN: 978-1-84104-183-4

Typeset by TW Typesetting, Plymouth, Devon
Printed by Biddles Ltd, Kings Lynn

Dedication

To the resuscitation of tolerance and conciliation in the
Church of England

Contents

List of illustrations

Between pages 132–133

27. Preaching at Enthronement June 1971
28. Blessing the City of Sheffield after Enthronement
29. Drawing of F.W. Robertson
30. Mandell Creighton
31. Dr Henry Major (from the archives of Ripon College, Cuddesdon)
32. & 33. Bishop Samuel Fallows, Gordon's American namesake; born at Pendleton 13 December 1835; died 5 September 1922 at Chicago; founded an Episcopalian Methodist denomination, described in posthumous biography by his daughter Alice, *Everybody's Bishop*. (Sears 1927) Friend of President Theodore Roosevelt. Reputation in Chicago dented when his approved Bishop's Beer failed to meet demand during Prohibition
34. Introduction to the House of Lords; supported by John Phillips, Bishop of Portsmouth and Eric Treacy, Bishop of Wakefield
35. Hetley Price, first Bishop of Doncaster; later Bishop of Ripon
36. Stewart Cross, second Bishop of Doncaster; later Bishop of Blackburn
37. Meeting the Queen with Edna at York, June 1972 (reproduced by permission of Newsquest York Ltd)
38. With Edna in the study at Bishopscroft (reproduced by permission of Sheffield Newspapers Ltd)

Acknowledgements

The largest portion of ingredients for this episcopographical pie were provided and mixed between 1998 and 2000. The final seasoning with a liberal helping of Fallows' home-brewed beer was not added until 2007 when the crust was put on the pie ready for baking.

My primary 'thank you' goes to Mrs Edna Fallows and Geoffrey Fallows. There would have been no pie at all but for their generous agreement and willingness to help in every possible way. I hope their faith in me may be confirmed by the finished result. They provided all Gordon Fallows' surviving papers. My visits to Mrs Fallows' home at Carter Knowle Road, Sheffield were always a joy. No request was too much for her. On arrival I descended into the basement where the papers were kept and emerged for lunch preceded by a welcome glass of remedial mixture. A guide through her lovely and perfectly kept garden lifted the spirits.

When I approached people for their recollections of Gordon Fallows they responded with alacrity and great pleasure. My considerable gratitude goes to all those people who wrote to me. Only extracts from a number of them appear by name in the biography, but all were vital in helping my portrayal and appraisal of Gordon Fallows.

Finally, if Gordon Fallows had his Edna, so John Peart-Binns has his Annis, who is the enabling foundation of my life. To her – my love, as always.

JSP-B July 2007

CHAPTER 1

Barrow-in-Furness and Oxford

WILLIAM GORDON FALLOWS was born on 21 June 1913 at 16 Settle Street, Barrow-in-Furness, then in Lancashire now in Cumbria. Barrow, at the western tip of a peninsula jutting onto Morecambe Bay, was an industrial and ship-building nineteenth-century town. Before the First World War the output of coal in the area had increased, but that of pig-iron fell, as did the amount of iron-ore being mined. The war created an artificial but temporary demand for iron and steel for ships and munitions. By the late twenties and early thirties the industrial glory receded, the slump came and one third of the population of Barrow was unemployed. Distress and disillusionment were widespread.

The red sandstone ruins of Furness Abbey are two miles from Barrow. This twelfth-century Cistercian foundation was endowed by King Stephen. Even today the ruins resonate a past great, rich and powerful religious house where the abbot ruled the district as a feudal lord.

The Fallows family originally came from Calder Bridge in Cumberland. Fell-walking was embedded and described by Gordon Fallows as, 'What it boils down to is tackling anything you can tackle without actually rock-climbing.'

Gordon was the second son of five children (Eric, Gordon, Joyce Millicent, John – known as Jack – and Winifred) of William (born 7 September 1890) and Ann Joyce (born 11 October 1890). William Fallows rose to the position of head foreman brass moulder at the Vickers shipyard. Their house at 16 Settle Street was a typical northern terrace close to the road, originally with an outdoor toilet at the end of the small yard. With five children home life was a mixture of essential routine and discipline within a loving embrace. The firm foundations of family, school and church were interwoven and essential for Gordon Fallows' future.

Fallows attended Oxford Street Infants and Junior School; Victoria School; and, in September 1924 he entered Barrow Grammar School for Boys. The school, established in 1880, was not in the best of surroundings with the constant din of riveting and the noise of tramcars waiting for the traffic rush from Vickers. A new school was long in the planning and in 1927 an agreement was signed for a new building on the hill at Risedale. This school was opened on 6 May 1930 for 500 pupils. It was a notable and well-proportioned building with spacious quadrangles and corridors, a show-place visited by committees and administrations from far afield who were planning similar developments. Thus Fallows experienced contrasting environments for his education.

Two headmasters influenced Fallows in different ways. Mr F.R. Barnes (1922–1928) had a Manchester history degree and is described as a 'young, slender business executive in spotted bow tie, pince-nez, with a seemingly inexhaustible energy and a ruthless determination to carry into practice the ideas that he thought the school needed to bring it up-to-date'. Modernising the school was crucial and this included expanding extra-mural activities such as drama and music, rambling and wireless clubs, and a historical society was encouraged. Perhaps for his future Fallows also learned how to be smartly and dapperly dressed. In 1928 Barnes was appointed Headmaster of the new Heaton Secondary Boys School, Newcastle-upon-Tyne.

In 1928 Mr W.D. Fraser of the Perse School, Cambridge, previously a master at Batley Grammar School in the West Riding of Yorkshire, was appointed Headmaster. A graduate of Glasgow and Cambridge Universities he had the unusual combination of a chemist who also read the historical tripos. He was solidly mature, deeply religious and with an all-round approach to education. He lived the words he spoke: 'The chief purpose of any school is to turn out young people with high ideals and a broad outlook on life who will give of their best towards the promotion of the common good.' It is not difficult to understand the impact of Fraser on Fallows who, for a period, contemplated the teaching profession as his career. Would he heed Fraser's advice to all boys: 'Get rid of your accents; get to university but do not form a coterie of Barrovians when you are there.' Fallows had no trace of a regional accent, speaking and writing the purest King's English. There were students at Ripon Hall who described their Principal as somewhat suave in manner, but there was no evidence of this at Pontefract or Sheffield.

There is considerable evidence from his contemporaries that Fallows was popular with staff and boys. Although hard-working, determined and ambitious he was not regarded as a 'swot'. His thirst for most branches of knowledge was guaranteed by discerning masters. He was a keen sportsman, liked drama, music and history. Eventually he was Captain of Fell House.

The school, auspiciously, if inadvertently, featured in Dorothy L. Sayers' crime novel *Unnatural Bodies* published in 1929. She mentioned that Inspector Parker received his early education in the Barrow School. Replying to a letter of Miss Maxwell Fraser on 13 December 1926 Sayers wrote:

As regards Barrow-in-Furness, I do not know that I had any particular reason for placing Parker's child there as I do not know the town at all; I rather felt it to be the kind of industrial place which gave Parker a background as far as possible unlike Peter's (Lord Peter Wimsey) and further than that I can hardly find any good reason for my selection.

In another letter Sayers expanded this observation:

My idea was this; having got my Lord Peter with his rather cynical attitude to life as of the young man to whom all things had come easily, and having furnished him with the appropriate Eton and Balliol career, I wanted, as a contrast to him, a thoroughly nice man of middle-class parentage who had made his own career by hard work. Native surroundings of docks and iron works seem to provide the right sort of contrast with the landed estates on which Lord Peter would be brought up. I wanted Parker to have a solid, well-furnished mind and a thoroughly sound education and it appeared to me that the right school for him would be a good Grammar School because I believe that for real, solid learning and efficient work, a Grammar School education provides about the best training a boy of that sort could possibly have. The result of these meditations was, accordingly, the Barrow-in-Furness Grammar School.

Inspector Parker's background and education were matched by Gordon Fallows'.

Between 1928 and 1936 twenty boys went up to Cambridge colleges and eight to Oxford, many on open scholarships. It was clear that Fallows would be one of that number, as intimated by Headmaster Fraser in this commendation of 3 March 1932:

William G. Fallows has been a pupil of this school since Sept 1924. In July 1929 he gained the matriculation Certificate of the Northern Universities' Joint Board with Distinction in French & Chemistry & in July 1931 the Higher School Certificate in Modern Studies. Since then he has been working for Scholarships.

In 1929 Fallows was appointed a School Prefect & gave such excellent advice that last September I appointed him Head Prefect. He is also Captain of the Football 1st XI.

He is a young man of the highest character, thoroughly conscientious in all his work & duties & in my opinion a thoroughly suitable candidate for admission to Oxford or Cambridge.

Fallows was fluent with pen, full of ideas, always extending his imagination. One fragment from his school years entitled *Child Laughter* carries its own interest:

The scene is any music hall on any evening. The house is almost full and the audience is composed mainly of grown ups with some adolescents and a sprinkling of small children, many of them under the age of eight. A few babies are whimpering annoyingly. They are probably hungry.

In addition the atmosphere is oppressive and stifles them while some of them are thrown into fits of violent coughing by the pungent aroma of their neighbour's tobacco.

The comedian enters the stage acting the part of a drunken man. His antics amuse the sophisticated portion of the audience who smile or chuckle with amusement. The children under eight have no idea what it is all about. They are profoundly perplexed. If you watch intently their puzzled brows you will realise that they cannot understand – which is not at all surprising. They glance round the audience inquisitively – daddy is laughing now – there must be something extremely funny going on somewhere. They gaze expectantly towards the stage again, the comedian is still trying to find the electric light switch, he continues to hit the wall within six inches of it with a shaky hand and then as if some magic wand had been suddenly waved over their intellects, it dawns on the mystified children that this is the subject of their parents' amusement. Whereupon they laugh uproariously. The drunken man's wife enters the stage. A quarrel ensues. The sophisticated audience are again moved to voluminous laughter, the children under eight, this time determined not to be left behind, enter into the laughter immediately, not from a sense of humour but from a sense of duty. If you watch them carefully you will realise that although the laughter in the end is spontaneous, it is nevertheless forced laughter. It is not that wonderful laughter which bursts inevitably from a young child when under the influence of the proper emotions.

Children are by nature imitators and if their parents persistently find the ugly and sordid to be amusing, it is certain that if present their offspring will follow their unfortunate example.

To the child with its sensitive imagination everything is real. The comedian is not acting, he is an actual drunken man. The marital upheaval is not a means of satisfying the perverted sense of humour of their parents, it is a piece of real life.

It is a tragedy that adults can find humour in such circumstances, but it is an infinitely blacker tragedy that young children should feel compelled to laugh at ugliness they cannot understand, for it will nurture in them a craving to understand and their mind will become obsessed with a picture of what is only a small and unpleasant side of life. They will begin to lose their sense of the beautiful just as they are beginning to develop it. Real child laughter, that is the unrestrained laughter of an infant which is incited by certain personal emotions, is stimulating and refreshing. The laughter in itself is a thing of beauty which we are indebted to Swinburne for immortalising when he wrote:

If the golden-crested wren
Were a nightingale – why, then,
Something seen and heard of men
Might be half as sweet as when
Laughs a child of seven.

The third element guiding Fallows to the future was the church. There were nine churches in Barrow and he attended the Parish Church of St George the Martyr (population 11,600) where he was baptised by the Rev. Robert ('Robin') Hawkins, vicar from 1927 to 1934, who later prepared sixteen-year old Fallows for confirmation. Hawkins regarded him as a 'boy of outstanding brains and ability and with a keen sense of vocation'. At seventeen Fallows was a Sunday School teacher and generally supported parochial events. One boy from a deprived home recalls Fallows buying him an ice-cream at a parish 'do', and there are other practical examples of his help and generosity. A cousin recalls 'a tall solemn dignified chap at sixteen passing my home on his way to school.' He was a handsome boy, capable of turning a girl's eye! Hawkins was succeeded by the Rev. Frank Meyrick Beddow in 1934 by which time Fallows was in Oxford though Barrow was still his valued home. Both Hawkins and Beddow graduated in theology from St Edmund Hall, Oxford.

If a career in teaching was one possibility for his future, ordination was another. Fallows visited Rose Castle, the home of bishops of Carlisle. There he met Henry Herbert Williams (1872–1961) who is little remembered today. Williams regarded his vocation as that of a teacher of philosophy. It is claimed that, in the paper in the final Honours School, he answered only one question – but his answer to this later became an article in the *Encyclopaedia Britannica*. His professional life was equally divided between twenty-seven years at Oxford (Hertford College, and from 1913–1920 Principal of St Edmund Hall); and twenty-six years as Bishop of Carlisle (1920–1946). At first he refused the Prime Minister's nomination to Carlisle and it was only by the strenuous intervention of the Archbishops of Canterbury (Randall Davidson) and York (Cosmo Lang), and a visit from Prime Minister David Lloyd George's emissary, that he was persuaded to accept. It is an example of the Church of England occasionally doing what it does least best – making a 'successful' man in one sphere a bishop. He would have possibly persisted in his refusal but for his wife who came from a Cumbrian family, the daughter of a Fellow of Hertford College, Oxford. Together they made Rose Castle a place of liberal hospitality.

Williams had a stern countenance and the sharpest of minds, neither of which precluded humour and wit. He may have had the qualities of being an outstanding bishop but there were personal, natural and temperamental handicaps, chief of all, he did not want to be a bishop and did not feel 'called' to be one. On a practical basis he disliked writing letters, fixing dates for committees for the year ahead, making appointments, and being asked for advice. He was always willing to give his judgement on the advisability or otherwise of a course of action, but would never make up a person's mind for him. Although he was not a pronouncing prelate this did not prevent him making searing comments on gambling and the activities of youth organisations which interfered with the proper keeping of the Sabbath. During his time as Principal of St Edmund Hall he worked through the councils of the university for the admission of women to degrees, and following the 1930 Lambeth Conference distinguished himself as Chairman of the Archbishop's Commission on the Ministry of Women. At assemblies where bishops met it was said he was the best man to quiet Hensley Henson of Durham. Together with Arthur Cayley Headlam, Bishop of Gloucester, Williams had the rare twentieth-century distinction of being made a Companion of Honour.

Williams somehow made his name as a heavyweight without publishing anything. His faith was simple and solid. If Fallows had served in the diocese he would have harmonised with his bishop's belief that the character of God is essentially goodness, beauty and truth; and that man is endowed through reason and conscience with a capacity to recognise these when he sees them, often finding them in the most unexpected people and places. Williams was a 'behind-the-scenes' bishop, a real father-in-God to his clergy, and shrewd in his estimate of them. He could be very stern when reproof or correction was necessary.

As he came to the end of his Barrow school days Fallows was encouraged to aim high and look to Cambridge or Oxford for his continuing education. Ordination was his most likely choice of profession, but he had no wish to dive into the theological pool at university. He had no difficulty in accepting advice to study modern history. He returned to his old school on several occasions, notably for the dedication of the School War Memorial 1939–1945 on 20 October 1948, the year in which he was President of the Old Barrovians Association. As Bishop of Pontefract he was guest speaker at an annual dinner, and was in touch with contemporaries to the time of his death.

Whether Cambridge or Oxford, Fallows needed a scholarship. His parents were not poverty stricken but money was tight with other children in need of education. In 1931 the school appealed to the Bishop of Carlisle to throw open more scholarships at Oxford for boys of the grammar school. However, Fallows went first to Cambridge to sit for an open scholarship and lodged at Sidney Sussex College. 'It was all very strange and wonderful. I made the most of my spare hours and went to Evensong at King's by candlelight.' Unsuccessful at Cambridge, he turned to Oxford with equal delight. He secured a George Moore scholarship, a Cumbrian Foundation, given by George Moore, a native of Wigton. In addition he obtained an Exhibition in history; and a Dean Rashdall Exhibition. Hastings Rashdall (1858–1924) was a tutor in philosophy at New College, Oxford, Dean of Carlisle and a leader of Anglican Modernists. There was also a Carlisle diocesan grant for Fallows. Officially he was an ordination candidate of the diocese. Now his destination was St Edmund Hall, Oxford, he was understandably proud to be at 'the world's most famous university.'

Fallows was an assiduous letter writer to family and friends. Extracts from two of them to his parents reflect the heady atmosphere of a northern lad's arrival in Oxford:

(16 October 1932 written on headed paper – St Edmund Hall)
Last Thursday the first Oxford Union debate was held on the motion, 'That this House has no confidence in HM's Government.' The son of Isaac Foot and the son of Arthur Greenwood were the chief speakers for the motion and the son of Sir Arthur Steel Maitland spoke against. Oxford is a hot-bed of politicians' sons. The President of the Oxford Union this year is the son of General Smuts. The speaking was more clever and witty than sound and David Lloyd George came up for a large dose of abusive rhetoric.

I am extremely glad to report that I was selected right-half for the Hall 1st XI in the first League match against Trinity College. We drew 2–2. We are now definitely settled down to our work which occupies the few idle moments we can find. It is very interesting and it is just possible to keep up to scratch.

Thursday last was degree day on which occasion John Heaton had his degree conferred. His mother and an aunt who were staying in London came to Oxford for the ceremony and he asked me to conduct them to it. It is a very impressive ceremony all of which is spoken in Latin. After it was over we all had a tea in my room and my tablecloth first saw daylight. (I had been using the supper cloth for all purposes).

I think I will use the tablecloth again today as I am doing tea today. Four of us all North Countrymen are very pally. My particular friend, a man named Cook, is from Sheffield. He is a state scholar and a good outside-left. I teaed with him on Friday and today he teas with me. Two other fellows form the quartet. One named Burnett from Seascale. He is the nephew of the Manager of the Barrow Electricity works. The other man is one Wall from Bradford which gives Yorkshire rather a bias. We are thinking of forming a North-Countrymen's Club.

We freshers have been deluged with trade circulars and various clubs and societies. So we have been invited to join The Irish Club, The Communist Club, the Labour Club, The League of Nations, The Oxford Union Society, The Student Christian Movement, besides a number of exclusive College Societies. I have joined the League of Nations and the Oxford Union.

(23 October 1932 – written on headed paper – Union Society)
I am writing this letter on my knee in front of my fire . . . Everything in the garden proceeds to be lovely . . . The chief news is that we have received from Cambridge the arrangements for the inter-varsity Old Barrovians dinner. It is to take place on Friday next at Cambridge. It will cost in all about £1. Will you let me know at once if you think I ought to go. I think I should really because

next year it will be in Oxford and I think Mr Fraser will be coming down this year. If I do not hear from you I shall go. I will try to write to Mr Foster sometime during the week. The number of letters I have to write still seems formidable. I wrote five last Sunday and I want to get three more away today.

About provisions. There is no point in sending such stuff as tea, sugar, cheese which I can get at standard prices here but if you want you can send an occasional box of food. This will keep down my tea expenses . . . I'll tell you what though – there is one thing you might send me and that is an old umbrella. They are very fashionable here. Another thing – can I grow a moustache?

On Wednesday morning just after Pat had called me at 7.30 a.m. another of the servants came into my room and said, 'The Principal's Compliments sir, will you please have breakfast with him?' And so I was the Principal's guest at breakfast in his own dining room. It was a great breakfast and all went swimmingly until the fruit came at the end. How do you eat a raw apple with a knife and fork? He is a very fine man, much more in touch with world affairs than is usual for a scholar.

Fallows' time at university was full and fulfilling, a medley of study, meeting and making new and lasting friendships, listening to some of the great people of the land in Union debates, the privilege of hearing great preachers, extending his knowledge and interests in the arts and culture, imbibing social life, and there was always an abundance of sport. In sum as with any promising undergraduate, broadening his mind. He graduated in 1935 with a Second Class in Modern History. He should have got a First but for his embrace and distraction of everything Oxford had to offer! By this time his vocation to the ordained ministry was firmly planted. He was not a person lying awake at night, one eye open waiting for a tap on the shoulder. The lesson of the Incarnation is that God works through normal human channels and situations except in rare cases. The lingering experience of church life in Barrow and friends and lecturers at Oxford were paramount in gently pushing and convincing him that the ordained ministry should be his life's work.

The next step was theological training. What are the primary strands? First, adequate theological knowledge is, clearly, a fundamental. In some colleges there was beginning to be a shift from the study of Higher and Lower Criticism to a presentation of biblical and religious truth which related to contemporary philosophic, moral and social problems. The Hebrew prophets and our Lord Himself should be the model, not the mediaeval schoolmen and their latter day successors. There should be an advantage when theological colleges are sited cheek by jowl with universities, where a dynamic relationship might develop between the theological colleges and the secular faculties, with the latter providing factual, critical data on the world, its experience and problems, and the former offering intelligent Christian comment.

Secondly, theological colleges should be concerned to foster the devotional life and the establishment of a spiritual discipline which cannot continue to develop in the rush and isolation of a parish. Yet so often the addiction to offices and set patterns of prayer and meditation had precisely the opposite effect: prayer became a grim battle instead of a relationship of the soul and God, and the offices, if relied upon exclusively, stifled spiritual growth and the soul's adventure. Moreover the quasi-monastic pattern of spirituality presented so often for the ordinand was often completely impractical – a much watered-down version – for the lay person fully engaged in the working world; and so if it was all that the priest knew, how could he possibly be expected to help the laity to deepen their devotion?

Thirdly, ordinands needed to acquire a realistic grasp of the problems and predicaments of the secular world. In particular, they needed to know how society worked, and the main problems which affected individuals and families, and the ways in which society, through central or local government agencies or voluntary bodies, could help men, women and children. In concrete terms this postulated a broad working knowledge of the educational, housing, social security and general social services' work, and where to look for help – and how to identify that help in the kind of case in which the community could do little or nothing.

Fourthly, there needed to be a greater emphasis upon preachers training for parish ministry and in particular upon techniques of communication, including preaching, teaching and work in, for and through small groups. Should not an ordinand spend part of his time in theological college in a parish, where he will learn by doing, analagous to teacher training. This should be carefully supervised and scrutinised.

Fifthly, many Church of England ordinands suffered from partisan bias and theological colleges confirmed them in their blinkered view of Anglicanism. Broadening not narrowing of minds was needed. A student should be led to a position of evaluating and valuing the comprehensive nature of Anglicanism and discovering principles which should guarantee both the integrity of the tradition and authenticate the process of indispensable change.

Where would Fallows receive this kind of education? He was persuaded to go to Ripon Hall which described itself as 'a Graduate Theological College established to provide a training on modern lines for those seeking Holy Orders in any diocese of the Anglican Communion' and it purported to secure 'a broad-minded, sympathetic, and well-educated Clergy.' This may appear to be a suitable place for Fallows until one appreciates that he has no academic theology. And, however bright and intelligent, it seems nonsensical that he will be only at Ripon Hall for fifteen months.

Alone of English theological colleges Ripon Hall represented the determinative principles of that type of Anglicanism which has persisted and developed under the successive designations of Broad, Liberal, and Modernist Churchmanship. There were great distinctive strengths in the Liberal emphasis on reason and rationality, in contrast to the Evangelical emphasis on scripture and the Catholic on tradition. However, not all liberal-minded scholars were modernists. Some mistrusted a tendency among a number of self-styled 'Modernists' to jettison old beliefs and to exalt into the position of infallible dogmas what may be only the passing hypotheses of a continuing developing science. There is a wise saying of Erasmus, which was quoted on the front page of every issue of *The Modern Churchman*: 'By identifying the new learning with heresy you make orthodoxy synonymous with ignorance.' Modernists themselves needed sometimes to be reminded that to identify orthodoxy with ignorance was not always the best way of commending their religion to the new learning. The Presidents of the Modern Churchmen's Union – Dean W.R. Inge, Dean W.R. Matthews, Sir Cyril Norwood, Sir Henry Self, Bishop Leonard Wilson, and Dean Edward Carpenter were truly Broad and Anglican and Fallows met or knew each of them. An examination of their convictions shows that the things which our Lord taught mankind as necessary for its salvation are few, simple and profound. They are neither easy to believe nor easy to practise. They make all the difference to the individuals and the societies who try to live by them. The Church should concentrate its authority upon its witness to a few essentials, staking all upon its faith in the Christ-likeness of God. And in other matters it should trust in the glorious liberty of God's children. 'For freedom did Christ set us free.' This is something Fallows took away with him from Ripon Hall, much less other of the five strands.

Above all else there was Henry Dewsbury Alves Major, 1871–1961, (usually known by his initials H.D.A.M.) who *was* Ripon Hall! His omnipresence affected all staff and every student, first as Vice-Principal from 1906, then as Principal from 1919 to 1948 and continuing to be felt as he intervened in the college's day-to-day affairs until his death on 26 January 1961. Concurrently he had incumbent status from 1929 until 1960 in the parish of Merton, Bicester, Oxford. He was Editor of *The Modern Churchman* from 1911–1957.

Major had a massive influence on students many of whom regarded him as a hero. He had his 'favourites' and one of these was Gordon Fallows, who, in turn, regarded Major as the greatest single influence in his life. Delivering the address at the funeral service at Merton Parish Church on 31 January 1961, Fallows, by now himself Principal of Ripon Hall, paid tribute as a disciple:

> If we seek a phrase that sums him up, surely it would be that triad – the moral, the rational, and the spiritual – which was always on his lips because it was written on his heart. When we mimicked him – as affectionately we often did

– we used to make play with these words, each of which, in isolation, is incomplete, but in harmony they take us to the heart of the Christian religion as he lived it and taught it. It was the essence of his teaching as it was the essence of the man.

His public life was a life of conflict – a conflict against obscurantism and a conflict against those who – in the word of one of his favourite quotations from Richard Baxter 'are always making more fundamentals than God ever made'. In all his conflict he was a model controversialist. Certainly in his hand the pen was mightier than the sword, and his writings, if often trenchant, never bore a trace of acrimony or bitterness. I once heard him described as 'the most pilloried cleric in the Church of England'. Yet no son of the Church of England had a greater reverence for it or a deeper devotion to it. And so, as Mr Valiant for Truth passes over to the other side, we salute today a great English Churchman. It is a sad reflection on our Church that it treated him with such scant recognition. With his learning, his literary grace, his historical and antiquarian interests, his business ability, and above all his engaging charm of manner, how well and with what distinction he would have filled the deanery of one of our ancient cathedrals. Not that he ever sought recognition or ever cared about it. It was indeed the true mark of his greatness as a Christian that it never entered his head. What is so surprising is that it never seems to have entered anyone else's head. He honoured the Church he loved; the Church he loved did little to honour him. This *enfant terrible* – as he seemed to some – was, to all who knew him, one of the Master's truest disciples. Of course he was honoured, honoured in the devotion and admiration of those (and there were many) who drew their inspiration from him. But he himself would have repudiated even that honour so conspicuously free was he from every trace of vanity.

There was a second name by which he was known – Henry. This was the name his students used among themselves when speaking of him. I sometimes ask myself what was the secret of his great Principalship. It was not primarily his teaching, fresh and stimulating and vigorous as that was. But the secret of his greatness as Principal was his reverence – reverence for the person and teaching of our Lord. To be present with him when he was the Celebrant at the Holy Communion was a memorable experience. It was this reverence for the person of Jesus Christ that manifested itself in those many courtesies which made him the man he was. There was yet a third name by which he was known – the name Hal. This was the name used by Mary, his devoted wife, who meant so much to him, who was in fact his eyes and ears, and without whom he could have achieved nothing. Those of us who saw this partnership of Mary and Hal at close quarters will always count it one of the greatest privileges of our lives.

The use of a pulpit at a funeral service is not the place for absolute candour. For that we turn to Canon J.S. Bezzant, Dean of St John's College, Cambridge, a Ripon Hall Governor and modern churchman. Albeit regarding Major as a 'great and good man' he recognised paradoxes. As with a number of controversial figures and mavericks Major was an ogre to some people who read his trenchant editorials and articles in *The Modern Churchman*; they felt some issue of identity when they met the quiet, rather shy, soft-speaking, easily embarrassed, but always courteous and kindly man, apparently with nothing to do (though his large writing table could have provided the original for the lawyer's *Bleak House),* who often astonished visitors when, whom in writing he would have called 'traditionalists', by commending to them some fact or other consideration which he knew to support their theological outlook but of which they had never heard, prefaced 'As you will remember . . .' his enthusiasm was matched by his patience, and it was prudent not to call on him if one had another pending engagement. Bezzant included a note on perspective:

The 1938 Report of the Doctrine Commission Major rightly regarded as recognizing as legitimate in the Church of England the position for which he had long contended. The 'Signs of the Times' in *The Modern Churchman* were nearly all his own work, and he frequently wrote articles for it . . .

He was the life and soul of the annual conferences of Modern Churchmen and the mainspring of their Modern Churchmen's Union. His Noble Lectures on *English Modernism,* provide the best summary of his position and ideals. His frequent pronouncements that 'Modernists hold' this, that and the other, often brought protests from those no less 'Modernist' than himself that they held nothing of the kind, and led to the suspicion that he desired to establish a 'Modernist' orthodoxy. He was adept at getting his own way in everything with which he was concerned, with few departures from gentleness, though in doing so he was often not over-scrupulous . . .

As Vice-Principal of Ripon Hall (1925–1933) I was responsible for the extremely mild discipline of the Hall; but he could not believe that any young man who chose Ripon Hall as his Theological College could be other than 'a good man'; and mature reflection has convinced me that this kindly error led to him palm off on some bishops candidates who ought never to have been ordained.

Ripon Hall was Major's life. And here, and not as a polite tail-piece, it should be said that Mrs Major's co-operation enabled him to do as much for it as he could have done had he been unmarried. She knew all about it, but never intervened. Her support, in every respect, was unqualified except that she would, occasionally, comment with acidulated truth upon some of its students, knowing that it would have no effect. In term-time she seldom saw her husband except on Saturday and Sunday afternoons and evenings, when he would take with him two or more students of the Hall to his homes, first at Kennington, then at Eastleach Turville, and finally at Merton Vicarage, where they might stay overnight and assist with the Sunday services. Students would be received there for a few days' rest after being unwell. Mrs Major generally read the proofs of

The Modern Churchman and for several of the latter years read to him when his sight made it impossible for him to read, and with her hand wrote his letters at his dictation. She also often played the harmonium in Merton church and he conducted services and 'read' lessons which he could not see but knew 'by heart'. No man could have had a more devoted partner.

Honesty requires a word which I regret. He remained Principal of Ripon Hall after his physical defects made it impossible for him to be as effective as the changed conditions during his last years required, and students who had not known him earlier sometimes failed to appreciate his greatness as those who did know him before his powers began to fail. When he resigned the Principalship – as a governor of the Hall and its treasurer he continued, in my judgment, to intervene in its day-to-day affairs in ways and to a degree such as he himself, while Principal, would not for a moment have tolerated from any governor or from the whole body of them. . . . He was a most genuine Christian gentleman.

Fallows embraced Modernism and joined the Modern Churchmen's Union. But he digested it, not swallowing it whole. He was committed to Carlisle and looked forward to ordination there. But as the time for leaving Ripon Hall drew closer no firm offer of a curacy came his way. Granted that Carlisle has no history of extensive scope for training curates as there is a paucity of large parishes, although there are some eminently suitable ones. Fallows' anxiety surfaces in a letter to his parents:

(4 November 1936)
My exams took place last week. I am very relieved to get them over. There is no definite news about the future yet. But I have received a definite offer outside the Carlisle diocese which I shall accept in the event of no vacancies in the diocese. I hope to let you know exactly what is happening within the next week or so. In the meantime this is not for publication.

Fallows' next letter was written in the Newdegate Arms Hotel, Nuneaton, Warwickshire.

(15 November 1936)
You will no doubt, be surprised by the above address. The fact is that I have come here to look over a job. The Carlisle diocese has not succeeded in finding me a place yet. So I have decided to get a job independently so as to be safe. The Carlisle authorities are extremely unbusinesslike and discourteous in not letting me know something definite before this. However, if I accept a job provisionally they will be forced to make a decision and they may leave me free to go where I choose. Yesterday I spent time at Leamington Spa interviewing a Vicar there. I am glad to say that he had the intelligence to offer me a job on the spot. Today I have come here to see another one. If I am offered this one I will have to choose between the two. I have seen the Vicar tonight for a short time and am seeing him again in the morning. The Leamington Spa job seems

very promising. It is a fashionable place and residential town but it is large enough to have all sorts of people in it. The Vicar is pleasant, is married, and has 3 children. The Leamington Grammar School is only 100 yards away from the Church. Altogether I was pleased by the prospects.

CHAPTER 2

Leamington Spa

FALLOWS ACCEPTED A CURACY at Holy Trinity, Leamington Spa. Leamington Priors, now Royal Leamington Spa, owes its royal prefix to the town's greatest benefactor, Dr Henry Jephson, a brilliant physician. Had it not been for Jephson and the passion for taking the waters, which was at its fashionable height in the later eighteenth and early nineteenth centuries, there would have been no Spa. It followed in the wake of Bath and was contemporaneous with Matlock and Buxton. Some of Leamington's streets and crescents are reminiscent of Bath. Jephson was responsible for the planning of the town and drew to the Spa Queen Victoria, the Duke of Wellington, Longfellow, Sarah Bernhardt and many more of the famous and fashionable to take its waters.

In 1936 the total population of Leamington was approximately 27,000. Eight churches had been built between 1825 and 1879. The notably proportioned and spacious parish church of All Saints was 'high church' and associated with it was the Anglo-Catholic church of St Alban the Martyr. The other churches were 'low church' which is an accurate description of its time. Current ecclesiastical terminology of evangelical would not accommodate all the degrees of churchmanship embraced by 'low church'. Holy Trinity was commendably free of labels.

Holy Trinity had an unusual history. The original building (1847) was one of a number of proprietary chapels built during the early part of the nineteenth century. Their erection was the result of Leamington's rapid growth and the need for additional church facilities. But the principle of these chapels was faulty. They were churches without parishes and as such not within the normal structures of the Church of England. There was a freelance element to them and they attracted some outstanding clergy but also ones who knew they were outside the parochial system and also, unfortunately, thought they were above it too. Headaches for bishops! The history and controversies were brittle, bitter and lengthy. It was not until 1899 that a new church was consecrated, a large and worthy building.

Fallows was made deacon on 20 December 1936 in the Cathedral Church of St Michael, Coventry, and ordained priest on 19 December 1937 at All Saints, Leamington Spa, by Mervyn George Haigh, Bishop of Coventry. We have Fallows' appraisal of Haigh provided to F.R. Barry, Bishop of Southwell for his biography of Haigh (1964). They carry additional interest as they were written when Fallows was Principal of Ripon Hall, before he himself became a bishop:

> Very few of his clergy came close enough to Mervyn Haigh to know him well. They respected him but the ties of affection were tenuous. To the junior clergy he seemed remote. I don't think any of us would have found it easy to unburden ourselves to him. Even so he took a real interest in his clergy, especially his junior clergy. He was assiduous in his attendance at the Junior Clergy Association in the Coventry Diocese. His amazing facility for keeping his finger on things enabled him to know more about us than we realised at the time. In later years I came to realise that this was more than administrative efficiency. It was a reflection of his real concern for people. I am sure he *cared* even though he often gave the impression that he only *ruled*. He never seemed to let his hair down, was never found off his guard, seemed to surround himself with an impenetrable wall so that no one would invade the citadel of his inner-being. That, at any rate, is how he struck me, and I think many of the clergy had a similar mental picture of their Bishop. But we did admire him and his seemingly effortless and superb management of men and affairs.
>
> He was certainly a commanding figure, but as a Church leader he seemed to me (and I think to other junior clergy) to be cautious. He was liberal and broad in his outlook and sympathies but there was nothing of the radical in his make-up. No doubt his caution was the caution of statesmanship rather than of timidity. Whatever it was he never seemed to put a foot wrong.
>
> He was impressive in appearance and bearing and always immaculate, whether taking his walk in the Memorial Park near to his Coventry home or on some more formal occasion.
>
> After a Confirmation or an Institution parishioners would line up outside the church to watch his departure as though he were a royal personage. He was in a way a Prince bishop rather than a 'bun-fight' bishop, and the laity revered him from a distance.

The Vicar of Holy Trinity was Malcolm Parr, a man of energy and leadership. He had some scholarship but never used it to browbeat parishioners or preach above their heads. Congregations were large. Parr was a Proctor in Convocation, Rural Dean of Leamington, Honorary Canon of Coventry Cathedral and, after seventeen years at Holy Trinity, was appointed Archdeacon of Warwick. He was a good training vicar for a curate even if Fallows slipped out of his grasp too quickly.

In view of later controversy in Fallows' ministry it may be here recorded that on his first Sunday at Holy Trinity, 20 December 1936, he solemnly declared as by law required:

> I assent to the Thirty-nine Articles of Religion, and to the Book of Common Prayer and of the ordering of Bishops, Priests and Deacons. I believe the

Doctrine of the Church of England, as therein set forth, to be agreeable to the Word of God; and in Public Prayer and Administration of the Sacraments I will use the Form in the said Book prescribed, and none other except so far as shall be ordered by lawful authority.

There was vigorous parochial activity at Holy Trinity but Word and Sacraments, preaching and worship, were always at the centre, not the periphery, of its life. It was here that Fallows learned lessons which he would not unlearn by future experience and the parish also learned something from this curate. The pattern of worship was common practice at the time for a church of this persuasion – Holy Communion every Sunday at 8 a.m., first Sunday at 11.45 a.m., third Sunday at 10 a.m. (Choral). Mattins at 11 a.m. and Evensong at 6.30 p.m. There were celebrations of Holy Communion on three weekdays. The worship at Holy Trinity showed it was possible to have dignity without stuffiness, and splendour with restraint. Fallows appreciated unfussy ceremonial as an aid not a distraction. He considered that services which were too informal tended to preclude a correct feeling of awe. He was adept at devising forms of service, a practice which began in this curacy and reached its fulfilment at Preston. He planned them in intricate detail, taking care of the balance of the words, pauses and silence, hymns, psalms and prayers for special occasions. Words mattered. He had poetry in him which found expression in this way. He became a master of restrained drama. But he always kept in mind: 'This is none other than the House of God, and this is the Gate of Heaven.' Holy Trinity was fortunate in having a large and good choir trained by a 'professional' organist, Dr Sydney Watson, more widely known through some of his compositions, and later Choir Master and Organist at Christ Church Cathedral, Oxford.

Parr placed great emphasis on the quality of preaching. Fallows was never a great or wholly compelling preacher but he was a good and effective one combining elements of teacher and pastor in the pulpit. People did not have to make a mental jump to understand him. Congregations never were sent empty away! He appeared to have a maturity beyond his years. When the congregation 'looked up' they saw a handsome young curate but the words came from one of riper years. He had natural gifts in the careful arrangement of material, reverence in phrase, a self-confident manner and a facility of speech which was attractive. To these gifts were added new skills learned at Ripon Hall, in particular that the secret of lucidity in language was clearness of thought. He was perceptively thought-provoking rather than deliberately controversial. Parr would have stamped on any personal idiosyncrasies in a curate. A member of the congregation says, 'I always found something to think about and discuss with others after listening to Gordon's sermons.'

Ripon Hall released many modernist preachers of radical convictions and intent. Here there are differences with Fallows. Although he was always a

'Modern Churchman' he held that the preacher should be sure that it is truth that he sets forth, not mere speculation, or improved hypothesis. He did not think the pulpit was the place for airing the latest critical theories, or for indulging in doctrinal speculations. The handling of the Word of God should be done honestly. People are saved by faith, not by doubt; and if the preacher's words disclose doubt rather than faith, how can they be other than spiritually baleful?

Parr liked courses of sermons, including topics which would not have been out of place on 'wayside' pulpits but also on subjects which would be expected outside Roman Catholic churches. Fallows was advertised to preach on 'St Francis, St Dominic and the Friars' and 'Thomas More and his Friends'. On other occasions people were invited to hear Fallows on 'Some Modern Adventurers' such as Elizabeth Fry, Robert Raikes, Lord Shaftesbury, Lord Lister and Albert Schweitzer.

Visiting was a key and compulsory ingredient in Fallows' training. He was taught the importance of offering and taking Holy Communion to the sick. There were frequently devised, printed and circulated cards advertising services and events which went to every house in the parish. There were 'Resolutions for Lent' and on Good Friday the Three Hours' Devotion attracted large attendances. Fallows observed that the conductors were not limited to any shade of churchmanship but were well-known priests used to retreats and quiet days. One year the parish priest of St John the Baptist, Coventry, the most notable Anglo-Catholic parish in the diocese, conducted the Three Hours at Holy Trinity. These were valuable lessons for the future in Preston, Wakefield and Sheffield.

Another of Parr's strengths was allowing ample room and freedom for Fallows to develop. This happened in two ways: the Junior Church Service held every Sunday afternoon, and the Young People's Association (Y.P.A.). His impact was immediate, massive and permanent. He lost no time in devising a service book for the Junior Church Service.

Fallows was full of ideas for the Y.P.A. and not afraid of experimenting whether they would succeed or fail. But nothing failed at Holy Trinity. He avoided the usual fayre of finding speakers for meetings. It was more important to build up real fellowship and friendship between members, emphasising the importance of worship and stimulating activities away from themselves. His style of leadership was neither from the front nor pushing from behind but in the middle. In this way everyone was carried along and no one left behind and no one so far out in front that they lost sight of the others. A member captures the atmosphere:

> We had lots of fun in a simple way, going for rambles, then a snack supper. We were responsible for the Christmas Crib and the Easter Garden. We took the

Sunday School on outings. On Gordon's birthday we had a Young People's Meeting finishing with a strawberry and cream tea. He was wonderful! There was also a Tennis Club. It was a melancholy experience when a War Memorial Plaque was unveiled in Church in memory of the young men of the Tennis Club who were killed in the Second World War, all of them friends of Gordon.

When Fallows left Holy Trinity, Malcolm Parr paid tribute: 'The young people of the parish have found him a true friend as he always sought their highest interests rather than mere popularity.' His easy manner appealed to all parishioners, and the older ones noted that he was the first person to take off his coat and roll up his sleeves when there was practical work to be done. Parr also encouraged Fallows to attend diocesan gatherings, to make himself known to clergy and laity, and not to be afraid of speaking in discussions and debates. Fallows was soon 'noticed' and although recently ordained he was considered to be a clergyman who 'would go places.'

In 1937 the Archbishop of Canterbury, Cosmo Gordon Lang, made an appeal called 'A Recall to Religion'. Parr and Holy Trinity responded to the challenge and Fallows was placed in the organisational forefront. It was necessary to identify the Church's faults before it could consider any move forward. The findings were salutary. The Church had been too subservient to the State and to public opinion and paid a cowardly respect to the supposed exigencies of public policy, and had not discharged a prophetic role with regard to the sins of social, industrial and international systems. Had the Church itself been unduly influenced or even succumbed to the nation's political and economic values? Were party divisions and social snobberies to blame for a low coefficient of fellowship in many parishes? Was the impact of the Church's public teaching and preaching manifest or did it remain conventionally doctrinaire or rested on the lower levels of commonplace morality?

Fallows, planning to react to the 'Recall', was influenced by his experience, albeit short in duration, of working in a parish. He thought – and continued to think – that the real value of the Church of England is in its parishes. Its strength is not in the great deeds of bishops and the work of assemblies, conferences and synods, but in the ubiquitous ministry of the parsons in the parishes throughout the land. He had witnessed this in his native Lakeland diocese of Carlisle, where Christ and the things of Christ had the opportunity of being proclaimed and kept in remembrance. Shepherding the sheep of Christ, dispensing His grace, proclaiming His gospel and holding up the lamb of faith and worship in a world that easily and actually fails to heed it is central in the pastor's task and service. However, even in 1938 it was not so easy to formulate the work of a vicar in an urban setting and that also applied to

Leamington as it did more obviously to densely populated Coventry. Although Fallows appreciated the opportunities for leadership available for clergy in any parochial setting it was more difficult when there were numerous Anglican churches, as in Leamington, rather than a single parish church.

The 'Recall' was not well timed as people's thoughts were preoccupied with the probability of war. After only two years at Holy Trinity Fallows' own thoughts were also elsewhere. It had been a period of continuing growth and maturity for him. Many years later the Bishop of Pittsburgh, Austin Pardue, preached at the Consecration of Mervyn Charles-Edwards, Vicar of St Martin-in-the-Fields, Trafalgar Square, as Bishop of Worcester. Leaning over the pulpit he looked the bishop-elect directly in the eye and gave him some advice: 'Grow ... but don't swell.' This is sage advice for any young clergyman to follow.

CHAPTER 3

Styvechale

A SHORT CURACY was sufficient to convince the Bishop of Coventry that Fallows was ready to spread himself as a vicar. Without delay he was offered, accepted and then instituted as Vicar of St James, Styvechale on 3 April 1939. Styvechale, formerly Stivichall, is two miles from the city centre of Coventry. There was a settlement in Saxon times and a church in Norman times. Priests and parsons can be dated from 1275 onwards. But by the nineteenth century the Church of St James was in a serious state of disrepair and demolished by 1810. It was five years before there was a new building, much smaller but adequate to meet contemporary needs. Behind the church was Styvechale Hall with its distant glory and by 1939 that too was in a dilapidated state. The village had had a feeling of idyllic remoteness, unhurried, undisturbed and unruffled by the busyness around and near it, a place where parishioners walked across the fields to the church.

Fallows lost no time in describing his first parish:

> There are streets and houses now, where, until a few years ago there were fields and footpaths. The tiny hamlet is bounded now by a vast estate and the population of the parish has increased a hundred times in little more than a decade. This vast estate has a shopping centre. Can we make Styvechale Church its spiritual centre? The door is ever open and an invitation is extended to all, no matter to what denomination of the Church they belong, to join us in our worship and our witness to that way of life revealed by Jesus Christ which alone can bring salvation to a disordered and disillusioned world. Although tarmacadam and bricks and mortar have appeared where once there were fields and hedgerows the Church itself retains some of its rustic charm and simplicity. But its exterior is better known than its interior! Some of those who go into rhapsodies about 'little Styvechale Church' are indulging in sheer sentimentality. To love our church in deed and in truth is to give it our active support.

Fallows had a sense of urgency and adventurousness in making changes and enlarging people's vision. The year before he arrived there were plans for a church hall to be built under a diocesan new area scheme. Fallows pushed these plans into action and the hall was opened on 24 January 1940. The church itself was too small for a rapidly growing population and congregation and some services were held in the larger hall. An enlarged church was dedicated on 25 January 25 1956.

Fallows did not act before ascertaining the views of the church officials. He was assiduous in visiting all the people of the parish and not simply those who were known to be 'Church of England'. After all he was the vicar of the whole parish. With his attractive persona he was not the kind of parson who is seen approaching a house, giving the person behind the curtains time to hide and become invisible when he knocks on the door. He was welcome wherever he went. When he introduced his own ideas they were received with acclaim. He wanted to bring fresh vision into the parish and introduce people to a less narrow view of the church. The parish magazine was altered to provide more space for views as well as news. His friends from Oxford and elsewhere were easily persuaded to write thought-provoking articles and this led to parishioners writing too. He introduced more services including a celebration of Holy Communion after Evensong for Sunday workers. It was unwise for anyone to complain that they could not get to services or meetings at inconvenient times. Fallows altered the times. When a point of view was expressed that there was no proper opportunity for discussion of a sermon or how religion affects life, he immediately formed a discussion group which met periodically at the vicarage after Evensong. He never feared experimenting and if an initiative did not work then it was dropped without fuss.

It was a foolish person who stressed the importance of youth work to Fallows saying, 'They are the Church of tomorrow!' His response and rebuke was such a view was a blasphemy against Baptism. 'They are the Church of today' was the instant retort of their twenty-six year old vicar. Styvechale was not a sleepy parish. There were active branches of Scouts and Guides and a lively 'Children's Church'. Fallows saw a gap and inaugurated a Youth Fellowship which became a focus of interest throughout the diocese and beyond it. Mrs Stella Grosse (neé Lord) is best placed to recount the story:

The families around had plenty of teenage people and Gordon Fallows was just what they needed, especially at the time – he was young, enthusiastic, very understanding and good looking. The Youth Fellowship which Gordon started soon thrived and it became the centre of life for many. Meetings were held in the church hall, but Gordon and Edna (they met and married at Styvechale) whose vicarage was a fairly small modern house, always welcomed us all into their home and comforted and supported those with anxieties and losses.

The Youth Fellowship was run on very democratic lines with a committee, and chaired by an industrial chemist in his early twenties. The age-range of members was about sixteen to twenty-five, though one or two could not bear to leave when they reached the top limits. It was open to all, regardless of whether they attended Church or not or whether they were confirmed. It was hoped that they would be influenced, as members, by the Church atmosphere. I had just spent two years in a Yorkshire training college for teachers and came home full of enthusiasm. I spent my time at YF committee meetings thinking out new ways of entertaining and educating members – some worked and some failed. Gordon had many original ideas as well. As secretary of the YF I wrote minutes of the previous weekly meeting and it was Gordon's idea to put them into a book to help many other churches who found there was a need and demand for youth organisations at that time. He was the one who brought the 'published' book into being.

It was not so usual for the laity to take part in the church services in those days, but we, as members of the YF were asked to read the lessons at times and occasionally to preach. Many young people went to church regularly, but they were not forced to. After evensong we always held a discussion group. Sometimes we studied parts of the Bible but often current problems were discussed. People were never afraid to voice their doubts. Gordon's approach was always practical and helpful which made these evenings enjoyable too. Gordon wrote or edited several publications on the Church's approach to current social problems for the Modern Churchmen's Union.

Holidays were not an important feature during the war but as a YF we did plenty of walking and cycling. One summer Gordon had the idea of acquiring an empty Georgian rectory in Northamptonshire for a long weekend. We transported mattresses in a lorry, and parked them for the boys in one room, and the girls in another. Everything was very basic. No one complained very much. Of course boys and girls paired off – some even married at a later date, but we never had torrid love affairs or illegitimate babies, as might be the case today. Our entertainments were simple and unsophisticated. We went to the village fete and won a piglet at skittles – this caused us problems for twenty-four hours until we sold it to a villager. My brother, who did not have too much experience of the YF because he was in the Air Force most of the time but who spent that weekend with us says he was amazed to see the Vicar (Gordon) as soon as he arrived at the rectory, with his sleeves rolled up, puffing at his pipe and cleaning out the lavatories.

A local private school had a tennis court which the YF was allowed to use in the evenings. As there was double summer time during the war we could play until 11 p.m. quite easily. No one seemed to want to play football in the winter. We had a weekly 'hop' in a larger hall not far away – we rarely missed that.

Of course, YF members, when they were old enough were called up to join the Forces. Those of us left behind because we were in reserved occupations or not old enough, kept in touch with them and they always visited us when on leave. It was Gordon who kept us together, as a friendly, caring, Christian community in difficult times during the war. He, and his family, were loved by us all.

Youth Fellowship Programmes by Fallows and Stella Lord was published by SPCK in 1945. Each of the 128 pages was crammed with suggestions for YF programme makers. They included topics serious, sublime, fun, idiosyncratic, recreational, debates, drama, dance, music, film appreciation, concerts, camping. Fallows advocated a youth fellowship with an open membership with a nucleus formed of young communicant members of the Church. Around this a larger group should grow, including some with little Christian background, and, at first, no allegiance to the Church. In a good fellowship the nucleus will set the standard and those on the fringe will gradually be drawn in. The book was widely and favourably noticed throughout the Church and such was its practical appeal that, to the surprise of its authors, it was quickly reprinted and in response to a demand a revised edition was published in 1951 by SPCK with a subsequent reprint in 1957. It had become a text-book for youth programmes and it sparkled because very many of its contents had been tried and tested at Styvechale. Its effects went beyond church auspices for Fallows was appointed chairman of the Coventry Federation of Youth Organisations and of the local youth committee.

There was another permanent bonding. Fallows' ministry covered the war years and his relations with members of the YF were deep and permanent. Letters have survived as a moving, and in some cases a melancholy, testament to that bond. Men serving in the Forces throughout the war kept in touch with Fallows. They were desperate for news of other members of the YF who had been called-up. They gave as much information about themselves and their 'doings' as they were allowed to do under conditions of war. In this way Fallows became both focus and conduit for spreading their news among people at Styvechale. Whether ominously 'somewhere in Europe' or in the British Isles, in India or Sierra Leone, each serviceman said they were bereft without the YF. Besides letters from Fallows and YF members food parcels and Christmas presents were sent to serving personnel. Fallows was also in regular touch with members who had gone to university, answering their questions, encouraging them in their studies and was generous in his loan of books to them.

Fallows arrived at Styvechale as a single man but with a very conspicuous and alluring companion – a flashy number – namely, a used Swift 2-seater car WM 3351 which he had purchased from the Rugby Autocar Co. Ltd. in Coventry 'as seen and approved' for £3 10s in January 1939. It would be replaced!

The car was nudged from its pivotal position of affection within months. Any handsome, intelligent, single young curate or vicar will never starve as invitations for meals come thick and fast. Miss Madge Blakeman writes:

Gordon was an extremely popular and hardworking man and good friend of the family. My parents, whose home was opposite the Church, were very involved with church affairs – Parochial Church Council, Choir etc. – and from my diary it appears he (Gordon) came to supper after Evensong on a good many Sundays and after choir practice on Thursdays.

And there is a diary entry for 11 July 1939: 'Mr Fallows took Edna (my sister), Tom (my brother) and me to a pageant at Kenilworth Castle in his ancient car.'

It was Edna Mary Blakeman to whom Fallows became unofficially engaged in November 1939 and officially on Christmas Day. They were married on 3 September 1940. The service was conducted by the Rev. J.D. Pearce-Higgins, then curate of Malvern Priory, and later a controversial Vice-Provost of Southwark Cathedral. Aid-raid warnings had been recurrent for months and the local public air-raid shelters were too frequent places of essential meeting. At the time of the marriage the marquee in the garden of the Blakemans' home could not be erected until the morning of the wedding in case it would be a target for German bombers. Their first child, Geoffrey, was born on 28 September 1941. Fallows was also a chaplain of the Municipal Hospital which brought him in touch with another side of life in the city. He had an empathy with those who were sick and suffering either mentally or physically. His seemingly natural companionable presence and unhurried conversation were appreciated as was his ability to be silent when words may not be the best form of communication. There were times he must have been in a hurry between appointments, but it never showed. Yet whether in hospital, officers' mess or with soldiers or airmen (he was a chaplain to the Royal Air Force personnel stationed at the balloon sites at Coventry), in houses in the parish or anywhere he visited, there was never any false bonhomie or back-slapping heartiness. He was wary of those clergy who acted as mouthpieces for the 'war effort', rather like those at the time of the First World War who were active recruitment sergeants in clerical collars. Visiting troops around Coventry or leading or participating in discussion groups he was fully aware of issues troubling men. In June 1943 he addressed a 'Letter to the Forces' urging those men who were weary or 'browned off' not to despair of the future:

> Great hopes were never born of despair. Make up your mind that you who fight to destroy Fascism will also destroy unemployment, bad houses, economic privilege and the old cycle of booms and slumps in which the booms grow shorter and slumps longer. The opportunity will come but we shall have to be very wide awake to seize it. You have not failed us. We must not fail you.

At Styvechale church services a few moments of silent prayer were observed for all those serving in the Forces. Fallows had already an astonishing range of friendships and was able to provide the people of Styvechale with experiences and viewpoints not easily available to others. At the Patronal Festival in 1941 the preacher was Rev. Dr C.G. Schweizer, a refugee pastor of the German Confessional Church, who was also a member of the World Council of

Churches. Dr Schweizer was imprisoned in Germany for his denunciation of the Hitler regime. After his release he found refuge in England. How to keep the torch of the Gospel alight through grim and evil days was a recurring theme and to hear from someone who had been persecuted for his faith was privilege and challenge alike.

Fallows thought reflectively. A single example is revealing. Following the 1943 R.A.F. raids on the Ruhr dams there was confusion, accidental or deliberate, on civilian casualty figures. It transpired that the loss of German women and children who had been swept away with their homes was not slight. This provoked a moving and unusual article from Fallows entitled ' . . . Shall PITY also die . . .' This extract conveys perceptions not too common at the time:

> What are we to say? (About the Ruhr dams raid). Certainly we must recognise the heroism of those who took part in the raid, nearly half of whom did not return. Their courage and devotion to duty were superb and worthy of the highest praise. Secondly we must recognise that the water power which supplies munition factories is a military target and that the destruction of the dams will reduce the German capacity to make war. But the vital question is this, are we to let human pity be destroyed? Shall we set aside for the duration the fairest flowers of the human spirit – mercy, pity and sympathy, and allow only the weeds of hate and malice and vindictiveness to grow? Are we to sink to the Nazi level to rescue human society from its Fascist chains? Do two blacks (morally speaking) ever make a white? Shall pity also die? Upon the answer to this question the whole future depends. No wise decision was ever made in white heat. Hate never inspires a sound policy, whether in peace or war. To take a leaf out of the Nazi copybook may be the easiest way to settle difficult problems but it is also the most perilous and one that is certain to fail and to fail disastrously in the end. Setting aside, for the moment, all Christian claims, it remains true that the wise man will not be zealous to preserve pity and sympathy in all his dealings. The fool calls this 'being soft.' It is, on the contrary, being strong. For the Christian's duty of preserving this delicate but lovely flower of pity is imperative. Others may be content to follow the dictates of what they misname common sense and to dismiss the Christian ideal as irrelevant for the modern world. But one thing is certain. There can be no mistaking what the Christian faith teaches about the conquest of evil. The New Testament is clear about this and those who claim to follow Christ, however, imperfectly, must pity all who suffer.

Fallows was always 'professional' in his character and demeanour, without sacrificing friendship and greatly respected for it. The clergyman is a conspicuous figure on the parochial stage. He is always in view, for whether at work in the parish, visiting the parishioners, taking the lead at parochial functions, officiating in the parish church at baptisms, marriages and funerals, he stands out to the general view. His official character implies a personal discipleship. He is assumed to be a good Christian because he is known to be a Christian minister. Accordingly, his behaviour is expected to be congruous with this assumption. In some sense he becomes the authorised commentary on the message he delivers. Little wonder that 'Who is sufficient'? is on the lips of clergy who at least endeavour to be true to their calling. But the clergyman's work lies mostly outside the view of critics. Yet it also has the handicap that much of his daily work can be done without the normal conditions of efficiency. His personal duty is largely unconditioned by routine, lacks the oversight of superiors, or the close continuing criticism of colleagues, and can never have the sure and relentless verdict of results. In a measure which has no parallel in the case of lay people, the clergyman arranges his own work, goes his own way, and takes no account of the consequences of his efforts. That is why, from the outset of his ministry, Fallows was steady and business-like in the way he approached everything that crossed his desk. His reading was never neglected so his library shelves grew in ever-increasing weight of volumes on which dust never gathered.

In 1945 Fallows was invited by the Minister of Labour and National Service, R.A. Butler, to act as a chairman of an Appeal Tribunal set up under the Unemployment Assistance Act, for Coventry, Nuneaton and Leamington districts. The appeals related to unemployment assistance and supplementary pensions under the Old Age and Widows' Pension Act, 1940. This was an early example of a future predominant skill of being able to hear evidence, make a rigorous assessment of its merit and proceed to make a decision which was manifestly fair and just.

Other interests which had already emerged including writing short plays were further developed at Styvechale. They included *The Truth about Furness Abbey; The Shadow Falls; Tea for Two;* and *Death in a Train*. This was straightforward entertainment, not plays with hidden meanings or morality tales. He wrote for local newspapers and early showed a 'knack' or adroitness of being reformist, radical and adventurer in theological exploration yet in a way as to appeal to a general readership. His robust common sense was aided by telling phrases to illustrate points he was making. It is sad that pressures at Preston obliterated this side of Fallows' skill. It had a substantial effect on people on the fringes of Christianity, gave him standing in the wider community, and an avalanche of articles and reviews in religious periodicals. This was effective witness!

Styvechale warmed to Fallows' persuasive way of presenting and commending the Gospel. The merit of his approach was proven by the number of lasting friendships he made. How different were the stories which reached him from

Ripon Hall contemporaries who were chaplains to the Forces. One friend had been posted to West Yorkshire and recounted his experiences:

> But having been inhibited by the Bishop of Bradford (Alfred Blunt) from preaching in any church within the diocese – on account of a modernist sermon which I preached at a service in one of the Bradford churches to a congregation of several hundred of my own men & about 6 civilians – mentioning the Virgin Birth and being far too racy – as it – subsequently appeared – the army moved me up to Catterick where, thanks to the Bishop of Ripon (Geoffrey Lunt) – bless him – I am in a position of far greater influence than formerly.

Another chaplain (ex-Ripon Hall) was taken to task in a similar way and inhibited for dangerous opinions. Heresy lurked in the wings depending on the particular diocesan bishop. At root there was probably little difference between Fallows and them except that Fallows would never have made the mistake of propagating such views to soldiers at war. He strengthened and encouraged them, not planting seeds of doubt in their minds when he would not be able to tend their growth on the battlefield. Fallows thought it was wrong for modernists to parade before the people any doubts and perplexities that shadowed their own minds. It was imperative for clergy to preach the truth, placing their emphasis on the Church's faith. Theological disputation was for study groups and specialist outlets such as *The Modern Churchman* for which Fallows was beginning to write.

Fallows was also making a name for himself in the diocese where his ideas and integrity were recognised across the spectrum of churchmanship and theological outlook. There was nothing remotely parsonic about him in speech or gesture. He broadened the outlook of many people at Styvechale by involving them in diocesan activities, albeit limited in wartime. He threw himself into Coventry's Religion and Life Week in 1942 which brought to the diocese the Archbishop of Canterbury-elect (Geoffrey Fisher), Sir Richard Livingstone, Miss Dorothy L. Sayers, Dr J.H. Oldham, Mr Rowntree Clifford and Dom Bernard Clements O.S.B. He seized every opportunity to meet ministers of other churches. Wherever and whenever possible he participated in joint worship and meetings which was easier to do in wartime. If his actions were questioned he quoted the ninth aim of the Modern Churchmen's Union – 'To maintain the historic comprehensiveness of the Church of England and to foster fellowship in Word and Sacrament with other Christian Societies.'

Fallows was already achieving notice in the Church and marked as an 'up-and-coming' talent. His name was increasingly appearing in print, for example, an article on 'The Jubilee of Phillips Brooks (1835–1893)' in *The Modern Churchman* June 1943. In July 1943 he presented a paper at the Twenty-Seventh Annual Conference of Modern Churchmen in Somerville

College and Regent's Park Baptist College, Oxford. The theme was 'The National Church and the National Life'. Fallows' subject was 'National Christian Reunion' which caused flutters in ecclesiastical dovecotes. He advocated receiving nonconformist ministers into the Church of England without re-ordination, backed up by sound historical sources! He also wanted greater facilities for 'open-communion'. It was published in *The Modern Churchman,* September 1943.

In 1942 the Bishop of Coventry, Mervyn Haigh, was translated to Winchester. Before he left a concentrated air raid destroyed most of the cathedral. The diocese had Czechoslovakian troops stationed near Leamington and there were war factories in abundance between Coventry and Nuneaton.

The new bishop was a complete surprise for Coventry and the wider church. Neville Vincent Gorton was Headmaster of Blundell's School, Tiverton and prior to that appointment was for twenty years chaplain at Sedbergh School. He was nominated by the Prime Minister (Winston Churchill) on the sole say and persuasion of Brendan Bracken, then Minister of Information, who had been a schoolboy at Sedbergh! In 1945 Brendan Bracken was also responsible for the translation of William Wand from Bath and Wells to London. Wand, previously Archbishop of Brisbane, had been the champion of the war effort in Australia. At Coventry the Bishop's Throne had been destroyed so at Gorton's enthronement on 20 February 1943 he was seated in an episcopal chair in the ruins. The Cross of Coventry carried at the head of the procession was made from three large nails found among the ruins.

When Gorton died in office on 30 November 1955 the Archbishop of Canterbury (Geoffrey Fisher) evoked the man and portrayed the bishop:

> There was a time when our Lord said He was not going to Jerusalem to die, and Peter said, 'That must never happen to You.' Neville would not have said that. He would have said, 'How splendid, I will go and die with You!' It was by his total self-forgetting, sincerity and devotion in the cause of Christ that made his impact like a lovely, loving, burning flame of God's compassion and God's fellowship with us, on the city, on the diocese, on its clergy and people and on the Church outside. He has gone like a comet leaving streams of colour and light and exhilarations behind, into the consuming glory of God and His Kingdom, and His burning majesty and love, and there at last Neville will be fully at home and perhaps at last fully at peace.

Neville Gorton was not an easy man to work with. He was untidy and disorganised in his habits; impulsive; prophetic. He stumbled into controversy rather than courted it. If he rumbled complacency he shook and exposed it. Hypocrites feared his coming. To him fell the task of suggesting a scheme for a new cathedral. When his views became known there was uproar. He wanted the cathedral precincts to include an interdenominational Christian centre. (It could have been Fallows talking.) A chapel of unity was at the heart of the plan. When the first set of architectural plans was published in 1945 the ideal appeared to have diminished. The cathedral was intended to be both the symbol of an inspiration and the disclosure of a policy. The 'high altar' in the centre would provide the first; and the 'four pulpits' placed around it in the corners would illustrate the last. Yet for many people the plans seemed rather to emphasize the exclusive claims of an episcopally ordained ministry than to remove the historic scandal of that calamitous exclusiveness. If those plans were accepted, a new cathedral was in danger of delivering a message which was incoherent and, perhaps, self-stultifying. Could not Coventry be genuinely different? If the spirit of discerning charity, which recognised in the four pulpits, 'diversities of ministration but the same Lord,' could recognise also the identity of divine commission in the Lord's ministers, albeit ordained in varying modes, when at the Lord's table they bring to His true servants the life-giving sacrament of His Presence in the Lord's Supper, then the witness of Coventry Cathedral would truly be precious, timely, and widely effective. This was pure Fallows. Otherwise why attach any importance to the novel architectural arrangements? These were not the first plans to be sacrificed. Basil Spence's design is some time distant and that, despite controversies surrounding it, was of the older pattern of cathedral architecture.

The plans outlined are not inserted for idle curiosity. Fallows followed the debate closely as it accelerated in speed and crescendoed in argument. On the surface the Bishop and Fallows had little in common except for a love for the Lake District. Gorton had a house in Patterdale. However there was a strong bond between them and Fallows was known to be the Bishop's 'blue-eyed' boy who would go far in Coventry. The Provost of Coventry (Richard Thomas Howard) from 1933 to 1959 was already a friend of Fallows. Howard was a liberal evangelical who had been strongly influenced by Frederick William Dwelly, Dean of Liverpool, who made the life and worship of Liverpool Cathedral inspirationally different from any other English cathedral. How wonderful if Howard could have Fallows as a colleague. The bishop wanted Fallows to have a diocesan position. With the two united the bishop wrote to Fallows in July 1945:

> I have determined to appoint a Residentiary Canon on the following terms and conditions:
> (1) He will hold the title of Director of Religious Education for the Diocese of Coventry
> (2) His functions will be (a) to carry into effect, under general directions from me in consultation with the Diocesan Education Committee, the whole work

of Religious Education . . . and (b) to work in relationship with the Cathedral
Christian Service Centre when that body shall come into action in this field
(3) His salary will be £600 per annum
(4) The Canonry will be for a period of three years
(5) There is no house available for residence
. . . I now offer you the Canonry. You have already heard from me in
conversation how greatly I hope that you will see your way to accept it.

There would be help in finding a house. But despite the allure of what
appeared to be an exciting and important job and one which Fallows could
make his own within certain parameters, there was a snag. The job was an
itinerant one of perpetual travel in the diocese and would possibly involve
committee work at Westminster. Fallows was now married with a young
family, Geoffrey and Angela. Accommodation was problematical and the
cathedral connection was more loose than fixed and secure for only three
years, although there could be no doubt that it would be extended if Fallows
wished. It was work better suited to a single man or whose children were
older.

Meanwhile Fallows had been encouraged to apply to Hulme's Trustees for
the major benefice of St John the Evangelist, Preston, the parish church of this
Lancashire town. The net income was £900. Surely this was far above his
level of reasonable expectations at this stage of his ministry? Would it not be
an act of audacious folly to apply? But he was pressed to apply by those who
intimated that Preston needed him. Did this reflect Fallows' self-assurance or
arrogance or had he a sense of vocation to an enlargement of his ministry in
a major town-centre parish? He was thirty-two years of age.

Fallows was accepted and his six years at Styvechale came to an end. The
people had watched his progress in the parish and diocese and knew they could
not keep him for much longer. Naturally they hoped he would remain in the
diocese. Unfortunately Coventry shared with a number of other dioceses, for
example, Leicester, Carlisle, Bradford, Derby, Guildford and Hereford, that
there were few major towns and large parishes to which a bishop could move
promising priests. Bishop Gorton had recognised Fallows' increasing responsibilities in the diocese by providing him with a curate in 1944. Thomas Bland
had been a curate in Bristol and went on to succeed Fallows as vicar of
Styvechale. There was a farewell party on 20 September 1945 a week before
his last Sunday in the parish. The bishop wrote to Fallows on 3 October:

Have I missed seeing you to say Good-bye? I am terribly sorry. I would have
liked to have seen you to say God Bless You and to thank you for all the grand
work you have done here. You will be missed by us all. You have got things
going in that parish and elsewhere which will last.

It should be an interesting job at Preston. I should not get too much tied up at the start with extraneous organisations. If you are going to make a city church come alive again I should concentrate initially on the services and the layout of the people round you. Use the patronage powers that are especially yours. They are your strong gift. Do not be distracted by external things, and do not worry about pistols being put to your head concerning the need to organise and administrate. I hope you will both be happy. All blessings to you.

CHAPTER 4

Preston

C ANON JOHN EYRE WINSTANLEY WALLIS was Vicar of Whalley for fifteen
years before moving to Preston as Vicar of St John the Evangelist, the
parish church of the town. He was well known in the diocese as a former
editor of the *Blackburn Diocesan Leaflet* and for his book *A Short History of the
Church in Blackburnshire* (1932). There were other works notably *English Regnal
Years and Titles* (1920) and *Verbi Ministerium* (1930). During his Whalley years
the diocese arranged to purchase Whalley Abbey and Wallis directed an appeal
for funds to enable it to be a conference and retreat centre for the diocese.
Wallis was a diligent and respected vicar of Preston and had to cope with the
disruption of the war years. In 1945 he was appointed a Canon Residentiary
of Lichfield Cathedral.

Preston has a fascinating past. In 1648 Cromwell's army routed twenty
thousand Scots allies of Charles I in three hours. In 1745 it was occupied by
Bonnie Prince Charlie on his march south from Scotland. Basically it is an old
market town and borough which developed into an important centre of the
cotton industry in the eighteenth and nineteenth centuries. It is the birthplace
of Richard Arkwright (1732) who invented the spinning water frame in 1769
which cheapened cotton production and powered much of the Industrial
Revolution. John Horrocks set up the first cotton mill in the town. In front
of the former Cotton Exchange there is a reminder of the twelve cotton
workers who were killed by the military on 12 August 1842. The Temperance
Movement was founded in Preston. The abstainers' paper, *Preston Temperance
Advocate* was published by Joseph Livesay. In 1834 there was a note in the
paper 'It is said that the word teetotal came from a stammering friend of
Livesay's when he tried to take the pledge of t-t-total abstinence.'

The original layout of the streets survives but all the old buildings have gone
and architectural interest dates almost entirely from the nineteenth century.
There are some fine public buildings radiating and still sustaining a sense of
civic pride. The magnificent Greek Revival style Harris Museum and Library
dominates the Market Square.

Today if you asked to be directed to St John's you would probably find
yourself in a shopping centre. In 1945 if you enquired as to the whereabouts
of the parish church it is not certain that you would arrive at St John's. Any
signs of its one thousand years of history have been many times obliterated.

The most recent manifestation dates from 1853 when the building was completely demolished and a new building raised on the old foundation at the cost of £9,500.

That Preston was a religious town was evident by the prodigality of churches and chapels, nineteen Anglican churches alone in 1945. Although there were churches of architectural note and worth a visit, the Church of England and the gambit of nonconformity did not feature in the pages of guide books. Why? Preston was a Roman Catholic town, a striking testimony to Lancastrian religious recusancy. The Roman Catholic Church was powerful and pervasive. The crowds entering their churches for Mass left all other Christian denominations puny by comparison. The influx of Irish workers who came to work in the mills and to escape the potato famine breathed further numerical increase into Catholic pews. And they worshipped in many noteworthy Classical and Gothic buildings. The old church of St Mary was founded in 1605, rebuilt in 1761, wrecked in an election riot and reconstructed in 1856. St Augustine of Canterbury in classical design is reminiscent of nineteenth century French church architecture; St Wilfrid's, the finest of Preston's classical churches, red brick with yellow terracotta decoration could have been transplanted from the Italian Renaissance era, monumental with a richly decorated interior. For Gothic impressiveness turn to St Ignatius; or to St Thomas of Canterbury and the English Martyrs, the latter by E.W. Pugin. St Walburga's is Gothic at its most confident, a church without aisles, 165 feet in length and 55 feet wide.

In 1945 the Vicar of Preston Parish Church occupied a central yet lopsided position in Preston. He was the pre-eminent figure of the Established Church of England and in civic society recognised as such. But he was not the major religious figure in the town. To his credit Fallows was fully aware of this and from the outset of his ministry in Preston went out of his way to meet Roman Catholic priests and if the result was a little one-sided it was not without warmth. An insight comes in a letter to his son Geoffrey, after attending the Catholic College for a performance of *Hamlet*:

> The visit gave me the opportunity of being gracious to the Holy Fathers & I am always glad of such opportunities. They give me V.I.P. treatment – front row centre – next to the Father Rector of St Wilfrid's. They are very kind though a Cleric's wife causes them a bit of confusion &, of course, Mummy was with me. The Priesthood is so exalted that the V.I.P. priests are front row & the V.I.P. Laity second row. The front row was solid with Jesuits – Benedictines – Secular priests – Me & Mummy.

That is in the future. In 1945 St John's needed a new vicar and on 10 April the Select Vestry and the Parochial Church Meeting appointed a deputation to meet the Hulme's Trustees to explain the needs of the parish. (The Hulme's Trustees were the patrons of twenty-three benefices in Lancashire). The Select Vestry of 'Twenty-four Gentlemen of Preston' is a historical curiosity. The Minute Books date from 1645. When the powers and responsibilities of the Select Vestry declined especially after the abolition of compulsory church rates in the nineteenth century, most of the Select Vestries fell into abeyance. The Preston Select Vestry was an exception. It met at least annually although its sole function was to elect the churchwarden. But there were still twenty-four members: eight appointed by the Mayor and Corporation of Preston, eight appointed by the Lay Rector, Sir Cuthbert de Hoghton, who was responsible for the maintenance of the Chancel and who, on special occasions, occupied his own stall. Vacancies in the remaining eight were filled as they arose by co-option. The three groups of eight Vestrymen represented the three divisions of the ancient parish of Preston. The upper division comprised Elston, Grimsargh and Fishwick; the lower Ashton, Ingol, Lea and Cottam; the middle, Preston town. That is why there were six churchwardens, two for each of the three divisions of the ancient parish.

At the April 1945 meeting the Mayor of Preston, Councillor J.E. Gee; Sir William Ascroft; Alderman Mrs Pimblett; and Mr G. Bradbury, were deputed to visit the Hulme's Trustees. St John's attracted a congregation from outside the parish boundary, some travelling long distances for Sunday services. The Electoral Roll was usually in the region of 400. St John's was a repository of funds from ancient charities and continuing bequests for the poor. The staff was meagre with a haphazard succession of curates, and though commensurate with the size of the parish of some 3,500 souls, it did not allow for the extra duties required of a vicar of the parish church of Preston. The need for time and impact of the church on the leading figures of Preston was in the bishop's mind when appointing Fallows. One of the parish's benefactors, Sir William Ascroft, created the W.W. Galloway Church Worker Trust for the poor of Preston. Deaconess Elsie Tongue was the Galloway worker and attached to St John's. She was a friend and counsellor to many in need and distress but had always nursed an ambition to go to Canada to serve the Canadian Sunday School Caravan Mission. The Mission maintained thirty vans and sixty honorary women workers. It was, in fact, a travelling church and in remote districts the only link that people had with the church. After fourteen years in Preston Deaconess Tongue left for Canada in 1954.

The Hulme's Trustees had a major concern. The vicarage contained some twenty-six rooms and presented a very difficult problem in housekeeping. It was likely to be an obstacle for anyone contemplating the living. On 12 June the Parochial Church Council agreed to divide the house into two. As for churchmanship there was no partisan stamp. Sunday worship was Holy

Communion at 8, Mattins 10.30, and Evensong at 6.30 with additional celebrations of Holy Communion at different times on three Sundays of the month. Mattins and Evensong were said daily with the Litany after Mattins twice a week. And placing St John's within its time there were Churchings on Tuesdays and Fridays.

Fallows was polite and courteous, usually charming, knew how and when to be formal as well as friendly. It was unlike him not to observe customary procedures. But that is what he appeared to do in his eagerness to accept the living of St John the Evangelist, Preston. Conceivably and understandably he would have assumed that the Hulme's Trustees would have informed and cleared their choice of incumbent with the Bishop of Blackburn, before offering him the living. That is far from the case as was made clear in a letter from the Bishop to Fallows, 12 July 1945:

> I hear from the Secretary of the Hulme Trustees this morning that they have offered you the Benefice of St. John's, Preston. This is one of the most important and difficult pieces of work in my Diocese and I had asked the Chairman of the Trustees to give me an opportunity, before they reached a decision, of meeting any man whose appointment they were considering. I was able to interview one of the candidates yesterday but I had no idea that you or others were to be there.
>
> I must ask you not to make any announcement about the appointment until I have had time to write to your Bishop and also have met yourself.
>
> Could you come up here to see me next week, say on Tuesday or Wednesday at any time convenient to you?
>
> I do not want to appear unwelcoming, but the situation at Preston is so difficult that I am even more anxious than usual to be quite sure that I am satisfied with any appointment that is made there.

This was an early lesson for Fallows who will exercise patronage as Vicar of Preston and later as Bishop of Sheffield. Some patrons do not scruple to have recourse to methods of advancing religion which pays little heed to the system and authority of the Church of England. In identifying Christianity with their own understanding of it, they yield to a temptation which is never far from dogmatic confidence, and rarely resisted by religious zeal. This applies particularly to Party Patronage Trusts propagating and perpetuating types of Anglican churchmanship of crypto-Papists, diehard Protestants and fundamentalist Evangelicals. They clothe their patronal privilege with respectability. Totally divorced from diocesan responsiblities, they have notions about the spiritual requirements of the diocese divergent from those of the Bishop who is legally and pastorally charged with the duty of spiritual government, and who cannot delegate his responsibility. Hulme's Trustees held advowsons of livings including Accrington Parish Church (St James) whose vicar was patron of three other churches in the town: St Mary the Virgin and All Saints,

1. Ann Joyce Fallows, Gordon Fallows' mother

2. William Fallows, Gordon Fallows' father

3. Gordon with elder brother, Eric

4. Barrow Grammar School soccer XI; Fallows seated second from left

5. Fallows performing in school play

6. Quadrangle at St Edmund Hall, Oxford

7. *Ripon Hall from the lake*

8. *The Dining Hall at Ripon Hall*

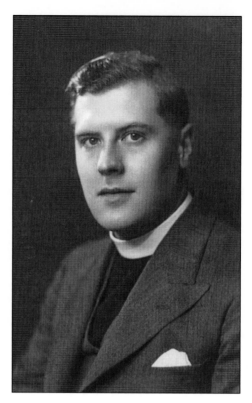

9. The young curate, Holy Trinity, Leamington Spa

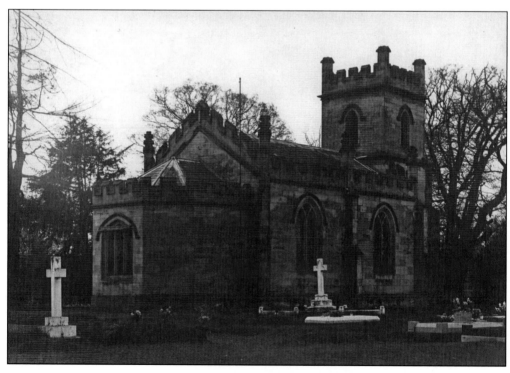

10. St James Church, Styvechale, Coventry

11. *The Youth Fellowship, Styvechale*

12. Marriage to Edna Blakeman; 3 September 1940

13. Great Gable and Wast Water – Edna's initiation into lovely Lakeland

Whalley; and Holy Trinity, Habergham Eaves, Burnley. Fortunately these Trustees were unencumbered with proselytising or partisan views.

Wilfred Marcus Askwith was consecrated Bishop (of Blackburn) on 30 November 1942. He was in great contrast to Fallows in appearance, character, background and churchmanship. Of Yorkshire ancestry, after serving his title at St Mark's, St Helens, he was chaplain of Bedford School followed by a chaplaincy to Europeans at Nakuru, Kenya, thence successively vicar of Sherborne Abbey and Leeds Parish Church. Physically he was a giant of a man with a powerful voice and remarkable presence matching his honour as a Knight Commander of the Order of St Michael and St George! His churchmanship was soundly Catholic without any esoteric trimmings. At Leeds one parishioner spoke for many in offering the view that he 'was a bit too 'igh for me.' There was never any doubt where he stood on any issue. He was a vicar – and bishop – who pronounced. There was in his public utterances no pretentiousness or cant, no facile use of clichés, simply unadorned speech. Yet often there was a sad reflective smile on his face. Blackburn welcomed a bishop who was a protagonist of church schools and a majority supported his traditional stance on moral issues such as marriage and the blight of divorce. To the eight curates living at Leeds Clergy House and the clergy of the Blackburn diocese he was understanding and pastorally helpful when personal problems surfaced but he was not entirely easy of approach. Askwith was also a sturdy believer in the Church as England as the ancient Catholic Church of the land and thus an opponent of exaggerated Roman Catholic claims.

Askwith's own experience would probably have led him to appoint a mature priest to Preston, probably from the North of England who had knowledge of ministering in a city or town centre. It reflects favourably on bishop and vicar-elect that he could write to Fallows on 24 July 1945:

The Provost of Coventry was away when I wrote to him and I have only just had his answer to my letter.

I write now to say that I very much hope you will accept Preston. What I saw of you the other day made me very clear in my own mind about your fitness for this important work, and the Provost's letter has confirmed my own impression.

There is, as I told you, a great deal to be done in the Parish and town. The links between the Church and the Civic authorities need to be extended and in particular I am anxious that on the side of education and work among youth, the Church should be enterprising and alive. I am also anxious to see the Clergy more united and working more with each other. I hope, too, that the Parish Church will become a centre for good solid preaching and teaching. I believe we have a great opportunity at the present moment for this. People are conscious of a need of something and they are prepared to listen if we will speak clearly and with conviction. I hope the problem of the Vicarage, or a substitute for it, may find a solution. The sooner you can get to us the better and I should like if possible to get you instituted towards the end of September or in October.

Gordon and Edna Fallows arrived with their children: Geoffrey (born 1941) and Angela (born 1944). David was born in 1946. Fallows was inducted and instituted on Wednesday 3 October 1945 at 3.0 p.m. It was attended by members of the Town Council and civic officials in their regalia and the bishop's watchword was 'I pray that this Church may become a new centre inspiring common action.' In common with all churches St John's was recovering from the war. Parish organisations which had been mothballed were resuscitated. Fallows was a vicar in a hurry, wanting results, determined to impress. Within six months he formed a youth fellowship for young people over the age of fifteen who immediately made their presence known by staging a one-act play at the January 1946 Annual Congregational Gathering, already a feature of the parochial year. These 'gatherings' were rollicking, side-splitting, entertaining events, when two hundred people or more sat down to a substantial 'Lancashire tea.' A constellation of activities for young people, including residential holiday courses and camps were held; plays and operettas were performed by the Parish Church Fellowship; The Friends of Preston Parish Church was launched enlarging its profile and extending its influence; the Men's Bible Class was strengthened; and a group was formed to study *Towards the Conversion of England*, a plan dedicated to the memory of Archbishop William Temple. Other activities followed, for young wives, an adult dancing class, study groups. It was not a parish where charity was made at home and never left it. For forty years St John's had supported an Indian nurse at St Luke's – 'our' Hospital – at Nazareth, South India. The Sunday school sent bandages and medical supplies to St Athanasius Mission, Lukamba in Matabeleland. Further help was given to the Mosse Memorial Hospital at Ta 'Tung, North China. This was in addition to regular support given to missionary societies – and to the Church Missions to Jews, and the British and Foreign Bible Society. One of Fallows' resolutions which he commended to the parish was, 'I will look for the job that needs doing and get on with it.' This applied to giving of self and giving of money. Emergency appeals were launched; for example, parcels of clothing were sent to relieve distress in the Greek earthquake disaster of 1953; and the response to need was immediate for the Hungary Relief Fund in 1956. Sunday School teachers were well trained forever expanding classes and the bishop authorised Miss Hilda Goodwin to do voluntary work under Fallows' direction, having particularly in mind the work of the Sunday School. She was qualified in educational method and technique through correspondence courses and a short residential course at St Christopher's Training College for Sunday School Teachers at Blackheath.

There had been a parish magazine for over fifty continuous years. Time for revamping. In January 1947 a specially designed new magazine appeared with the symbol of its patron of lamb and flag and the letters P.P. on the cover. P.P. – *Princeps Pacis* – was Preston's motto. In the Middle Ages the letters were invariably inscribed under a representation of the pelican feeding its young from its own crop. The 'Vicar's Notes' in the magazine were always of interest and reports of organisations were as helpful as occasional teaching articles by curates were illuminating. Infrequently Fallows provoked his readers and the local newspaper took note. But there was little rich meat from him so readers had to be satisfied with nibbles in his 'Notes.'

He was busy writing and reviewing for journals, and preparing sermons and addresses. However, there were several times when the magazine carried provocations by Fallows. When he was prompted into the public arena of debate his views were candidly expressed. His language was not headline-grabbing but neither was it colourless. If he intentionally provoked it was an endeavour to make people think for themselves. When the controversy on the question of whether Preston should have Sunday cinemas or not arose in 1946 he pleaded that Christians should not take a negative attitude. With the cessation of war attendance at cinemas increased. Fallows wondered if:

a legitimate and healthy form of relaxation is becoming, for many people, a soporific. Enquiries in schools reveal that many children attend three, four or five times a week. School teachers in some of the poorer areas of most large towns are alarmed at the bad effect of an excessive dose of films on the minds and health of their children.

Ample opportunities were afforded during the week to attend the cinema, so the closing of them on Sunday would therefore be no serious deprivation of liberty. Although Sabbatarianism was dead how far was Sunday a day of rest, a day of worship and a family day? The breakdown of home and family life and the erosion of religious practice, if not belief, gathered momentum. Fallows urged people to face facts and recognise that many homes are not places where a pleasant Sunday evening can be spent. We must also recognise that young people will not want to stay at home, and that, in fact, they will drift about the streets unless some alternative and better form of recreation is provided.

A more controversial intervention came in November 1946 when he would ruffle Roman cassocks. Fallows used the Presidential Address of the

Archbishop of York, Cyril Garbett, to the Convocation of York in which he issued a warning to Anglicans contemplating marriage with a Roman Catholic against signing away their rights over possible children. It gave Fallows the opportunity of making his own position known which he might not have done otherwise with such force and clarity in a Catholic town. He was riled by the Roman Catholic position. Anglicans should not sign a document that solemnly promises that all the children, of both sexes, who may be born of the marriage 'shall be carefully brought up in the knowledge and practice of the Catholic Religion;' or that the Roman Catholic promises to do all within his or her power to induce the other party to 'embrace the true faith.' As Garbett said, 'It means that while freedom is secured to the Roman Catholic it is denied to the Anglican.' Neither Anglicans nor Roman Catholics should be intimidated by any warning or threats that a mixed marriage in an Anglican church would be invalid. It would be marriage in the sight of God and in accordance with the laws both of the Church and the State of the realm. Much misery was caused in mixed marriages in Preston and elsewhere when the Roman Catholic promised to do all within his or her power to induce the other party to convert. When Anglicans were encouraged to stand firm by their clergy and refused to give a pledge or sign a document, there were times when the Roman Catholic authorities did not insist upon it, or, more frequently, the marriage took place in the Anglican parish church.

In 1947 Fallows advocated taxing the gambling trade by the Chancellor of the Exchequer, Hugh Dalton:

> because some people argue you are giving official recognition to a social evil and giving the State an interest in the prosperity of the gambling trade . . . Are we to be content as a people to waste and fritter our limited resources in such a fashion and at a time when our economic condition is so perilous? Will the future historian of Britain say not that 'she wants to go down fighting,' but 'she went down betting.' Are there not better uses of our time and leisure; better ways of deriving pleasure and entertainment?

If the foregoing gives the impression of a whirling of constant and consuming activity it cannot be denied. Yet Fallows was also wise and cautious. He recognised that 'activity is not always a sign of movement'. After one year as Vicar he referred to 'signs of renewed activity and new life. But the real pulse of the Church is to be found in its worship, in its concern to relate worship and life, in its efforts to extend the Church and spread the Gospel at home and overseas.' That is what mattered. It is something he never forgot. He was conscious that Christians should not take time too seriously. Fullness of time is not measured by an hourglass or a diary. He liked Robert Browning and quoted with approval and effect:

We live in deeds, not in years; in thoughts, not breaths;
In feelings not in figures or a dial.
We should count time by heart-throbs.
He most lives who thinks most – feels the noblest – and the best.

To assist in his largely self-motivated and unremitting ministry Fallows secured
a curate in July 1946. Unfortunately there was not a direct succession or
overlap of curates throughout his Preston years. There were woeful gaps of up
to six months affecting vicar and parish alike. Too frequently there was a
melancholy note from his pen:

> The search for an assistant curate goes on. The only way we shall be able to
> manage in the coming months is by concentrating on the essentials and leaving
> the non-essentials. That will be a salutary exercise in itself. I am quite clear what
> some of the essentials are – the visitation of the sick, and bereaved, and those in
> trouble or distress of any kind; the teaching of the children and the care and
> guidance of the young; the preparation of the Sunday services. I am also quite
> clear what some of the non-essentials are. I leave you to guess them and I hope
> you will encourage me to neglect them for the Kingdom's sake.

Fallows' choice of curates is interesting. All were married, usually with
children, and only one followed the direct route from school, university and
theological college and even for him Preston was his second curacy. All the
others were mature men from a variety of backgrounds and proven gifts. For
example, one man, after graduating, joined the Metropolitan Police Force.
When the outbreak of war changed his plans he joined the Army and spent
four of his six and a half years in India, before returning to university to
prepare for the ministry. Another man worked as a chaplain in Patagonia and
Buenos Aires; another had experience with the Tyneside and then the
Lancashire County Education authority. They brought other skills including
a flair for working with young people, a grasp of administration, leadership
among contemporaries. Sporting prowess was not overlooked by Fallows.
There was some help from retired priests whose pastoral and spiritual qualities
were valued, and a 'lecturer' was appointed whose full-time work was teaching
scripture and English at Worsley Technical College.

At first the curates and their families lived in the converted half of the
vicarage but moved into a separate curate's house when, in April 1949,
Fallows moved from East Cliff House which had been the home of vicars of
Preston since 1904. Their new domicile was 13 Ribblesdale Place at the
entrance to Avenham Park, a better house in more congenial surroundings,
easier to find, and easier to keep clean! The family relished the change.

Fallows lost no opportunity of making himself known to civic, professional and business leaders in Preston. His masonic connections helped. In 1946 he was invited by Sir Percy Macdonald, the new High Sheriff of Lancashire, to be his chaplain. Each year the church bells 'ring in' the Mayor when elected to office and when he made what was referred to as a 'state visit' to the Church. Fallows enjoyed these grand occasions and took great care with preparing the 'Orders of Service'. Fallows was chaplain to many of the mayors. As the Bishop hoped he took inordinate care in courting and cementing relationships. There were the 'duty' meetings held in a convivial atmosphere, like having the rural deans of the archdeaconry of Lancaster to his home for conversation when Edna Fallows, a superb cook, provided a buffet lunch. There was lunch at the Bull and Royal Hotel when he entertained some twenty-eight Savings Bank officials from all over Great Britain. The 'off duty' meals with 'interesting people' and scintillating conversation, at home or elsewhere, were regular entries in his diary, for example, supper at Whalley with the vicar and a doctor and their wives: 'Our talk ranged over questions of world population, Wolfenden Report, female emancipation.' He was fortunate that Edna was often at the driving wheel of the car. Fallows became an ecclesiastical dignitary without ever being a 'churchy' person. He did not enjoy everything he did or had to do and admitted that he was over-booked at events that did not require a cleric. When he was archdeacon he spoke and spread himself in light-hearted post-prandial vein, not least at after-dinner speeches.

Fallows knew how to relax without wasting time. He snatched a short walk in the Park most days when he was at home, but when travelling carried notepaper with him so he could write letters in spare moments between appointments. If there was an aspect of ease and informality about him was it because he was a pipe-smoker? Those who were inclined to be sceptical of his Modernism could hardly take umbrage from the seemingly collected contentment of a pipe-smoker, rather like Tony Benn and the mainstream Labour Party. There is a photograph of five off-duty, casually dressed clerics, four of them, including Fallows, puffing their pipes. When he achieved gaitered prominence there was usually a light suit in the boot of his car ready for a quick change.

The supremacy of worship was always central in his ministry. There was never any doubt that he was the Vicar of Preston but as a parish priest he had the ability to be formal and calm at the same time, reassuring to his congregation and welcoming to strangers. He was quick to notice visitors in church. The dignity of worship was enhanced rather than distracted by good music well sung. Fallows introduced courses of sermons during the year and on weekdays in Lent he preached on themes, for example, 'Our Lord Jesus

Christ. Incidents in His holy life', 'Hymns in the English Church', and a memorable series on 'Men of Vision' explaining the religious significance and message of the influences of Richard Baxter, William Blake, William Wordsworth, Robert Browning, and Francis Thompson. Research and preparation involved reading and time. He attracted many outstanding visiting preachers. To the pulpit came Canons Edward Carpenter of Westminster Abbey, C.J. Stranks of Durham Cathedral, W.J. Phythian-Adams of Carlisle Cathedral and Rev. F. Paton-Williams, rector of Prestwich and one of the leading personalities of the annual Blackpool Mission; Rev. C.O. Rhodes, Editor of the *Church of England Newspaper*; Dr Charles Foster, an educationalist, scientist and lay theologian. There were visitors from America notably Rev. Dr George Gibson, Professor of Preaching at McCormick Theological Seminary for Methodist, Congregational and Presbyterian students in Chicago; J.W. Visser, Presbyterian Minister of Westminster Church, Detroit; and Rev. Wilbour Eddy Saunders with four earned doctorates, President of Colgate Rochester (Baptist) Divinity School which trained men of all denominations. The Bishop of Blackburn was a regular visitor to Preston buttressing his support for Fallows. Fallows introduced a bookstall, including the publications of visiting preachers, and encouraged people to buy the *Church of England Newspaper*.

There was a box at the west end of the church marked 'Messages for the Clergy' which was normally used by newcomers asking for a visit or the sick to be visited. Fallows extended its use by encouraging people to pose questions they would like discussed in a sermon or simply matters puzzling people. He was delighted when this was used. One note enquired about the use of praying for the dead to which Fallows responded:

> It is not wrong to remember in our prayer those who are passing out of this life, to pray for others and especially for those who have no-one to pray for them is acceptable to God.
>
> On the other hand the Church of England does not include prayers for the dead among its teaching. There is no mention in the New Testament of such forms of prayer for the dead and it has no part in the teaching of Christ. The practice grew up in later centuries and was the cause of serious abuse. Experience shows that there is a danger of creating the impression that God can be cajoled and bribed. But it is equally true, and experience endorses this view, that there is a real need in the spiritual life for a prayerful remembrance by the living of those who have passed on.

The increasing number of children attending services with their parents was 'a very healthy sign of a return to the goodly custom of the family pew.' The number of confirmation candidates was high, up to thirty each year. He thought the minimum age for Confirmation was thirteen or fourteen. For Fallows the separate Adult Confirmation was 'one of the most impressive services of the year.' These services included those being received into the Church of England from the Roman Catholic Church. There was a greater emphasis on receiving Holy Communion and opportunities for doing so. Fallows did not 'finger-wag' but persuaded people to be regular in their reception of the Sacrament. On Christmas Eve a Midnight Communion service was introduced, and one on New Year's Day, another mid-week service at 11.30 for the elderly and infirm. Prior to Easter 1954 he made this plea:

> Will those who have lapsed or grown careless and indifferent make a new beginning at Eastertide and having begun again, endeavour to keep it up by regular attendance at the Holy Communion Service. There could be no greater blessing for our church than the recovery of fellowship of the 'breaking of the bread,' as the Holy Communion is called in the Acts of the Apostles. Young people especially, should come early and regularly to this service. It is indeed a sad state of affairs when, as sometimes happens, young people who should show most vigour are the ones who grow lazy in this respect, and are conspicuous by their absence from the early service.

Fallows was mindful of the changes in custom in the Church of England where many parishes were laying chief emphasis on the Parish Communion with hymns and short address, held at about 9 or 9.30. He admitted 'That is not the ideal solution for a central town parish. It is much more suitable for a parish with a large population living near to the Church.' Nonetheless he challenged the congregation, 'Is our own arrangement for Sunday morning services the best we can devise? How can we best render the praise and honour due unto God's Holy Name? How can we best bring others, through the worship of the Church, to know, to love and to serve the Lord?' When he left Preston in 1959 the Sunday services remained unaltered. During his time there were four BBC broadcast services from St John's.

Great events in Preston included the visit of King George VI, Queen Elizabeth and Princess Margaret in 1951. It was also the year of the Festival of Britain when the combined parishes of the Deanery held a Church of England Exhibition in the Public Hall illustrating the worship, history, organisation, social services and witness of the Church in the past. Prominent speakers testified to the power and life of the Church. Thousands visited the Exhibition and people were drawn to services and pageants. This was not the Church stagnant but militant, alive and moving forward. The Preston Guild was initiated in 1179 when Henry II conferred it by charter upon the town. It was held every twenty years but the 1942 Guild had been cancelled as a result of the war. The year 1952 was extra special when Prestonians from all over the country returned for the historic celebrations. The parish church played its traditional role in the events of the week not least by the Guild Court, the very essence of the Guild. The magnificent and memorable procession was unequalled in the north-west of England. The parish church had its own dressed lorry and tableaux. There was a Guild Grandstand in the churchyard with preference given to regular members of the congregation. Vast crowds thronged the church night after night and also by day. Some forty thousand 'pilgrims' made their way through the church during Guild week. To mark the end of Guild Year the Archbishop of York, Cyril Garbett, visited Preston. At the age of seventy-eight he remained a person of great stature, a commanding figure. It was a glorious civic and religious occasion and the Church had the rare experience of witnessing an archbishop in scarlet chimere and a train, carried by two choirboys. The year 1955 was the centenary of St John's, another occasion for special services attended by numerous bishops and another pageant. Abbots and bishops, beggars and builders, soldiers and statesmen, kings, mayors, councillors, blue-coated school children, fair ladies and prisoners, lords and warriors, homeless townsfolk and noblemen, all coming to life in their time and place in the scroll of parish history, under the inspired direction of the Rev. F.C. Morgan, a curate, who was endlessly innovative with teenagers.

One regret was the disappearance of the Church School. Education was an imperative throughout the diocese. It was hoped that St John's School would be retained in the Education Development Plan for Preston which included four primary Church of England schools and one secondary modern school, all of which were to be new buildings. St John's would be closed as a day school. It was in need of major alterations and refurbishment and the one question Fallows had to face was, 'Can we afford to keep the school for parish purposes?'

Fallows had a feeling for beauty in nature and an eye for beauty in architecture. He was not bracketed to the past and appreciated many modern architectural developments. There was an uproar when, following slum clearance in Preston, it was planned to build eleven-storey blocks of flats. 'Manhattan comes to Preston' was his off-the-cuff remark but he did not join the protestors as he thought it could be an interesting development. 'Mixed in with other buildings and other sizes it should certainly make for a varied sky-line.' However, his particular vision was used to excellent purpose at St John's. Gifts were regularly received enabling him to make substantial improvements to the interior, in conjunction with the architects. In 1950 the whole of the chancel – the sanctuary and a chapel – was re-decorated. The sanctuary tiles were replaced by two-foot squares of Hopton Wood stone. The altar itself was enclosed by riddel posts and curtains, above them a frieze in oak bearing carved and armorial crests of all the dioceses in which Preston had been included, York (in the Middle Ages), Chester (after the Reformation), Manchester from 1847 and Blackburn from 1926. The chancel screen was removed, resulting in a lighter and brighter appearance. Removing the reredos revealed the whole east window not seen in its entirety since the 1870s. The opening of a Memorial Chapel by Lord Derby, its dedication by the Bishop of Blackburn, and laying-up of the colours of the First Batallion on 1 June 1950 was a magnificent occasion, with three Chelsea Pensioners in their scarlet uniforms adding lustre. The motto of the Regiment, *Loyauté m'oblige* (Loyalty binds me) was everywhere apparent. There were many other embellishments over the period including a magnificent new pulpit on a Longridge stone base in 1952. Treasures of silver included a rare gift. At Christmas 1914 Queen Mary presented to Miss Mary Fielden, a descendent of two ancient and famous Preston families, a reproduction fourteenth century silver gilt incense boat. Miss Fielden was at the time Secretary of the Queen's 'Work for Women' Fund, and in 1956 she presented the gift to the church.

The most conspicuous and controversial alteration to the church came in the wake of the Centenary celebrations. A booklet to commemorate the event was read by Mr T.S. Wilding, an old friend and former worshipper, who was struck by a reference to 'that blank west wall which now cries out for some bold painting.' After consultation with Fallows, Mr Wilding expressed a desire to provide a mural painting as an act of thanksgiving and also in memory of his parents. Who would be commissioned to do this?

> To stand before an empty wall as in a trance, to let shapes cloudily emerge, to draw scenes and figures, to let light and dark rush out of the surface, to make them more outward or recede into the depths, this was bliss.

These potent and cogently expressed words came not from the ever-increasingly inventive vocabulary of an art historian but from the lips of an articulate practitioner of mural painting who was also an easel artist, sculptor and lithographer. Hans (Nathan) Feibusch was born in Frankfurt in 1898, the son of Liberal Jewish parents. As a child he preferred paint to toys. His consuming ambition was to paint. He studied art in Munich, Berlin, Rome and Paris, toured Italy and was drawn to and influenced by the works of Giotto, Masaccio, Mantegna and Piero della Francesca, and the twentieth century German Expressionist painter, Max Beckman. Feibusch studied under Andre Lhote in Paris who inspired him to seek a style that was both simple and monumental. But Germany in the 1930s was no place for innovative artists, particularly Jewish ones. He came to England in 1933 leaving behind much completed work, some of which was seized and declared decadent and included in the Nazi-sponsored Degenerate Art Exhibition in 1957. Once in England, Feibusch came to the attention of two substantial patrons of the arts, Kenneth (Lord) Clark and George Bell, Bishop of Chichester. With the latter there was mutual reverence. Thenceforward we find murals and other works of great significance. His deceptively gentle and retiring nature camouflaged flair and boldness in his art as he mounted scaffolding. His mind was reflective and subtle and he steeped himself in the biblical or other stories he was to portray. Fallows admired Feibusch and got to know him well and he repaid the compliment with a very good sketch and later a bust of Fallows. After Fallows' death Feibusch reflected: 'We found it easy to talk to one another and I remember our strolls through the park and how I enjoyed his elegant choice of words and diction.'

A muralist is involved in physically demanding work, never more evident than in, for example, the sequence of scenes from the Nativity at St Wilfred's, Brighton; and pre-eminently his greatest and largest mural, *Trinity in The Glory* which takes up the whole of the east wall of St Alban's, Holborn. His first ever Stations of the Cross were also for St Alban's. Amongst his murals there are ones at Chichester Cathedral; Goring by Sea, about which there was a major controversy; St Elizabeth, Eastbourne; Christchurch Priory, Hampshire; St John, Waterloo Road, London; St Mark, Coventry; and in the Bishop's Palace, Chichester. His *Crucifixion* at St Ethelburga's, Bishopsgate perished when the I.R.A. blew up that church in 1993. In secular buildings there are murals at Dudley Town Hall; and most notably at Newport Town Hall/Civic Centre, six paintings each 18 ft. high, on the two 50 ft. walls of the landing which contain 120 figures slightly bigger than life-size, an illustration of life in Newport since Roman times. There are sculptures at Ely Cathedral and a 'St John the Baptist' at St John's Wood Church in London, where he worshipped. He also designed dust jackets for books and posters for Shell and London Underground. That is the measure of the versatile artist who accepted the Preston commission.

The subject for the west wall of St John the Evangelist, Preston was the Beatitudes, 'The Sermon on the Mount,' measuring approximately 6 × 4 metres. The following is Feibusch's own account of his painting:

The great events narrated in the Bible have been depicted over and over again for many centuries, and every one of thousands of artists has tried to represent them in his own way. The results have been widely divergent, so that neither the figure of the Lord, nor those of other biblical persons, nor their dress or the scenery ever repeat themselves. Every artist is of his own time and has to express the ideas and habits of his period: but he has also to reach out towards the eternal truths and so reach the continuity underlying the constant change. Every painter, while using the colouristic language of his own years, must try to use certain traditional forms which to the beholder are inseparably associated with the sacred personages.

The artist commissioned to paint a mural has to satisfy two demands: he must tell a story, and he must do it on a given surface. In this case, the story, the event, was 'The Sermon on the Mount'; it shows Christ as the Divine Teacher talking to disciples and other followers. The scene is a hillside with trees; the afternoon sun shines; big clouds sail over the mountain; everybody listens quietly while Christ addresses not only those around Him, but the whole of mankind.

This scene had to be portrayed on a wall much higher than wide, a wall overhung and over-shadowed by a hammer beam ceiling, which meant that the action had to be spread vertically instead of horizontally, and that no important part of it could be placed at the top of the wall. The arrangement finally achieved shows the figure of Christ seated where there is the maximum of light, about one-third down the wall, with the other figures spread out above and below. The trees high up serve to detract the eye from the roof beams which would have shown up far more against a clear sky and to cast a shadow over the upper part of the picture, thus throwing forward, by contrast, the centre figure. The wall is of asymmetrical shape, the left half wider than the right. The grouping of the figures follows this in a broad curve on one side against a straight vertical on the other. Both sides are drawn together at the bottom and anchored in the large figure from the back. This kind of planning lies behind every painting or other work of art whatever it represents, and whether it is ancient or modern; but it is the test of the artist's skill to make the result look natural. That he must have sincerely experienced that which he wishes to express, is a matter of course.

Feibusch's vibrant use of colour is important. Colour is used for emphasis and effect. It is used to create an atmosphere of other-worldliness and transcendence. There are strange combinations in all his murals – who else would think of placing lime green, purple and a searing orange next to each other? Opposing colours created a bold chiaroscuro effect of light and dark, out of which form emerged. He knew how to project joy and sorrow in his paintings. The European conflict and fate of the Jews was only a little beneath his emotional surface.

The mural painting was dedicated on 10 June 1956 by the Bishop of Burnley, George Holderness. It was predictably controversial though much more admired than criticized. Religious art is difficult territory. In an article on 'Mural Paintings in Churches' (*Theology* January 1954) Feibusch had a challenge for his day and today:

What chance is there for the creation of inspired, vital, and truly contemporary work in a world where religion and art occupy only corners; where churchmen are usually without aesthetic interests and without knowledge of modern art, while artists are no longer inspired by the world of the Bible? How can a religious art be created which can spring only from a religious renaissance, while we live in times that seek salvation in the manufacture and accumulation of consumer goods?

Fallows inherited a dull church at Preston and left a greatly enhanced and beautiful one, well worth a visit! That was a legacy. There is a footnote to Hans Feibusch's life. He died less than one month from his hundredth birthday in 1998. He had converted to Christianity by Baptism and Confirmation in the Church of England, but early in the 1990s he left the Church and returned to his Jewish roots.

Holidays were paramount for Fallows. However hard-pressed and eventful his life, holidays were written into his diary as unmovable feasts. It was a time of complete focus with his family. He reflected:

> Periods of rest and withdrawal from the world's busy scene are essential if the fullness of life is to be experienced and enjoyed. This has been true all down the ages, but the tempo of the modern world makes it especially true of our time. As life becomes more and more regimented, and we are all in a measure slaves of routine, it becomes more important that we shall have one opportunity of carefree re-creation, of escaping from the office, the bench, the queue and the sink.

Twice he exchanged the vicarage of Preston, once with the Rev. W.V. Awdry, Rector of Elsworth in Cambridgeshire, and of 'Thomas the Tank Engine' fame and once with the Rector of Gosforth, Cumberland. Sunday services and dire emergencies were his sole duties. At Gosforth he thought 'the Rector must have warned his parishioners not to die or be born or even be sick during his absence for the amount of emergency duty I was called upon to perform was very little indeed.' For consummate bliss there were two particular holidays, conveyed by Fallows, 9 August 1954:

> Tomorrow we take our tent and iron rations and turn the nose of the 'Minx' due north to spend a few days exploring a little of the Scottish Highlands on our way to the back of beyond. On Saturday (August 14) we hope to come to rest in a farmhouse bed on a small island (Inchmarnock) off the west coast of Scotland. There we expect to be marooned for a fortnight before returning (gales, tides and fog permitting) to the mainland.

In 1957 the family went to Bassenthwaite, Cumberland, to a small cottage under the shadow of Skiddaw for three weeks:

> For quite long spells we have plotted our way through the clouds on the mountain tops aided by compass and sometimes by those cairns which other mountain travellers have so thoughtfully built for the guidance of those who might otherwise lose their way in the mists. We have often been drenched, but never depressed. There is an exhilaration in the hills which the fickleness of the

weather can never dispel. I am rapidly becoming domesticated and I shall never cease to wonder how much (and sometimes how little!) you can do for a family on one calor-gas ring. But the exigencies of the cooking plant do not matter for the cottage has the glorious amenity (for me) of not being on the telephone. That is a holiday in itself.

In 1959 they went to Grasmere. In Fallows' entry in *Who's Who* only one recreation is recorded – fell-walking!

Being Vicar of Preston Parish Church was only a portion of his work. For the rest we now turn.

CHAPTER 5

Venerable and gaitered

CONCURRENT WITH HIS DUTIES as Vicar of Preston and his primary work as parish priest of St John's, honours and increased responsibilities for Fallows came thick and fast, many of which took him away from the parish, far too often and for too long was the view of some parishioners. Relations between Bishop Askwith and Fallows were never likely to carry the intimate warmth of personal friendship for in theological and ecclesiastical outlooks they were transparently different. However Askwith was large-minded and recognised merit and potentiality when he encountered it. Within a year of Fallows arriving in Preston he was appointed Rural Dean of Preston. In 1951 he was invited to be one of Askwith's examining chaplains. The importance of this latter function depends on what the bishop pushes their way. Askwith's examining chaplains were not a coterie of like-thinking people but included priests of very different shades of theological opinion and churchmanship. In 1950 Fallows was elected Proctor for Clergy for the Diocese of Blackburn in the Lower House of the Convocation of York, which carried with it membership of the National Assembly of the Church of England (Church Assembly). This suggests a measure of trust and popularity among his fellow clergy in the diocese. Convocation met at York and Church Assembly at Church House, Westminster. This could mean an absence from the parish of up to four weeks in a year. Fallows was an assiduous attender though infrequent speaker but each provided opportunities for being near the pulse of the Church of Engand, and enabled Fallows to keep in touch with old friends and make new ones. He was present at Convocation in 1955, when something deep in his heart and striving moved towards fruition. Closer relations with the Church of South India were established. A report on Church relations in England was also considered, but he would live to see his hopes raised and dampened on unity with the Methodist Church. Visits to London enabled exhilarating treats to the theatre. On one visit he recorded:

> Monday night, Covent Garden, 'Salome' (Strauss). Tuesday, Sadlers Wells, 'The Flying Dutchman' (Wagner), and Wednesday, Sadlers Wells 'Falstaff' (Verdi). All quite different. Salome, perhaps the most horrific of Operas. In a week of rich musical expressions the Wagner night was outstanding. I am getting quite knowledgeable in this field & am certainly enjoying my education.

51

On another visit he got a seat in the 'gods' for the first performance of an opera – *Lucia di Lammermoor* by Donizetti, with an eighty-year old conductor and a tour de force by Joan Sutherland:

> I have never known so many curtain calls at the end or so many bouquets presented. After the performance I did something I have never done before in my life, namely, wait outside the stage door & see the VIP's departing. I even secured the heroine's autograph on my programme.

Fallows was receiving bouquets of a different kind. The constituent bodies of Church Assembly are always on the look-out for promising new talent. It was not long before he became a member of the Central Board of Finance which involved more journeys to London. In 1952 there was a vacancy in the Honorary Canonry of Haltun in the Cathedral Church of St Mary the Virgin, Blackburn. The Bishop deemed it 'right that the incumbent of one of the leading churches of the diocese should have this title . . . and I am conscious of a great sense of security about the leadership you are giving there and the counsel you are able to give myself.' Fallows was collated and instituted to the canonry on 31 August 1952, pledging to 'observe perform maintain and keep all the Statutes Regulations Ordinances Rules and Customs of the said Cathedral Church and as much as in you lies to maintain and promote the honor and interest thereof.'

In 1953 Fallows received a letter from the Bishop of Norwich, Percy Mark Herbert (previously the first Bishop of Blackburn 1926 to 1941), in his capacity as Clerk of the Closet, a position which Fallows himself will hold when Bishop of Sheffield. Bishop Herbert was responsible for proposing that Fallows' name should be submitted for possible appointment as one of the thirty-six Chaplains to the Queen, a very ancient office. In due course the Queen's command to offer him the position was notified by the Lord Chamberlain (The Earl of Scarborough) and duly Warranted and Certified on 3 November 1953. The duties are slender including preaching according to a 'Rota of Waits' in the Chapels Royal. The outward manifestation of a Royal Chaplain is the wearing of a red cassock and chaplain's badge. The badge embodies the Royal Cypher, of silver gilt, and is worn on the scarf.

There was one great compulsion on Fallows' time. The patronage of Preston parishes – eighteen in the town itself – was divided between the Vicar of Preston, Bishop of Blackburn, Simeon Trustees, Hyndman's Trustees, and some other miscellaneous Trustees. Of that number the Vicar of Preston had greater patronage than all the other patrons together. His own patronage extended to other parishes in the area. The prevailing churchmanship of Preston churches was 'low' and 'traditional' or 'evangelical', the three not necessarily coinciding. During Fallows' Preston years every parish, bar one, had new incumbents, and in several cases more than a single change. Seeking and finding clergy who will best fit a benefice, reinvigorate a failing one or enlarge ministry in a thriving one, is difficult. The amount of correspondence is considerable, lengthy interviews imperative, negotiations with the church-wardens and officers of the vacant parish often tricky and heated and, when an offer is rejected, the need to start all over again. A bishop has an identical problem but he has clerical and secretarial assistance. Any acceptance is subject to the bishop's approval which is not a rubber stamp and cannot be taken for granted. If the Bishop of Blackburn was uneasy with Fallows' choice he insisted on interviewing the candidate himself, as he had done with the Hulme's Trustees' appointment of Fallows to Preston. Generally, Bishop Askwith approved Fallows' choice without question but he was wary of controversial Modernism finding its way into the diocese. One exchange of correspondence between Bishop and Patron, is sufficient to amplify the point. These were the days of 'My dear Fallows ... Yours sincerely, Wilfrid Blackburn' and 'My Lord Bishop ... Yours obediently, W.G. Fallows':

(Askwith to Fallows:)
I have seen 'A' this morning and I am afraid he must have found it rather a trying interview.

One of the things which worries me about him is that he has not settled down anywhere for any length of time and I am always rather doubtful about putting men into benefices who have had as little consecutive practical experience as he has had.

I was also concerned to find out just how modernist he is. I believe in intellectual honesty, but at the same time I am rather strongly convinced of the necessity of clear confident and authoritative teaching with simple people. On the whole he was able to reassure me and I am ready to accept your nomination to St 'B', if you decide upon it.

(Fallows to Askwith)
I am glad to know that after consideration and enquiry you feel able to approve the Rev. 'A' to the benefice of 'B'. I am, however, disappointed to learn that the proposal has caused you some misgiving and concern. I am sorry about this and can only express the hope that the future will remove any doubts you may have.

I made careful enquiries about 'A'. Amongst other things I received excellent reports of his preaching from very reliable sources. His liberal theological outlook is confirmed with a real love of people and will enable him to stress the fundamental affirmation of the Christian faith in such a way as will help rather than hinder even simple people. This is the ideal I set for myself and for which I believe there is a place and need in the parochial ministry.

There were times when the Bishop would suggest clergy who needed a move to be considered by Fallows for a parish of which he was patron. There were only two churches in the Preston Deanery which could be described as 'Catholic' without the telling and ominous prefix of 'Anglo'. Fallows was content for the candle-power to increase modestly unless there was opposition by parochial officials. It would be many years before he received the 'ostrich feather' treatment, being processed and paraded in mitred glory amidst incense-laden churches in Barnsley and South Yorkshire.

There were other commitments including membership of the BBC Religious Advisory Council; Vice-Chairman of the Governors of Preston Grammar School for Boys; and he continued as a prominent and active Council member of the Modern Churchmen's Union. He did not have to sing for his supper as an avid supporter of Preston North End Football Club.

The physical health of Bishop Askwith did not match the robustness of his manner. There was so much concern for his health that he was offered the large and significant bishopric of Salisbury in 1949 on the grounds that a warmer climate may be better for him. But he preferred the bracing air of the north to the prospect of the 'damp climate' of Salisbury. How a diocese with 426 benefices, 525 clergy and one bishop suffragan would be better for his health than Blackburn with 256 benefices, 339 clergy and two bishops suffragan, stretches credulity. However, in 1954 he accepted translation to the See of Gloucester where he remained until his death in office in 1962.

Blackburn was not kept waiting for a new bishop. By the time Askwith was enthroned at Gloucester on 16 July 1954 his successor at Blackburn was announced. Walter Hubert Baddeley was Bishop Suffragan of Whitby, his least notable achievement. Born in 1894 and educated at Varndean Secondary School, Brighton, his further education was interrupted when he enlisted in the Army in 1914 and took part in some of the stiffest engagements on the Western Front with the Royal Sussex and East Surrey Regiments, serving throughout the war with distinctions and many acts of bravery for which he was awarded the D.S.O. and the M.C. and bar, and was four times mentioned in dispatches. On demobilisation he completed his education, graduating from Keble College, Oxford and then responded to a deep-seated vocation to the priesthood, training at Cuddesdon Theological College. Only tough jobs appealed to him which came with a curacy at St Bartholomew's, Armley, Leeds followed by eight years as Vicar of South Bank, Middlesbrough. His characteristics embraced zeal, impatience, bravery, imagination and forceful-ness. It was said he would go far but who could anticipate what that would mean? In 1932 at the age of thirty-eight he was consecrated Bishop of Melanesia, a diocese with a quarter of a million souls, scattered over widely separated Pacific islands. The mission ship was his episcopal palace as he moved among his Christian congregations. His energies were immense and his evangelistic outreach was both wide and deep. He had just got into his stride, with a scheme for increasing the number of native priests, and providing better medical services everywhere, when war engulfed the Pacific. Japanese troops were putting a stranglehold on Melanesia, so the Resident Commissioner went to the Bishop for advice about the future. 'My mind is made up; I am staying in the Solomons,' declared Baddeley with that forthright economy of words which dominated many an important and decisive conversation in which he was involved. Evacuation would be desertion. He lived in bush huts, on native food, and succeeded in keeping his situation secret. Under the noses of the Japanese invaders he organised a policy of resistance and carried on his ministrations, caring for sick and wounded natives, fighting for the Allied cause. He went about in his bare feet and the state of his bush shirt and shorts beggared description. After the war he sought funds in Australia and elsewhere for rebuilding schools – and an infant welfare centre. He was chaplain to the Fiji Military Forces, and was awarded the U.S. Medal of Freedom.

In 1947 Baddeley left Melanesia a hero and returned to England as Bishop of Whitby where his energy and plain speaking were appreciated. He was married with a family and also a man's man scoring a personal triumph when speaking to the Church of England Men's Society where his ability to reach the minds and touch the hearts of laymen was well attested. He was also a zealous Freemason, elected Grand Chaplain of the United Grand Lodge of England in 1949, served for a year at the end of which he was appointed Provincial Grand Chaplain of the Craft in the North and East Ridings. This was at a time when the Archbishop of Canterbury (Geoffrey Fisher), many diocesan bishops and other ecclesiastical dignitaries were Freemasons. Fallows was an influential Freemason. How different by the turn of the century when the Bishop of Carlisle, Graham Dow, received great support for an article: 'Arguments to support the view that Freemasonry is not compatible with true Christian Faith.'

Walter Baddeley was enthroned as Bishop of Blackburn on 28 October 1954 and was never happier than when reaching out in episcopal ministry in parishes. Every parish was visited within two years of his arrival and he once commented that he slept in twelve different vicarages on twelve successive nights. He was not a bishop to be directed or confined to 'officials'. He wanted to meet and be with lay people.

Baddeley inherited a diocese where there were pressing vacancies to fill. In this he was unusually fortunate for he was able to appoint people of his own choice for senior positions in the diocesan hierarchy. The Bishop of Burnley, Keith Prosser, had died on 27 June aged fifty-seven. It may appear odd to describe a bishop's character as Christian but it was that rather than 'Church' which best describes Prosser, encapsulated in the words:

Charity suffereth long, and is kind; charity envieth not, charity vaunteth not itself, is not puffed up, does not behave itself unseemly, seeketh not her own, is not easily provoked, thinketh no evil, rejoiceth not in iniquity, but rejoiceth in the truth.

Prosser had previously served as a parish priest to a scattered population in Canada and in an English industrial parish. Surprised at being invited to be a bishop he continued his patient, pastoral work on a larger scale.

In 1936 a new Suffragan Bishopric of Lancaster was created with Benjamin Pollard as its first Bishop. He continued as Vicar of Lancaster Priory and Rural Dean of Lancaster. In addition he was appointed Archdeacon of Lancaster in 1950. He was also the Prolocutor of the Convocation of York, Chairman of the House of Clergy of Church Assembly, and a Governor of the Church Commissioners. If he regarded his manifold duties as sublime, he moved to the ridiculous when he was appointed Bishop of Sodor and Man in 1954, a diocese founded in AD 447 comprised of twenty-seven benefices and thirty-eight clergy. It must have seemed like retirement, but he made his presence felt in government (where the bishop has a seat in the Manx Parliament), although in ways more party political than as an ecclesiastical statesman. He appointed Fallows as one of his examining chaplains.

Baddeley was determined to separate the archdeaconry from the suffragan bishopric of Lancaster. The diocese looked to three new appointments from within the diocese and there were numerous people wishing to bend his ear. Baddeley thought otherwise. He wanted 'new blood' and fresh approaches in the diocese. Accordingly, George Edward Holderness, Vicar of Darlington, and Anthony Leigh Egerton Hoskyns-Abrahall, Vicar of Aldershot, were appointed Bishops of Burnley and Lancaster respectively and were consecrated together on 2 February 1955. Both were trained at Westcott House and served as chaplains during the war, the first as an Air Force chaplain, the latter as a Naval chaplain. There the similarity ended. Holderness was also Rector of Burnley; Hoskyns-Abrahall had no parochial cure. Holderness relished his Yorkshire roots and had enjoyed exercising conspicuous leadership in Darlington of an ecclesiastical Rotarian variety. Eventually at Burnley he became deeply disillusioned and some bitterness entered his soul. Unfortunately he did not receive the preferment he thought was due to him, and for which the suffragan bishopric had been a preparation. He would openly say that he had been 'shunted into a siding.' After fifteen years he accepted appointment as Dean of Lichfield but by his episcopal background and temperament he did not take easily to the constraints of capitular life. He was not the complete master in his own household as he may have anticipated. He was hardly on speaking terms with one of the Bishops of Lichfield, Kenneth Skelton, with whom he served. Hoskyns-Abrahall was in the Royal Navy before ordination and afterwards served his title at that great priest-training parish of St Mary, Portsea, followed by a few years as chaplain at Shrewsbury School. He was always a good bishop because he never forgot that primarily he was a priest. Pastorally sensitive and trusted he was a real father-in-God to clergy and was happy and content in his service of episcopal ministry at Lancaster for twenty years, until his retirement in 1975. He had made the diocese of Blackburn his own! He was an effective promoter of planned-giving campaigns, always stressing that stewardship will not only increase parish giving but also create a deeper sense of personal commitment and responsibility to the community. His wife was President of the Mothers' Union in the diocese, and a strong opponent of the ordination of women to the priesthood,

The third vacancy was the Archdeaconry of Lancaster, which comprised the Rural Deaneries of Blackpool, The Fylde, Garstang, Lancaster, Preston, and Tunstall. Preston and Blackpool were heavily populated followed by Lancaster and Morecambe. There were many historic parishes such as Poulton-le-Fylde, Hornby, Goosnargh, Silverdale, as well as a large number of twentieth-century churches built to meet the needs of accelerating populations. Bishop Baddeley not only separated the bishopric from the archdeaconry, but also from Lancaster Priory, to which he appointed the Rev. H.A. Bland, who had been successively vicar of Whalley and Morecambe, and was well known in the Church of England as the editor of the magazine insert *The Window.*

By canon law, the office of archdeacon in the Church of England is styled 'the bishop's eye.' But he is also in hallowed practice the bishop's nose, poking it into all manner of parochial affairs where curiosity attracts him. A good archdeacon combines the tidy habits and business-like approach to ecclesiastical affairs with a rich pastoral, not necessarily a parochial, ministry. How that ministry should best be undertaken varies according to the wishes and whims of the diocesan bishop. There was never any doubt in Baddeley's mind as to whom he would ask to join the gaitered ranks of bishops (Right Reverend), deans (Very Reverend) and archdeacons (Venerable), as the new Archdeacon of Lancaster. Fallows was his first choice and there was a feeling of 'whoopee' when it was announced. One of his friends, George Frederick Townley, Archdeacon of York and soon to be Bishop Suffragan of Hull, wrote with a shade of disappointment: 'I thought it might have been to purple but you at least now must get into gaiters which will suit you admirably.' They did! Canon A.S. Picton, Vicar of St George's, Preston (later Archdeacon of Blackburn) and a respected leader of Anglo-Catholics in the diocese and beyond, wrote with satisfaction, although, interesting at this stage of Fallows' life, added a note of medical apprehension:

My hearty congratulations on your excellent news. It seems to me a most suitable appointment and I know you will do the job well. Our new Walter is showing his wisdom early. I do hope you will display yours by giving the medical factor in life a bit more sway than you have done in the past. Cautious archdeacons are of more value than ailing ones.

One question Fallows had to face was whether he should continue as Vicar of Preston. He decided to do this. One letter merits quoting in view of subsequent developments. It was from Eric Treacy, Archdeacon and Vicar of Halifax:

My congratulations on your elevation to Venerable rank – one of the worst things of being an Archdeacon is to be called 'Venerable'! I do not know whether you are holding on to Preston or whether you are going to be Vicar of Lancaster – I hope for your sake that you will have a parish as it makes a lot of difference to have your own pulpit and altar. On the other hand you will have all my sympathy if you are to have a double job. I am supremely happy here with the two, but I am sometimes torn to the point of real anguish between the claims of the two. Perhaps such tension is good for us. On the whole, I think people are ruder to and about Archdeacons than any other type of Church dignitary – probably because they are more in reach than the others – but for all that it is a grand job as it gives a wonderful pastoral opportunity with the clergy. I am sure you will enjoy it. I am sure you will like Tony Hoskyns-Abrahall. I have known him for nearly 25 years and he is a first class person. I imagine the appointment of these two suffragans from outside may have caused a little fluttering within the diocese – but they are good men and will quickly settle in.

Fallows referred to this duality in his 1959 Visitation Charge:

The Church of England has not yet solved the dilemma of an archdeacon who has also a full-time parochial charge. This combination of duties is, perhaps, not all loss. His preoccupation with his own parochial business reduces his nuisance value as an archdeacon. I am more than content that it should be so. In the words of the old nursery adage 'What the eye does not see, the heart does not grieve over'.

There is, however, another and more important gain arising from this dilemma of a beneficed archdeacon. It enables me to speak, as it were, from the ground floor, and to know first-hand and day by day the problems of the parochial clergy, it also means, as my brethren will appreciate, that even a charge like this has to be composed against the background of the unmelodious music of the telephone and the front door bell. No vicarage has an ivory tower. I share your trials and your joys. We know, each of us, in our hearts that though the disappointments in our work are many, and the sense of failure often strong, there is no more thrilling and rewarding adventure than that to which we have put our hands, so long as our sense of vocation is preserved. Churchwardens and all the lay people of our Church can help us to keep that sense of vocation bright and burning by sharing with us in the total ministry of the Church of God as members of one body and servants of one Lord.

Fallows was instituted as Archdeacon on 14 January 1955. He approached his new work with curiosity, seriousness and despatch. An archdeacon makes Visitations which are preceded by detailed Articles of Inquiry and followed by a Charge. There is no common form of Visitation Articles. Every archdeacon is free to follow his own inclinations but Fallows immediately consulted historical works and then, with care and deliberation, prepared his questions directed to churchwardens. They were printed in imposing form which emphasised both the seriousness of the questions and the importance Fallows attributed to this duty. Most of them were straightforward, matter-of-fact. A number were carefully composed to provide him with knowledge by which he could gauge the spiritual temperature and rhythm of church life. 'Is your church open daily for private prayer?' may suggest, if not, why not? Fallows read, digested and dissected the replies to the Articles of Inquiry.

Three lengthy Visitation Charges were delivered in 1956, 1958 and 1959. There was space for him to display his historical knowledge and his wry humour helped people to digest his words. Indeed, people enjoyed listening to him and a Charge never became a sermon. If he had pursued his academic studies he could have followed a university path in ecclesiastical history. But this would not have fulfilled his personal predispositions or, perhaps, his ambition. The Office of Archdeacon was a plateau not a summit, a stage on his continuing journey not a terminus as archdeacon. But this work provided invaluable insights into the organisational aspect of the Church of England. A few very brief extracts throw light on the matters which concerned Fallows at the time:

(A) The parochial clergy often bemoan the paucity of attendance at the Annual Parochial Church Meeting. Here is the principal business meeting of the year and how very few sometimes can be persuaded to attend. Although I share the disappointment which is widely felt in this matter we should remember that it is not peculiar to the life of the church but is characteristic of our age. It is ironical that in this time and this age of democracy there should be so little interest shown by the rank and file in, for instance, local government elections, trade union branch meetings and the like. Nevertheless however few there may be at our Annual Parochial Church meetings it is essential that they should be conducted in conformity with both the spirit and the letter of the law.

(B) Vergers or verger-caretakers. The conditions in the different parishes differ so widely that it is impossible to generalise from the replies you made. One fact however is reasonably certain, they are by and large ill-paid for the work they do and those who are employed full time in this work and are wholly dependent on it for their living must be amongst the lowest paid workers in this country today. Of a good verger we may say, as the writer of Proverbs says of a virtuous woman, his price is above rubies. But, we may add, his pay bears no relation to the value of his service. A theological college tutor used to advise his students in looking for a first curacy always to seek a parish with a good verger, he would say, who can teach and help you more than anyone. I have no hesitation in acknowledging my own indebtedness to several vergers – outstanding and colourful characters – worthy representatives of a noble breed of men whose service to the church is worthy of our highest admiration and praise ... Their work is often exacting, it calls for a wide variety of skills; it demands the utmost tact and patience. Let us see to it that no unnecessary hardship falls upon those who serve the Church so faithfully in this ancient office.

(C) (On the position of the laity and especially the churchwardens in the life of our church.) The greatest difference between the reformed and the unreformed churches of Christendom is to be found in the place and status given to the laity in the respective traditions. The Reformation in a nutshell was the emancipation of the laity. In this year (1956) of the fourth centenary of the martyrdom of Thomas Cranmer we do well to remind ourselves that the reformation which he adorned with his learning and ennobled with his death gave to the laity not only the Scriptures and the Book of Common Prayer in their native tongue but it also recognised their place and status in the government of the Church. To the medieval Christian a churchman was a cleric. That this view survived in the unreformed part of Christendom may be seen from a letter in 1867 by Monsignor Talbot from Rome to Cardinal Manning at Westminster. 'What is the Province of the laity?' (Talbot wrote) 'To hunt, to shoot, to entertain. These matters they understand but to meddle with ecclesiastical matters they have no right at all.' On the other hand the churches of the Reformation and not least our own Church of England asserted the rights and status of the laity in varying ways ... I hope those who are 'sworn in' as churchwardens and sidesmen today will be proud of their responsibility for leadership in the life of the church.

(D) I am disturbed at the number of parishes, and not only small ones, in which there are no youth organisations. The reason in almost every case is lack of leaders. Here is a harvest field crying out for labourers. All youth work has changed in the last generation, even in the last few years. The teenagers of our Church today are a generation born in wartime, children of a space age, whose whole lives have been lived so far under the cloud of nuclear extinction. One full-time youth worker with long experience recently told me that there is a ferociousness about all that young people do and want to do in these days. Our job is to direct this energy into the right channels. Ping-pong and other well-tried organised activities no longer do the trick. The need today is to give young people a challenge. Surely the Christian Church can issue the greatest of all challenges to young people.

Words of St Paul were carried on the lips of Fallows and guided his actions. 'Let everything be done decently and in order.' Nothing irritated and pained him more than public worship conducted in a casual or haphazard fashion with little consideration for careful diction of words and The Word. Vestments and surplices which needed cleaning and washing offended him and he let the guilty parties know of his displeasure. 'Only the best for God.' Those people who complained that the Archdeacon's visitation was outmoded, an archaism, an ineffective and inefficient survival of a bygone age with little more than antiquarian value in an age of modern communications, received a thoughtful response. Fallows mused:

> I ask myself whether the printing press and the post office and the telephone have not made this annual gathering an unnecessary farce. My reply would be that nothing can really take the place of personal contact. This is all the more important when so much of our communication with each other is distant and impersonal.

Visitations and meetings at rural deanery level were a way of helping people to feel that they were members one of another, concerned for each other. Anything which heightened the corporate sense of the Church, which extended a vision beyond the bounds of the parish, was a healthy and invigorating corrective to narrow vision and complacency. Fallows was as accessible on these occasions as he was when visiting parishes in the archdeaconry for the induction of clergy and when invited to take part in deanery events.

There is one diocesan figure who rarely makes an appearance in published works. He is the Diocesan Registrar. Lawyers have a reputation not much above accountants. Registrars are thought to be grey men in wigs wielding considerable power behind the drapes. Fallows had considerable praise for the Diocesan Registrars and Legal Secretaries to the Bishops of Blackburn, Wakefield and Sheffield. They were long-serving Christian-minded lawyers and fine people. Fallows referred to the most important quality of Reginald Clayton (Blackburn) who in 1958 had served twenty-five years as Registrar, as 'simple, unaffected piety, abounding faith, and love for the Church he served so well.' The story that he used to plug in a portable telephone in the bathroom may be apocryphal but it is symbolic of the fact that he was always readily available for diocesan business and that he was immersed in it even when he was immersed in something else. More generally Fallows noted:

> No Church, I suppose, is so dependent on legal officers as the Church of England. Some would regard that as an impediment and a defect in a spiritual society. I confess I take a contrary view. It is one facet of the close constitutional relationship between the Church and the State; it is also, in part, a consequence of the incumbent's freehold and a measure of the fact that once having been lawfully admitted to it, he can only be dispossessed by due legal procedure.

There are a myriad ways in which, by the very nature of the organisation of the Church of England, we need the services of those who are versed in ecclesiastical law.

In Shakespeare's King Henry VI, Part II, there is a discussion between the rebel Jack Cade and his friends. They are plotting to overthrow the constitution. In dealing with their programme for the proposed new order, one of Jack Cade's fellow conspirators says: 'The first thing we do, let's kill all the lawyers' to which Jack Cade replies, 'That I mean to do.'

Fallows was no Cade. He constantly sought guidance from the Registrar to confirm a proposed course of action and 'Many a time I have expressed an opinion in reply to enquiries from clergy and gone on to say, "But I think you would be well advised to have a word with the Diocesan Registrar".'

There is another aspect of Fallows' archidiaconal ministry which left an impression on many clergy. His personal perceptions and ecclesiastical antennae were ever alert to clergy in his area. He was often the first person to discover, unearth and bring to the surface, serious stress – not a twenty-first century malaise! He encountered theological perplexities, moral conflicts, confusions and crises, seeming irreconcilable problems and the incessant pressures on clergy, some of the latter having their origins in the diocesan headquarters. A number of priests and pastors were saved from folly, temptation and sin by the perceptive eye and wholesome heart of this particular archdeacon. Equally he was capable of stirring people from slumber and sloth to activity. Yet again, he was a great encourager to hard-working clergy. He knew when a situation should be referred to the bishop but usually that was avoided. Fallows was someone whom people felt they could talk with and it often started over a cup of tea or repairing to a public house for something stronger.

Not every clergyman was drawn to Fallows and neither he to them. If his theological liberalism or political conservatism or his cautious radicalism on Church reform was questioned he was able to give account of his views and himself, but could be surprised by the forthrightness of tone and language of others. Moral and ethical issues were not yet paramount. It should not be overlooked that Blackburn was a traditionally-minded diocese. It still is! In 2007 the Bishop of Blackburn, Nicholas Reade, is the only diocesan bishop in the Province of York who does not ordain women priests. Fallows was wary of the very few priests who appeared to be absorbed with vesture and gesture, smells and bells, though the majority of clergy in the Catholic tradition liked him. More difficult were biblical fundamentalists or narrow single-gauge conservative evangelicals who were strident in their beliefs with a cold-hearted intolerance. Not Fallows' glass of beer! The Charismatic Movement was not yet prevalent!

Ordinands came to his notice when he quizzed them about their interests. Those who already had a developing hinterland and were brimming over with ideas and enthusiasms and/or who were heading for academic achievement at university appealed to him. He would have agreed with Bishop William Wand of London who recalled an interview with a too-solemn ordinand at Fulham Palace. 'Do you smoke, do you go to the cinema, do you read detective novels?' he asked. And when the rather shocked young man gave a trinity of negatives, Wand responded, 'What a pity. I was only trying to discover your relaxations by posing to you my own.'

What in sum can be said of Fallows at this pivotal juncture of his ministry? In one sense his policy appeared to be to keep people reasonable, but with no ignoble ideas of living a quiet life. His character and power of persuasion succeeded in making people temporarily, at least, reasonable. With all the force of his clear and able mind he believed in moderation. Plans and policies that savoured of overblown extravagance or loose from historical moorings seemed to him impolitic and unlikely to be harnessed to any common good. He did not like sudden bursts of emotional energy in public yet he was a master of constant pressure. He was eminently sane and judicial, cold towards excessive fervour and condemnatory of stridency, but never cold towards ardent faith. Although he was comfortable with his views and beliefs there was no element of self-satisfaction in him. His views were expressed with modesty, usually with healthy good-humour, disposed to take life cheerfully – and family life was always pre-eminent. He never mistook a molehill for a mountain, always quietly certain that he was moving on the right road whatever critics may or may not have said about his direction and pace. Above all or, rather below all, he was a clergyman who both said and prayed his prayers. The daily Offices of Mattins and Evensong were his practice and provided the inner lining to his spiritual life.

In 1959 the Church of England was nearing one its periodic crises although this time one which would change the direction of the Church. Different kinds of leadership would be required. And Fallows? Would he make a captain or a good umpire? A judge or an advocate? Or was there emerging in his outlook and practice something of a statesman? It is a misused word. 'steersmanship' is a better one, the antonym of which is drifting. Steersmanship implies control, guidance, direction, and foresight. These garments would appear to be tailor-made for Fallows. It will be twelve years before he wears them.

What and where next for Gordon Fallows? His admirable qualities and achievements have been sufficiently traced and evinced. Little has been noted or explained about his weaknesses and impediments. His legacies at Pontefract and Sheffield will be largely and uniformly favourable and noteworthy. That is why opinions and judgements on his Preston ministry are exceedingly surprising. In 1959, the year of his departure for Oxford, he had been ordained for twenty-two years, thirteen of them as Vicar of Preston. He was forty-five years of age. Time to take stock! It is extraordinary that the views of people who knew him at Preston are diverse and extreme, from the savage to the sublime. Everyone is in agreement that he was a powerful and impressive figure but that is where concord ends. Observations from parishioners include 'his time seemed spent in empty promises and cultivating those people – and only those people who would facilitate his ascent of the greasy pole towards becoming a bishop.' Others recall his time as 'unmemorable and unremarkable.' Contrary recollections are 'He was a wonderful pastor who visited the sick, the poor, and absent parishioners. Nothing was too much trouble, and the poor always had help' and 'He put Preston Parish Church on the map' and 'He helped anyone in trouble or struggling with their faith' and 'He was so kind and warm, and I cannot think he had any weaknesses,' and 'He knew how to lead.'

Timothy Samuel Atkins, curate from 1951 to 1954, gives a curate's eye view. Prior to ordination he served with distinction as an officer in the Marines, taking part in the Normandy beachhead invasion and awarded the D.S.O. He came to Preston as a graduate of Emmanuel College, Cambridge, theological training at Ridey Hall and a curacy at Melton Mowbray. Mrs Atkins was a Mancunian. Fallows told his congregation they should have a 'gradely' welcome. Atkins has these memories:

> My time in Preston was one of sheer joy and happiness: partly due to the town and parish; largely to Gordon and Edna Fallows and their family. The Parish was recovering from the war years, but it was a war that had been won; and Preston's industries had been diversified. More impressionable perhaps than post-war austerity or exhaustion was that this was the first time of the post-war Preston Guild. This coincided with the Coronation and in a town with the civic pride of Preston, this made for an exciting time with much to prepare for and do. Incidentally, Tom Finney was at the height of his powers. He had an aunt in the Parish who could sometimes produce him to open such events as parish bazaars.
>
> The congregation tended to be eclectic from the whole town, largely 'middle' or 'upper middle class' as might be expected in almost a cathedral-like set up. As a curate visiting (with a bicycle – no car for another five years – and only once driven off the road!) I covered and knew reasonably well most of the topography of Preston. As a largely Roman Catholic town, there was a continual sense of competition which probably brought out the best in us. Gordon Fallows to all intents and purposes gave me a free hand, while keeping an eye on things. He gave me a very fair share and participation in the services. The Church was made available to Orthodox Ukrainian refugees from time to time.

Gordon not only permitted but encouraged me to play cricket for Preston (not generally 1st XI) and Blackburn clergy. He led and trained by personality and example, and by gifts of leadership and administration. He was a man of prayer, who never stopped or spared himself even when suffering great pain from a perforated duodenal ulcer. My impression is that he was an outstanding Vicar of Preston, building up the church. I had little part in administration in the parish. I think Gordon saw to this privately and personally with the churchwardens and P.C.C. who were obviously more permanent and durable than a two-year transient curate. He was a Freemason, which may have opened doors not available to everybody! He seemed to know all his parishioners personally and individually, and so could get the best out of us all. A lovely man and family: a good time: only happy memories.

If a perforated duodenal ulcer was the only item in Fallows' medical history, nothing further need be written. Alas that is not the case. In 1948 he was on the precipice as a result of overwork and the firm ultimatum by the churchwardens that he should take immediate leave prevented a full and major collapse. In 1954 he was sick-visiting among countless duties up to the moment when he was leaving for London to preach in the Chapel Royal in the morning and St Martin-in-the-Fields in the evening when he suffered a serious breakdown of health. The parish had been without a curate for nine months and the resulting heavy accumulation of work had further expanded with the departure of the Bishop of Blackburn for Gloucester and the death of the Bishop of Burnley. Fallows was suffering from a recurrence in a more serious form of an old trouble. In the December 'Vicar's Notes' he mentioned that he was picking up the threads again, but 'I confess that I am not, by nature, a good patient and that I find my incapacity for even a short time rather frustrating.' In March 1956 he was admitted to Preston Royal Infirmary for an emergency operation and it was six weeks before he resumed his duties. He was upheld by the prayers of the congregation and 'the experience has staggered me beyond comprehension. I have never known such generosity and kindness.'

In 1958 the following message appeared in the October parish magazine:

I owe you all – or nearly all of you – some explanation of my sudden disappearance from the parochial scene at the beginning of September . . . Most of you will know by now that I have just spent another spell under the hospitable and beneficial roof of the Preston Royal Infirmary. It was thither that I went, under my own steam and feeling wonderfully robust and fit, on Monday September 1st. On the following Thursday I had an operation for the removal of a long-standing source of trouble which has been nagging at me, off and on, for years. It was as long ago as mid-June that the medical pundits put their heads together and decided that the time had come for a radical solution, and that I was just cut out for some more table treatment. From that moment, of course, I felt completely fit and I did just wonder whether the June decision might be revised when September came. That is why I made no announcement of my impending fate, except to the Churchwardens. But how thankful I am now that I submitted to the experts and had the job done. The fact that I was in the pink at the time has contributed to a remarkably good and speedy recovery.

Two years earlier, in 1956, Bishop Baddeley conducted the Adult Confirmation at St John's. He was clearly unwell. Within a few days he was in hospital and seriously ill. Fortunately, he responded to treatment, enforced rest and returned to lead the diocese until 1960. Fallows had this to say:

One of the significant features of our high-powered civilization is the larger number of men in high and responsible positions who break down in health. The medical experts are deeply concerned about this and there may well be a connection between this incidence of sickness and the administrative burdens that are laid upon our leaders in Church and State.

It is a clumsy adage that if you want a job doing give it to a busy man. It is almost beyond belief and certainly incredulous to wonder why an already too-committed and too-busy Fallows was offered and accepted Bishop Baddeley's offer to be Archdeacon of Lancaster which came at a moment when Fallows was only beginning fully to resume his duties following major surgery. Moreover, he was not even guaranteed the immediate help of an additional curate. He retained all other ecclesiastical embellishments with the exception of the Rural Deanery of Preston which he relinquished.

This raises a wider issue, in no way limited to Fallows. Alec Hamilton, Bishop Suffragan of Jarrow, gave Ian Ramsey, Bishop of Durham, candid advice, that his first duty was to do the work he was paid for and only then to undertake additional tasks. This arrested Ramsey's attention – but the moment passed. But Fallows accepted a greatly increased workload for which he was paid. Was he sure he could cope? How many more spheres of ministry in the Church of England would satisfy him? Ian Ramsey could not help himself, but was there a more shadowy doubt about Fallows' motives? Or was he merely a glutton for overwork? Preferment is a virulently contagious disease in the Church of England. Once caught it is difficult to control and impossible to cure. It makes its presence felt by a constant nipping away at the interior self. A priest eagerly anticipates and notes episcopal retirements or deaths. His mental and emotional energies are swift to imagine himself filling a vacant bishopric. When he reads the appointment of his peer or junior (in age and experience) he is deflated and discouraged. There is the temptation to become half-hearted in his spiritual work. There is nothing that more effectually destroys pastoral efficiency than a divided mind and the restlessness of discontent.

Turn the coin over and acknowledge that a good priest is aware of his natural gifts, acquired skills and sheer, solid, proven ability. He does not obliterate future possibilities by limiting his horizons to his present parochial cure or other ministerial commission. An ambition to serve in a wide sphere is not unhealthy, but a wise spiritual director will be essential if the ego is not to lead to pastoral distraction and spiritual travail. Consider the hard-working parish priest with a combination of pride, longings, temptation and torment, of energetic striving and mental effort, back-breaking and heart-rending ministry, inflated by successes and coping with failure; of finding souls and losing some; of endeavouring to be holy and good; of holding in almost impossible equipoise the family of God of the parish with his own family of wife and children.

By 1959 it was evident that Fallows needed a change, a new sphere in which to exercise his ministry. It was too soon for him to be appointed to a diocesan bishopric. Seven fell vacant between 1956 and 1959 and were filled by men in their early fifties, with two exceptions, those of Bradford when the Principal of the London College of Divinity, Frederick Donald Coggan, was appointed aged forty-seven; and the Principal of Ripon Hall went to Derby aged fifty-seven. Fallows' historical research gave him a sense of perspective. He knew that not withstanding a large swathe of liberal-minded bishops in the Church of England, few subscribed to the tenets of modernism, and fewer still were prepared to call themselves 'Modern Churchmen' in public. It is to Fallows' considerable credit and integrity that he professed without wavering his commitment to modernism. Modernists were welcomed into a beneficial and non-rigid embrace which did not require its devotees to sign on the dotted line of a calculated and narrow version of theological outlook, Christian doctrine and ecclesiastical practice. There was an abundance of prominent and 'modernist' deans and professors, but few bishops. Indeed in the twentieth century up to and including Fallows' appointment to Sheffield in 1971 there were only thirteen 'Modern Churchmen' in the episcopate. Each was independently minded and fearless, some of them controversial, others outstanding 'rational' as well as 'diocesan' bishops. Those who were imaginative innovators could never be mistaken for museum attendants. This small number includes John Diggle of Carlisle, William Greer of Manchester, Leslie Hunter of Sheffield, Joseph Hunkin of Truro, Richard Parsons of Middleton, Southwark and Hereford, Ian Ramsey of Durham, C.S. Woodward of Bristol and Gloucester, Henry Wilson of Chelmsford, and Leonard Wilson of Singapore and Birmingham. Equally interesting is that during this period only three Ripon Hall students became English diocesan bishops – Geoffrey Allen, Ian Ramsey and Fallows.

If no diocesan bishoprics were on the horizon, and no invitation arrived for him to be a suffragan bishop, what would attract, satisfy and enlarge his experiences whilst mitigating his tempo – except his driving speed! – and complete his restoration to full health and, perhaps, lead to 'high office' in the Church? Above all he wanted to expand not retract. It was exceedingly fortunate that the choice of a perfect setting was at hand for his continuing ministry.

In 1959 Geoffrey Francis Allen, Principal of Ripon Hall, was appointed Bishop of Derby and left the Principalship in June. The following is the sequence of events in Fallows' own words in letters to his son, Geoffrey:

(8 May 1959)
An interesting and varied week. A good Mayor's Sunday 'do' with a civic preachment for me. I had a feeling that it might be some time before I did another (an RC Mayor next year & the future is always in the lap of the gods). On Sunday afternoon I baptised at Lytham & in the evening was chauffeured by Mummy to Coventry. Monday in Oxford for the Ripon Governors – a momentous & important meeting as I hinted to you. I have to go back again next Friday for further deliberations.

(22 May 1959)
It looks as though I shall become Principal of Ripon Hall (though this is still confidential). The balance in favour seems decisive & the few people I have been able to discuss it with in confidence have all been clear about it. Though we shall be sorry to be uprooted from here there are tremendous compensations and exciting new possibilities for us all. A change now solves many problems here arising from the unsatisfactory double burden of the Archdeaconry & Parish. If I miss the unsought opportunity I may drift on for years & really will only be marking time if not actually receding. So all in all I am beginning to think it is providential and a nettle to be grasped . . . Boar's Hill will be a wonderful place for hospitality in a way that Preston can never be. Last night I went to the Mayor-Making Ceremony here, and then to the Mayoral Banquet. The speeches went on till 11.30 p.m. & were not very scintillating. Yesterday afternoon I opened a 'Fair & Sale' at St John's, Blackpool. I couldn't help feeling that these two events absorbed a lot of time that could have been more profitably (not to say enjoyably) used.

(12 June 1959)
My appointment as Principal of Ripon Hall will be announced in Church on Sunday. All the people I have consulted are strongly in favour & I am more and more clear that it will prove beneficial to us.

(26 June 1959)
On Monday we left for Oxford reaching the Principal's House at 3.30 p.m. I chewed over many things with Bishop Allen and then I had a session with the Vice-Principal (J.F.B. Goodwin) & the Chaplain (R.J. McKay). The V.P. is a Cambridge graduate who has spent some time teaching in Nigeria. He is quiet

man, married with 3 children, aged 5, 7 & 9 (or thereabouts). The Chaplain is a chatty Irishman, a Dublin Graduate. I like them both & we should form a congenial and harmonious team. On Tuesday morning I went round meeting all the domestic staff – 3 resident married couples – 1 resident single woman (an ex-school matron) and 3 dailies. It was quite a business seeing them each in turn. There has been some friction on the domestic side & one of them will probably have to go if we are able to keep the others. Sufficient unto the day.

Fallows did not celebrate by having his head measured for a mitre. Much better, he changed his car to a Ford Consul Convertible. You can also feel the excitement as he describes his purchase: 'That is two years younger than the Hillman. It has a bit more elbow room & a lot more power. The bodywork is in excellent condition (ivory colour) & it is in good mechanical order. The hood is the one indifferent feature but I am assured that it is weather-proof.' After its first run, 'The car is a winner. It goes like a bomb & it is a joy to handle after the worn-out & sluggish Minx.'

When Fallows arrived in Preston a good Prestonian and devoted parishioner commented: 'He's nobbut a lad.' If that was disparagement it was soon extinguished. On 10 September the Assembly Room at Preston was filled to thank a mature man and to present Gordon and Edna Fallows with gifts. He preached his farewell sermons at Mattins and Evensong on 13 September 1959.

CHAPTER 6

Principal

D R HENRY MAJOR RETIRED AS Principal of Ripon Hall in 1948. As for the
succession the historian and scholar, Alan Stephenson, one-time Vice-
Principal of Ripon Hall noted that the person Major would have liked to be
appointed was Leslie Basil Cross, the Vice-Principal (1933–1953) and
Chaplain of Jesus College; and to attract him to Boar's Hill he had managed
to buy a delightful Principal's House with an equally delightful garden. But
Cross did not rise to the bait. However, in a letter to one of the Governors,
Canon J.S. Boys Smith, Fellow – later Master – of St John's College,
Cambridge, Major indicated that he had approached Geoffrey Francis Allen,
Bishop in Egypt about the Principalship even before Canon R.D. Richardson
consented to become a candidate (letter 6 October 1951). This was wishful
thinking on Major's part for two reasons. Allen had only been consecrated
Bishop on 25 January 1947; and the Archbishop of Canterbury, Geoffrey
Fisher, who was Visitor of Ripon Hall, would not have sanctioned such an
approach. Canon Robert Douglas Richardson, Vicar of Harborne, Birmingham was appointed Principal. He was a scholar in early liturgy for which he
had earned a doctorate in divinity. He also appeared to be an uncritical
enthusiast of the thought and writings of his bishop, Ernest William Barnes,
whose controversial book *The Rise of Christianity*, published in 1947 still
resonated with critical vibrations in the Church. Richardson was the choice
of a cabal not of all the Governors, who were a distinguished and
representative body. Unwisely Major remained Treasurer of the college. The
merits of Richardson for the post of Principal were negligible. College
numbers receded to a stage where there was even talk of the college itself
moving to smaller premises in Oxford. Richardson was persuaded to leave
before he was pushed and accepted the living of Boynton with Sherrington,
near Warminster, Wiltshire.

A Special Committee was appointed on 4 July 1951 to consider the
college's future and a selection committee formed with regard to a new
appointment. Major, interfering as usual, was not alone in unsuccessfully
pressing Fallows' name as a member of the committee. Ripon Hall desperately
required someone who would command respect beyond the confines of the
college so the position he already held was imperative. This time Geoffrey
Allen was the obvious candidate and his appointment was formally confirmed

by the Annual Meeting of the Governors on 12 October 1951. He was a former chaplain of Ripon Hall (1928–1930), went to China with the Church Missionary Society, before returning to England, eventually appointed Archdeacon of Birmingham by Bishop Barnes. The influence of Major on Allen, once strong, had faded. In his place came the strange duet of Frank Buchman and Karl Barth. Allen was less modern churchman than a penitent liberal. That he was a bishop was a key to his attraction for the post.

Geoffrey Allen was not available to take up his new work immediately so once again problems surfaced at the college. Richardson told Boys Smith (now Chairman of the Governors) that he was willing to carry on beyond 31 December, until the end of the Hilary Term 1952. This news filled the majority of students with deep dejection. Major wrote to Fallows (23 November 1951) 'that it would be far better for the Vice Principal (Cross) and Canon Ian Ramsey, (Nolloth Professor of the Philosophy of the Christian Religion, and Fellow of Oriel – who had just succeeded Major as Treasurer) and Rev. Denys Whiteley (Chaplain, Fellow and Tutor of Jesus College) to carry on from 1 January until Bp. Geoffrey Allen arrives.' Fallows informed Major that there would be a 'mutiny' of students if Richardson's tenure was extended. If this ran over into the public domain the college's precarious position could lead to its closure and its being deprived of its licence both by Oxford University and by the Central Advisory Council of Training for the Ministry. This focused minds. Moreover, it should not be overlooked that the Visitor of Ripon Hall was the Archbishop of Canterbury, and Geoffrey Fisher continued as Visitor throughout Fallows' time, under his new title, 'The Most Rev. and Right Hon. Lord Fisher of Lambeth.'

Under Geoffrey Allen's executive and tireless ability the fortunes of Ripon Hall were both revived and transformed. The internal organisation was strengthened and the financial affairs were sound. There was a 'full house' of students. In 1959 Allen was appointed Bishop of Derby and vacated Ripon Hall in June.

The college needed a successor in the Ripon Hall tradition, although someone who would bring different qualities and experiences to take account of the rapidly changing times both secular and religious. The signs of seismic upheaval in the Church were already evident. It was also important that the Principal should not be unknown in the institutional church not least in the passages of persuasion at Church House, Westminster. Fallows, a marked Ripon Hall man and Governor, was pressed to let his name go forward and his journey from Preston to Oxford has been explained at the end of the previous chapter.

Fallows was installed in September 1959. It was sufficient to lift his heart and bring a fresh spring into his step. The setting of Ripon Hall on Boar's

Hill was an idyllic environment, a college set in a large acreage, providing freedom and space both physically and spiritually, and a much needed all embracing restorative for Fallows. It was described as 'a perfect setting, a real academic island.' And the view from it? 'No place in the world looks more like the celestial city than does Oxford seen from Boar's Hill in the light of the evening sun.' (*The Clarendon Guide.*)

Fallows arrived when the student body was changing and enriched by a few older men preparing for ordination after years of service in other professions and occupations. The general trend of earlier marriage was reflected in a quarter of the students already being married and many of the others engaged. The Hall set a high value on academic distinction and deliberately sought students who would advance its reputation in this respect. Ordinands included most shades of churchmanship from a few Anglo-Catholics to Billy Graham converts but never from the extremities nor biblical fundamentalists.

Fallows' impact was immediate. No fanfare, no blueprints, no scroll of initiatives, just a kind of leavening and relaxing presence. In 1966 when the whole student body was assembled at the beginning of term, Fallows' first words were auspicious: 'The era of Law has come to an end, the era of Grace has begun.' He was not simply referring to the fact that it was the year which saw the first intake of women students, a unique occasion in the life of theological education. Of course they could not at that time train for the ordained ministry, but were reading for degrees of various kinds. Fallows also took the opportunity of pointing out that Chapel would no longer be compulsory, except for ordinands.

From the beginning to the end it was Fallows' humanity and caring which predominated. However, there is not a uniform view of his character and appraisal of him as Principal. Indeed there are paradoxes, contrasting and contradictory views. It should be remembered that, unlike his years as vicar and bishop, Fallows was daily exposed to students. Some student memories paint a portrait that would not hang or even be recognizable in an episcopal gallery! There are constants, most notably and consistently that he was a person of integrity, an able administrator, good fund-raiser, with a firmly gentle or gently firm hand on the overall direction of the college: more chairman than managing director. His lectures on church history were sound, on ecclesiastical law illuminating with a good story to illustrate a dull point and hold the attention of students. On pastoralia he spoke with a good deal of common sense supporting his words from his ministry at Styvechale and Preston. His sermons were interesting rather than compelling or profound, but students were treated to an array of visiting preachers – bishops, deans, regius professors and noteworthy members of the Board of Governors who always had something to say as distinct from having to say something.

Theologically, Fallows was held to be more broad than modernist. The formative influence of Henry Major was expressed less in theological than personal terms, although one student, David Agassiz remarks: 'It was as if Major's presence conveyed more of his theological stance than his writing. In a way Gordon was like that too.' Fallows was not theologically self-revealing. One student speaks for many: 'I doubt if Gordon believed in the virgin birth, but I would be surprised if he didn't believe the empty tomb, though his years as archdeacon had taught him to be diplomatic in revealing his own personal beliefs and doubts.' B.A. Mastin admits Fallows:

> was not a creative theologian – no sense of criticism. He was well read and would sometimes hint at unconventional views which he held, but, though he unquestionably belonged to the liberal tradition he was probably more conservative in his basic theology than he liked to admit. He was tolerant of men who had extreme liberal views.

Emeritus Professor Canon J.W. Rogerson writes with perception on one aspect of Fallows' stewardship:

> On my arrival for the Summer Vacation Term of 1961 I discovered that I was one of the four students who was to be housed in the Palace, that is, the wing of the Principal's house. This was for students who were doing courses in Oxford and who were thought to need a quiet environment. I did not know beforehand that I would be doing courses at the university, but Gordon had the unusual view that, whatever else the Church of England needed, it needed scholars, and he intended to see that Ripon Hall played its part in helping to produce them. I had just completed a four-year B.D. course at Manchester – probably the most comprehensive first degree course available anywhere in Britain at the time – but felt that I knew a little about much but not a great deal about anything. I therefore responded gladly to Gordon's suggestion that I do a course in Oxford during my two years at Ripon Hall, and asked to be entered for the Oriental Schools. I had done four years of Hebrew at Manchester and felt that I would like to do the subject properly. I had no wish at this stage to do anything other than enter the parochial ministry.
>
> My first Summer Vacation Term was characterized by two things: the regular afternoon activity in the garden, and the Modern Churchman's Conference. We were each expected to assist with maintaining the thirty-five acres of grounds, with Edna Fallows setting a vigorous example. Gordon's view was that maintaining a good vicarage garden was a good witness and a potential source of contact with parishioners. Gordon organized the 1961 M.C.U. Conference on *Christ and Human Need* and attendance was compulsory for College members, but with speakers such as W. Norman Pittenger, F.W. Dillistone and G.R. Dunstan, this was no burden. In the summer of 1962 a pilot project was carried out at St George's College, Jerusalem. The building of the College was not yet

completed, but the staff had been appointed and the Church of England asked each college to nominate a representative to spend the Summer Vacation Term in Jerusalem, with the participants being housed in the nearby St George's School. It was typical of Gordon that he should see this as a great opportunity for me, and I was accordingly nominated to represent Ripon Hall. I was the only person from among the representatives of nearly twenty Anglican Theological Colleges who knew any Arabic or who was specializing in Old Testament studies.

With the arrival of final year, Gordon began to make noises about me staying at Ripon Hall as a member of staff, with a title at a church in Abingdon. These plans were postponed by the fact that I had been urged by Professor Godfrey Driver, whose lectures on Ugaritic I attended at Magdalen College, to apply for a scholarship to spend a year at the Hebrew University of Jerusalem. The plan was that I should return to Ripon Hall as a tutor in 1964. While I was in Jerusalem, however, Driver wrote to say that I should apply for a lectureship in the University of Durham. Gordon was equally adamant that I should do this. When I met Gordon briefly in March 1964, having come, successfully, to England for the Durham interview, his comment was that he wept tears of joy at my not being available, after all, to go to Ripon Hall as tutor.

Following my ordination and the beginning of my work in Durham I had only occasional contact with Gordon. In 1973, however, he invited me to give a week's lectures at Whirlow Grange to Sheffield clergy. Apparently, he insisted that all clergy should attend one course of a week's study each year, and he made a point of being present himself. As a result of this visit to Sheffield, a link with St. Mark's Broomhill, Sheffield was made and I did a Three Hours' Service on Good Friday 1974 based on the Old Testament. Gordon was in my congregation for the whole of the service. In November 1978 I received to my surprise a letter from the University of Sheffield asking if I was interested in the Chair of Biblical Studies. The main reason that impelled me to take this seriously was the presence of Gordon as Bishop of Sheffield and, indeed, he was a member of the interviewing committee that I met on 21 December 1978. Alas, Gordon died before I began my work at Sheffield.

As a Theological College principal Gordon had two aims: to equip ordinands intellectually for their future ministry and to insist that if Christianity was concerned with the truth, then there was no place for an apologetic attitude towards what we were doing or for a retreating behind ecclesiastical barriers. There was a wonderful openness and breadth about what went on at Ripon Hall. Gordon tried to recruit ordinands who would make a contribution to the intellectual life of the church and the community, and of the students and staff present in my brief spell there four of us (John Bowker, Stephen Sykes, Tony Dyson and myself) would come to hold chairs, Brian Watchorn and Ian Clark would become deans of Cambridge colleges while Brian Mastin and David Selwyn would hold university posts in Bangor and Lampeter respectively. Gordon's philosophy was that two years at Theological College would be the last chance, perhaps for forty years (there were no clergy sabbaticals then), to read and reflect profoundly on theology and that this was necessary if ministry was to be effective. Events in Oxford such as Bampton Lectures (by Alan Richardson) or Theological Society Lectures (by S.L. Greenslade) were attended by Gordon with students such as myself in tow. The occasional quiet days at Ripon Hall were as much of an ordeal to Gordon, I think, as to the rest of us; and it was typical of Gordon that he should seek and act upon suggestions from the students as to who might be invited to conduct quiet days. Two of my own suggestions – Canon Hedley Hodkin and Professor Thomas Fish – were taken up and proved to be very popular. Hodkin was such a sincerely pious man that no one could begrudge the time spent listening to him, while Fish (a Roman priest and expert on cuneiform who became an Anglican in protest against the Italian invasion of Abyssinia in the 1930s) was perfect for Ripon Hall at that time, with a fund of amusing stories and profound observations, and a no-nonsense approach to spirituality and its artificially-enforced silences.

Withal, Fallows ensured the Ripon Hall tradition was maintained and upheld with a progressive feel to it, which set it apart from its closest neighbours, St Stephen's House ('Staggers') and Wycliffe Hall, under Derek Allen and David Anderson respectively. At Cuddesdon the era of Robert Runcie had dawned and Michael Hennell was Principal of Ridley Hall. Fallows was anxious that the candle-power of Ripon Hall churchmanship and its spiritual temperature should be kept in check. Moderation was his watchword. He was indignant when half the college petitioned for a daily celebration of Holy Communion which he thought would be divisive. He ironed out any possible conflict between the 'pious' and 'run-of-the-mill liberal' ordinand. Thus worship was unchanged and unradical, almost oblivious to what was happening in the wider church at the beginning of the turbulent sixties.

At times the environment appeared too idyllic and somewhat unreal. One student explodes:

> The arrival of Tony Dyson as chaplain in 1963 (and Fallows' successor as Principal) at least introduced us to the Liturgical Movement, centrality of the Eucharist, Taize, Vatican II, Series III. I'm grateful for that: it has remained central to my perception of Christian life and worship. Sadly Gordon Fallows was left utterly out of his depth, puzzled, suspicious, ill at ease. His idea of really radical 'reform' was omitting the bracketed verses in the Psalms at Mattins/ Evensong in the 1928 Prayer Book. I don't remember him ever asking a really fundamental questions such as: 'What the hell are grown men – there were no women at the time – doing, chuntering their way through "1662" services twice a day, and Cranmer's Litany sung on Fridays?!' Some of us had done two years' National Service by then. The 'Modern Churchmen' seemed to be stuck in a time-warp about Jonah and the Whale: I was being invited to sally forth into a tough North of England housing estate (and very educative it was too.)

Are such angry criticisms too harsh? Is there substance in them? Were they shared by other students? Stephen Lowe was one of four students from the Fallows' years to become bishops – he to Hulme and now Bishop for Urban Life and Faith. The others were Neville Chamberlain to Brechin; Stephen Sykes to Ely; and Anthony Edward Pierce to Swansea & Brecon. Bishop Lowe puts his finger on some strengths and weaknesses of the Ripon Hall experience, albeit of what for him were 'happy years.' He refers to the:

> wearing of gowns, the style of high table and the long table of students was very much reminiscent of the Oxford College and these things seemed to matter to Gordon. Breakfast was the easiest time for conversation with him, as small talk was not one of his greatest strengths. I used to sit quite close to the end of the table, one place away from Gordon's seat at the top of the top table. The Vice-Principal and the Chaplain would be dotted in appropriate places halfway down at the end. It was at these times that Gordon would comment at length about Preston North End Football Club, Preston Parish Church and Tom Finney, and make arrangements for the afternoon tennis. I was never a good tennis player and I do not think ever risked playing with him. There were those with whom an engagement and the possibility of beating young active students was a matter of great significance for him. An afternoon without a tennis match for him in the Summer was clearly an afternoon without meaning or purpose! He was always warm, kind and friendly, and, in fact, he conducted with another former Riponian my marriage – the first in Ripon College Chapel.

There is a strange blend here confirmed by others. Julian Scharf says, 'He was very good to me – unassuming and modest. He did not have a gift for small talk, and awkward empty seats at high table had to be countered to fill them up. On the other hand his friendships were prized.' David Agassiz remembers:

> As soon as I met Gordon Fallows we 'clicked'. He would often creep up at lunchtime and suggest an afternoon of tennis, and did not discourage people like me from spending a disproportionate amount of time playing games. I think this laissez faire approach was his way of allowing relationships to develop, rather than the more formal attempts at group work which was introduced in later years.

The corresponding defect of this approach was a shyness or institutionalism which could lead to insensitivity. Fallows rarely had individual students for a person to person creative, even liberating, pastoral chat. Thus, for example, a rather confused, worried and anxious student who was homosexual was not helped to explore and face his struggles and its consequences for his future ministry. Yet Fallows was pastorally focused when there was a marriage breakdown involving a third party student which he handled with deep care and considerable discretion.

It is easy to miss the great strengths of Fallows' approach and supporting authority to students. The key characteristic of Ripon Hall was freedom, nowhere better explained than by John Giles:

> I first heard of Gordon Fallows from Howard Root, the Dean of Emmanuel College, Cambridge, when I asked him for advice about theological colleges. Ripon Hall proved to be one of the greatest blessings of my life. Under W.G.F.'s wise and supporting authority, the place was a second home and family for all its students . . . There was no model of an ideal of super-clergyman hovering in the background. Hence, guilt at failing to emulate some imagined priestly role model did not undermine the proper sense of the calling of the students. Secondly, never was there any hint of spiritual arm-twisting, moulding, or hidden moral pressure-to-conform in the influences placed on the students. In all this Ripon Hall stood in a tradition of reasonableness all of its own in comparison with other colleges, of whatever persuasion. Outwardly and formally they might have appeared to be exerting stronger influence on ordinands. But that of Ripon Hall was no less formative for teaching its students the essentials of religious freedom. Humanly speaking this freedom was rooted in Gordon Fallows' own big-hearted support for every student, and indeed his pride in them. There is no doubt he loved the job and he rejoiced in the proper responsibilities he carried for those in his care. With this was a deep respect for the faith that they held whatever form it might take or wherever it might come from. Understandably this created a strong underlying confidence and security within the college community. Gordon knew that if you got the people as right as they could be, and the necessary understanding of the work of the church in the world sorted out, God could do the rest. Not that he would put it in those words. One of his deepest and most characteristic convictions was that 'you should not put all your best goods into the shop window.' It was like John Keble's tract: 'Of Reserve in Communicating Religious Knowledge'. But to those who knew the faith that underlay his almost suave or urbane outward manner was no less real for being hidden away.
>
> Warmth was always evident. He emphasized the Parson as 'the Persona', a ministry to all, and you knew he had practised what he advised for others to follow. He stressed a sense of proportion as far as the Church in relation to the rest of society was concerned.

John Giles had a pioneering ministry as chaplain of the University of East Anglia, and eventually he went to Sheffield as Vicar of St Mark's, Broomhill. Fallows instituted him on 23 April 1979 and his sermon had four headings: Shared Ministry; Intellectual Ministry; a Ministry of Healing; a Ministry of you and to the People. Is that a summary of his understanding of the ordained ministry?

Fallows – suave and urbane? A number of students thought so, but suave is usually used pejoratively, whereas urbane catches Fallows correctly as civilized and courteous. There was a certain degree of Oxford snobbery about him, for he held all things Oxbridge in awe and all things London University where some students were doing Bachelor of Divinity degrees in somewhat less awe. Nevertheless Ripon Hall was a college which allowed students to explore disbelief, as well as belief; to work with an understanding of the death of God, the John Robinson era, Form Criticism and both to break down and rebuild faith and spirituality. There was no 'party line', no one being told what to believe or what not to believe.

During Fallows' years there were three significant changes in staff. In 1961 Michael C. Perry was appointed chaplain and librarian. He arrived with academic credentials, a former senior scholar of Trinity College, Cambridge with three Firsts (in both parts of the Natural Science Tripos and Part II of the Theological Tripos.) In 1963 A.M.G. Stephenson was appointed Vice-Principal in succession to J.F.B. Goodwin who became Editorial Secretary of World Christian Books, and A.O. Dyson was the new chaplain. Michael Perry went to SPCK as Chief Assistant in Home Publishing. There was very great rejoicing when the Hall's Treasurer of fifteen years, Ian Ramsey, became Bishop of Durham in 1966, although he remained active and interested as a Governor. The Ripon Hall Common Room presented him with two mitres.

In 1962 the college was slightly over-full with forty-seven students with an additional one the following year, the highest number ever. There were more students reading for a second degree at Ripon Hall than in any other English theological college. In 1963 after three years of planning and negotiating, work began on the extension to the buildings, providing a lecture hall, a library building, six additional student rooms, two small houses for staff, and a small extension to the chapel. On 23 July 1964 the new buildings were opened by the Chancellor of the University of Oxford, the Rt. Hon. Harold Macmillan M.P. In his address he recalled hearing Bishop Boyd Carpenter, the founder of Ripon Hall:

> preach when I was a boy at school, and I can remember well the impression made by his extraordinary powers of oratory, at a time when rhetoric, both lay and clerical, was still respectable . . . In my recent capacity (as Prime Minister) I had quite a lot to do with bishops and deans as well as with the clergy as a whole. For my side I have much enjoyed that association. I do not feel, as one of my predecessors complained when he said about the bishops, 'I believe they die just to spite me'. Over the course of a long life I have had many friends among clergy of a great variety of points of view and function, from army chaplains to parish priests, and one or two hunting parsons, who, happily, still survive . . . No doubt the men of this college will find in the world, as their predecessors found, the same confusion, the same doubts, the same antipathy, or perhaps even worse the same apathy towards the basic principles of Christianity

as have those in the past. This takes different forms in different ages, but the truth remains the same, and in this college the love of truth is the fundamental ideal of its founder and is still pursued by you.

Fallows encouraged and enjoyed the temporary residence of priests and students from other Churches; for example, two Greek Orthodox priests, a Roman Catholic priest, two German Lutheran theological students. They enriched the fellowship of the Hall. The college was also a venue in vacations for conferences, notably in 1964 the Church of England Council on Foreign Relations and the German Evangelical Church on 'Authority and the Church', chaired by the Bishop of Leicester, Ronald Williams.

In 1965 the Church at large was noticing a marked decrease in the number and quality of candidates especially among graduates, and Ripon Hall was not exempt from this trend. There was a wider context and in the Annual Report of the Governors, Fallows had this to say:

Theological education in general and theological colleges in particular are under fire from many quarters. We wonder sometimes whether those who fire the shots have recent first hand knowledge of the rich and varied life of a college. Certainly there is no room for complacency but we can be thankful for the vigour and vitality of the life of the Hall during the year under review. The future is uncertain and the general decline in numbers of ordinands is deeply disturbing. It may be that we can make a virtue of necessity and provide a longer course of training than is at present required of graduates who have not studied theology, and perhaps also open our doors to a few clergymen who might value extended refresher courses.

Between 1964 and 1966 there was in the Church of England a forty per cent decrease in the number of candidates recommended for training. Although Ripon Hall felt the draught the drop in numbers was only slight. Throughout his tenure Fallows took every advantage of the Hall set in the milieu of the academic distinction of the University of Oxford. He invited scholars of theology and other disciplines to deepen and widen the students' knowledge. In the Hall itself the Norman Sykes Society was founded where papers were read on the study of ecclesiastical history, and the Hastings Rashdall Society was revived as a focus for theological exploration. The Visitor, Lord Fisher of Lambeth, gave a memorable talk on 'The Size of the Clergyman's Job.' Students went to Taize and supported 'Shelter', the recently formed charity for the homeless.

Fallows was keen that all students should have some practical experience of parochial life, if only briefly. There were many initiatives in parishes within reach of the Hall and in 1965 during the Easter Vacation he and six students spent a week in the parish of Slyne-with-Hest in North Lancashire. Fallows was watchful of older men especially those married with children of school age who were faced with serious domestic and financial problems. It was decided to rearrange the terms – three terms of ten weeks instead of three terms of eight weeks and one of six weeks.

The year 1967 was a difficult one in the life of the college. There were six empty places. Although it was soon full again the national trend was unsustainable with existing arrangements. There were three hundred vacant places in English theological colleges. Consequently the Archbishops of Canterbury and York appointed a small Commission (Sir Bernard de Bunsen, the Rev. Professor H. Chadwick, and the Dean of Salisbury, Kenneth Haworth) to investigate the number, size and distribution of theological colleges. Their report appeared early in 1968, recommending the drastic reduction in the number of colleges from twenty-five to fourteen; the increase in size of colleges to between one hundred and one hundred and twenty students; the siting of colleges, in the main, in university centres, with two or three detached colleges for non-academic type courses. Fallows' initial reaction was:

> It is too early to comment on the destiny of this report but not too early to say that one of the tentative recommendations of the report, namely that Westcott House, Cambridge, should be merged with Ripon Hall on the Ripon Hall site is not likely to materialise as Westcott House is exploring other possibilities in Cambridge.

In 2007 there are eleven theological colleges and one of them is Ripon College, Cuddesdon!

Besides sporting activities at the Hall the students presented concerts and plays. There were dances. There was a televised 'Seeing and Believing' programme on 19 March 1961. Its theme was 'The Gospels for Today' written by Fallows assisted by A.O. Dyson, J.W. Bowker and singers from the Hall.

Fallows' personal life was possibly richer than at any other time of his ministry. Any pressures on his time and commitments were largely self-imposed. He did not have diocesan responsibilities although he had some central national work. The Allans were near neighbours on Boar's Hill. Allan senior had been at St Edmund Hall and the families became very close, not least because of the proximity in age of their respective children. Richard Allan, a son, has these recollections:

> Gordon officiated at both my wedding with Diana in London and Elspeth's wedding with Roger in Cumnor, near Oxford. Geoffrey was my best man, and his family and mine continued holidaying together in the Lake District over Easter over a period of twenty-five years.
>
> My initial memories of Gordon are of his officiating at Holy Communion at Easter and Christmas in Ripon Hall – what I would describe as an 'orthodox

no-frills' service, which very much accorded with my parents' preference and my own experience up to that time. This approach was borne out in his astute handling of our weddings where, thanks to his having grown to know the partners very well, his discretion and pragmatism in the face of some agnosticism were very much appreciated. Tolerance always seemed one of Gordon's special hallmarks, and made it difficult to place him on either wing of the Church. He was never evangelical or hearty, nor was he interested in pomp and pageantry; rather he came across as a warm and generous theologian, who also loved nothing more than retiring to his study and immersing himself in his books.

Naturally most of my contact with Gordon was when he was off duty. Ripon Hall had a range of facilities which he and Edna allowed the Allans to share in. There were the glorious grounds where we often walked, the College hall where the Fallows and Allan families held joint dances, the tennis court where he and Geoffrey performed in tandem against all-comers (he had a unique call, 'drop', for a ball played out), and the Principal's House where he and Edna entertained us on countless occasions, normally with the aid of a seemingly limitless supply of home-brewed beer. This was when I saw Gordon at his most relaxed, at home with his beloved wife and family (all called by their first initials – 'G', 'A' and 'D') enjoying hugely the simple things in life – conversation, beer and young company. He always seemed equally at ease with our generation as with his own, and I fancy he liked the presence of Ripon Hall students around him. Nevertheless his intellect was equally to the fore, and my father used to return on occasions from a guest-night at St Edmund Hall and reminisce on how well Gordon had held his own with the College fellows – he once described Gordon to me as 'generous, but very sound', and that certainly accords with the Gordon Fallows I knew.

An American, Edward E. Wendell, Jr. was another friend of Geoffrey Fallows and has vivid memories from Ripon Hall days and onwards to Pontefract and Sheffield. He refers to 'Bishop Fallows' and although his vivid recollections refer to later times they are recorded here:

Geoffrey's father had an engaging countenance. When he looked at you, spoke with you, and listened to you, you had the feeling that your existence was consuming his business. My contact with Bishop Fallows was as a friend of his son – I was one of those folks that kept turning up via the kitchen entrance. Time spent with Bishop Fallows was warm and fulfilling. He had a tremendous sense of how life could be. A trip to the local pub was always a part of the day's routine. Typically just before dinner, we would wend our way to the local. On the first evening of a visit to Sheffield in 1973, the appropriate time arrived, and a trip to the Travellers Rest, the nearest pub to Bishopscroft and a 'hangout' for the Fallows was arranged involving the Bishop, David (Geoffrey's younger brother), Mary, my wife, and myself. As we were driving to the pub, the Bishop turned to us in the back seat. 'I must ask you not to refer to me as "Bishop" in the pub. You see nobody knows I am the Bishop and were they to find out it would upset the relationship we have.' Our pint was indeed quaffed with the locals, and there was no hint that his identity (known by all) was known.

Dinner by Mrs Fallows, always a many coursed, culinary delight, was often preceded by some sort of physical activity. On the Sheffield trip, we went to the dales and had a vigorous walk. Conversation was lively, but the pace was livelier, and the trip to the pub and dinner thereafter were always well earned. On one occasion, on my own, when the Fallows were in Pontefract, the athletic event was to be squash, since a gift to the Diocese from an industrialist's widow had a squash court appended to it.

Mrs Fallows was an able brewmaster, and part of my anticipation of a visit with the Fallows included having some of her fine home brew. There was a competitor for the good liquid in the house and Mrs Fallows disclosed to me that for days prior to my visit she would have to hide the brew from the Bishop, lest there be none available on my arrival. On more than one occasion, I was met with a shaking head and the explanation that there were but one or two left as her hiding place had been discovered.

Edna Fallows had a highly deserved reputation as 'green fingers'. She may have regretted that she also became an able brewster.

The 1960s were a wonderfully productive period for theological college principals. They were to provide a number of prominent and notable leaders in the Church – an Archbishop of Canterbury (Robert Runcie of Cuddesdon), two Archbishops of York (Stuart Blanch of Rochester and John Habgood of Queen's, Birmingham), Bishops for Ely (Peter Walker of Westcott House), Norwich (Maurice Wood of Oak Hill), Derby (Cyril Bowles of Ridley Hall) and Gloucester (John Yates of Lichfield), and Deans of St Paul's (Alan Webster of Lincoln), and Worcester (Tom Baker of Wells).

And Gordon Fallows of Ripon Hall?

CHAPTER 7

Broad Churchman

THE MODERN CHURCHMEN'S UNION was founded in 1898 as a group of scholars, students and clergy who were convinced that the findings of historical and critical study in their application of the Bible – particularly to the New Testament – were in conflict with some traditional presentations of Christian doctrine and that a new approach was necessary. They considered that if the Church of England was to remain distinguished by sound learning, it was urgent that people should be free within the Church to view orthodox tradition in this new light. It was also the year when Ripon Hall at Ripon was founded by Bishop Boyd Carpenter; and Hastings Rashdall, Fellow and Tutor of New College, Oxford, published his *Doctrine and Development*. The following year Percy Gardner, Lincoln and Morton Professor of Archaeology at Oxford University, published his *Exploratio Evangelica*, A Survey of the Foundations of Christianity; William Ralph Inge, Fellow of Hertford College, Oxford, published his Bampton Lectures on *Christian Mysticism*; and James M. Wilson, Vicar of Rochdale and Archdeacon of Manchester, published his Hulsean Lectures *The Gospel of the Atonement*. In their differing ways these were foundation documents of modernism. In his biography of Dean Inge (1960) Adam Fox makes a potent observation:

> Modernism has never looked like becoming a widespread attitude in this country, much less has it created a party. But in the years through which the Dean presided over the Modern Churchmen's Union there began to be in religion more tolerance without indifference, more respect for science without loss of faith, more truth without alarm. This change was to be found largely among people who had never read a word of *The Modern Churchman*, but it was a team of Modernists who brought it about, and the effects are by no means fully worked out yet.

The Conferences of Modern Churchmen began in 1914. The most famous and disputatious conference came in 1921 at Girton College, Cambridge, with its subject 'Christ and the Creeds.' Of the seventeen speakers at the seven-day conference the papers of Hastings Rashdall, J.F. Bethune-Baker (Lady Margaret Professor of Divinity at Cambridge), and H.D.A. Major were regarded as notorious and were widely reported in the press. It was not long before condemnation from pulpits and in print appeared not merely, as anticipated, from defenders of the faith but also from a number of modernist critics. Major was accused of heresy. There was a good outcome, when the Archbishops of Canterbury and York appointed a Commission on Doctrine in the Church of England in 1922.

Fallows mixed with the great 'modern churchmen' of his time, shared platforms with fellow speakers at a number of annual conferences. He was a member of the M.C.U. Council from his Preston years alongside, for example, A.C. Boquet, J.S. Bezzant, J.S. Boys-Smith, Marcus Knight, R.H. Preston, Ian T. Ramsey, Norman Sykes, Denys Whiteley and T.J. Wood. All this is impressive and Fallows enjoyed mixing with these people even if he could not match their scholarship. However, it was not from these living luminaries that Fallows drew greatest strength. The well down which he dropped his bucket for the intellectual water of life was not twentieth-century modernism, The seeds of Fallows' inlook and outlook were germinated in the nineteenth-century 'broad' church. He may have left comparatively little of a written legacy but there are traces everywhere of the roots of his thinking and churchmanship in the works of broad church leaders. They reveal most of where and for what he stood in the Church of England. Few of the major figures are recognisable as ecclesiastical or 'churchy'.

Samuel Taylor Coleridge (1772–1834), poet and critic, spoke of the need for a spiritual interpretation of life. His conviction that Christianity is primarily ethical led him to believe in the possibility of a unification of Christendom on a wide basis of common tenets; and earned him the title of 'Father of the Broad Church Movement'.

Thomas Arnold (1795–1842), was a Fellow of Oriel College, Oxford and Headmaster of Rugby School. His goal was to educate the sons of middle-class parents and to reform the school by introducing mathematics, modern history and modern languages, and by instituting the form system and appointing prefects. Arnold believed in the essential unity of the secular and the religious, of Church and State, and in the universal priesthood of the laity. His ecclesiastical ideals were epitomised in his *Principles of Church Reform* (1833). He was the author of six volumes of sermons. Fallows called him 'a prophet for today.' (John) Frederick Denison Maurice (1805–1872), the son of a Unitarian minister, continued as a Dissenter at Cambridge, leaving without a degree when he began a literary career in London. Influenced by Coleridge he was ordained in the Church of England and was successively chaplain of Guy's Hospital, of Lincoln's Inn, Professor of Literature, then of Theology at King's College, London. The publication in 1853 of his 'Theological Essays' dealing with the atonement and eternal life lost him his professorship, but in 1866 he was appointed Professor of Moral Philosophy at Cambridge. With Thomas Hughes and Charles Kingsley he formed the Movement of Christian Socialism in 1848. His most enduring book was *The Kingdom of Christ,* or

14. St. John the Evangelist, Preston Parish Church

15. High Sheriff's chaplain with Assize judge, Mr Justice Sellers, Liverpool 1947

16. *The 26-room vicarage (until October 1949) at East Cliff House, Preston*

17. *Gaitered; the new Archdeacon tries his skills at the parish garden party*

18. The Sermon on the Mount – mural painting on the blank west wall of Preston Parish Church, now The Minster, by Hans Feibusch – June 1956

for Gordon
from Hans
22nd Nov 1956.

19. Drawing – for Gordon from Hans Feibusch, 22 May 1956

20. Ripon Hall: the new buildings – Civic Trust Award 1964

21. The Ripon Hall students (including the first four women admitted to a theological college) summer 1968; with Gordon Fallows, Principal; Alan Stephenson, Vice-Principal, and Tony Dyson, Chaplain

22. After tennis with elder son, Geoffrey

*23. Consecration at Wakefield Cathedral, St Barnabas Day, 11 June 1968
with Archbishop Donald Coggan*

24. Fallows' family at his Consecration − L. to R. younger son, David; son-in-law, Richard Orchard; daughter, Angela Orchard; Gordon and Edna Fallows; elder son, Geoffrey and daughter-in-law, Carolyn Littler (Angela died of cancer in 1978; Gordon in 1979; David in 1982; Carolyn in 2000)

25. Brothers-in-law Maurice Millard and Eric Woodend; sisters, Joyce Woodend and Winnie Millard; Fallows' mother; sister-in-law, Hilda and brother Jack Fallows

26. *Sheffield Cathedral*

Hints to a Quaker concerning the Principle, Constitution and Ordinances of the Catholic Church (1838). Benjamin Jowett (1817–1893), variously Master of Balliol, Regius Professor of Greek, and Vice-Chancellor of Oxford University, was 'broad church'. For his contribution *On the Interpretation of Scripture in Essays and Reviews* (1860) he was tried but acquitted by the Vice-Chancellor's court. Thereafter he ceased to write on theological questions. Arthur Penrhyn Stanley (1815–1881) was Canon of Canterbury, Professor of Ecclesiastical History at Oxford and Dean of Westminster. He advocated toleration for both Tractarian and liberal extremes. His aim was to make Westminster Abbey a national shrine for all, irrespective of dogmatic creed. Archibald Campbell Tait (1811–1882) Dean of Carlisle, Bishop of London and Archbishop of Canterbury was also influential; 'The Tracts for the Times' began as Tait took his degree, and from that time he had to measure two contending religious-intellectual forces, the Catholic and Liberal Movements. Against the Catholic Revival he sternly set his face. When Newman wrote *Tract 90 (Remarks on certain Passages in the Thirty-nine Articles)* in 1841 Tait, then Fellow and Senior Tutor of Balliol College, was one of four Oxford tutors who publicly protested against it. With liberalism and 'broad church' Tait's relations were closer. He was selected to succeed Thomas Arnold at Rugby, and he had first-hand acquaintance with Liberal Protestantism in Germany. He hoped to see 'a deeply religious Liberal party' formed in the Church of England, but to an extent his hopes were disappointed by younger liberals who, unlike Maurice, lacked piety. As archbishop he had but one aim, to strengthen the hold of the nation upon the eternal verities of the faith. *The Dangers and Safeguards of Modern Theology* (1861) and *Harmony of Revelation* (1864) were two of his published works.

The greatest glory of the Church of England is its comprehensiveness. That was Fallows' unerring conviction. It may be pulled or pushed, to or by, its narrow-thinking adherents towards extremes but they are not representative of its *via media*. There is a doctrinal and clerical fundamentalism as certain as a biblical one. Fundamentalists cling to dogma and unravelled certainties. They measure their influence by decibel rather than by dialectic. Comprehensiveness is not an untroubled path to follow. Its journey is demanding. Stability is constantly a stumbling block as each age brings fresh insights and consequent challenges. Part of the lessons in Fallows' lifetime was to be fully aware of what was happening without losing perspective or loosening moorings. To many onlookers the Church of England seemed to be adrift, like a rudderless derelict on an uncharted sea, where precedents were valueless, and principles hard to disentangle and apply.

Under scrutiny it is clear that Fallows was more a 'broad 'churchman than a 'modernist' one. Modernism as it was often perceived and sometimes accurately portrayed from the 1960s onward could be flighty, ready to jettison the articles of the Christian faith in order to suit the successive fashions of modern teaching. The *dernier cri* of intellectual modishness was not to be mistaken for the last word of truth. For Fallows it meant rather a continual re-presentation of the spiritual truths which are the essence of the Christian gospel, in such guise and under such forms as would bring its message home to the minds whom modern thinking might otherwise bemuse. It meant learning to emphasise and expound the old facts – of the reality of God, of man's place as the child of God, as Christ as the Word of God, and the Church as the focus of His Spirit – in such wise as to commend them to the mind of the present generation. For such work the guiding inspiration for Fallows was less a curiosity for new theology, more a pastoral desire to make truth come home to the souls of people in parish, theological college, and diocese. And the conviction which governed was that truth is always justified of its faithful disciples. Truth is one. But it has not only many facets but many ways of presentation. As a teacher Fallows knew the need for constant restatement in order to ensure that the truth which he knew should be fairly set out so as to get over unperverted to those to whom he was speaking, lecturing and preaching.

Views of Fallows' preaching vary from lukewarm to effective. But there was always something sufficiently digestible and nourishing for people to take away, to think about. Thoughtfulness rather than provocation motivated him. He was in little danger of falling into either of the different yet allied errors which threaten a preacher. On the one hand, he did not think meanly of his office; on the other hand, he did not exaggerate the value of his personal contribution to the ministry of preaching. Straining to reach the highest conceivable standard, he never acquiesced in any version of duty less than the best of which he was capable. Neither did he sink to the sham humility which excuses the preacher's ignorance or indolence by the plea that in conversion God must be all in all. The question for the honest preacher's conscience is not how little use he may be, but how much he ought to be, when God is working through and with him. This will be the spur of unceasing effort – not pride, or ambition, or professional zeal, but with the conviction that 'it is required in stewards that a man be found faithful.'

Fallows was a great reader of other people's sermons, as his bookshelves bore witness. To whom was he drawn? Did any of the nineteenth-century preachers speak to his condition and that of the mid-twentieth century? He read the sermons that had them rolling in the aisles in Spurgeon's Tabernacle or bringing a gentle tear to the eyes of the more decorous congregation of St Mary the Virgin, Oxford, during Newman's incumbency – the sermons that drew thousands to St Paul's when Liddon was Canon-in-residence – do not excite or even interest the congregations of today. And yet there is one exception – one nineteenth-century preacher whose words still ring a bell, whose sermons can still be read with profit and inspiration. He is Frederick William Robertson (1816–1853) usually referred to as 'Robertson of Brighton.'

Fallows was entranced and magnetised by Robertson. He collected everything published by and about him, travelled to read unpublished material held in libraries and had access to his diaries. He had begun assembling material for a biography and written preliminary notes. Why Robertson? At first and second glance the reason is illusory. Robertson started with no special advantages of birth or wealth; he gained none of the academic distinctions which sometimes take their place; he won the patronage of no great men and secured the public interest by no great book; he received no preferment; he formed no party; he never preached to the University either in Oxford or in Cambridge; he was never invited to occupy the pulpit of Westminster or St Paul's; he never preached at Court; no bishop complimented him with a chaplaincy; the only honorific position he ever held was that of High Sheriff's chaplain; he was the recipient of no honorary degree. Born into a military family he had an unusually varied education: Beverley Grammar School, Tours, the New Edinburgh Academy, Edinburgh University, and Brasenose College, Oxford. Ordained in 1840, and married the following year, he served in a poor Winchester parish, living an ascetic life. After thirteen months he had a breakdown and went to the Continent for recuperation. Returning to England he went to that paradise of evangelical churchmanship, Cheltenham, as curate of Christ Church. In 1846 he had another and more severe breakdown and went to the Austrian Tyrol, then to Heidelberg where the English colony requested him to be their regular pastor. By this time he had thrown off the tight shackles of evangelicalism and on 15 August 1847 became Minister of Holy Trinity, a proprietary chapel in Brighton where this tall, spare and active cleric remained until 15 August 1853 when he died of a brain haemorrhage. He was thirty-seven!

Robertson's clerical career failed as a career through some defects of his qualities. His nature shrank from the requirements of social life. Oxford was too 'donnish' for his liking and his friendships were few. In his home life he was what those who talk biblically described as unequally yoked. Brought up as an evangelical he eventually found himself mentally and theologically uncomfortable in the Cheltenham milieu. But what his personality could not do because of its weaknesses – a nervous vehemence, a portentous lack of humour, an inability to suffer fools – his Brighton preaching easily accomplished. His sermons made him universal, a power over all parties because he was entirely independent. At Trinity Chapel every seat was occupied, many stood and some sat on the floor. Such was his reputation that Gladstone and

Lord Shaftesbury journeyed to Brighton on Saturday to sit under Robertson on Sunday. Robertson was a wonder and a whirlwind. Yet he had known abasement and scorching inner travail. Fallows was struck by Robertson's self-candour and doubly underlined a passage of his writings:

> It is an awful moment when the soul begins to find that the props on which it has blindly rested so long are, many of them, rotten, and begins to suspect them all; when it begins to feel the nothingness of many of the traditional opinions which have been received with implicit confidence and in that horrible insecurity begins also to doubt whether there be anything to be believed at all. It is an awful hour – let him who has passed through it say how awful – when this life has lost its meaning, and seems shrivelled into a span; when the grave appears to be the end of all, human goodness nothing but a name, and the sky above this universe a dead expanse, black with the void from which God Himself has disappeared. In that fearful loneliness of spirit, when those who should have been his friends and counsellors only frown upon his misgivings, and profanely bid him stifle doubts, which for aught he knows may arise from the fountain of truth itself; to extinguish, as a glare from hell that which for aught he knows may be light from heaven, and everything seemed wrapped in hideous uncertainty, I know but one way in which a man may come forth from his agony scatheless; it is by holding fast to those things which are certain still – the grand simple landmarks of morality. In the darkest hour through which a human soul can pass, whatever else is doubtful, this at least is certain. If there be no God, and no future state, yet, even though, it is better to be generous than selfish, better to be chaste than licentious, better to be true than false, better to be brave than to be a coward. Blessed beyond all earthly blessedness is the man who, in the tempestuous darkness of the soul, has dared to hold fast to these venerable landmarks. Thrice blessed is he who – when all is drear and cheerless within and without, when his teachers terrify him, and his friends shrink from him – has obstinately clung to moral good. Thrice blessed, because this night shall pass into clear, bright day. I appeal to the recollection of any man who has passed through that hour of agony, and stood upon the rock at last, the surges stilled below him and the last cloud drifted from the sky above, with a faith, and hope, and trust no longer traditional, but of his own – a trust which neither earth nor hell shall shake thenceforth for ever.

One wonders if Gordon Fallows found a kind of solace in these words. We do not know if Fallows had spasmodic deep doubts of faith which he could not share. We do know that he had breakdowns in health, underwent crippling surgery, suffering from Parkinson's Disease and malignant cancer, and experienced impenetrable grief following the death of a daughter.

There are six footnotes to the Robertson story. First, Robertson's reputation was almost entirely posthumous. In his lifetime he published only one sermon, but after his death five volumes of sermons were published and a considerable number, enough for two volumes, were mislaid on a railway platform and despite the offer of reward were not recovered. The published sermons sold in vast numbers and the publication in 1865 of Stopford Brooke's *Life and Letters of F.W. Robertson* established a permanent and abiding reputation. The centenary of his birth in 1916 was much celebrated by admirers and critics alike. Secondly, Robertson combined originality, piety, freedom of thought and warmth of love. His repeated admonition was, 'Feel God, do His will, till the absolute Imperative within you speaks, as with a living voice, Thou shalt and Thou shalt not, and then you do not think, you know there is God.' Thirdly, there was his mesmeric language and cogent lucidity, sometimes colloquial, always scriptural and compelling. He also preached to the times, for example, on the opening of the Crystal Palace on a Sunday afternoon and the first Sunday mail trains to run out of Brighton inspired two outstanding sermons on Sabbath observance. In 1852, when the policy of Napoleon III aroused much alarm in England, Robertson said, 'I am still in many cases for the Christian virtue of an English oak stick, with an English hand to lay it on, and show mercy when you have done justice.' Fourthly, is Robertson's self-deflating view on preaching. 'Sermons are crutches. I believe the worst things for spiritual health that were ever invented.' Fifthly, thousands of people in Brighton crowded the streets on the occasion of Robertson's funeral. Among them was his friend and confidante, Lady Byron, the poet's widow, who discarded her carriage, considering herself not worthy even to walk behind the hearse of one so gifted and holy.

There is a sixth footnote with a tantalizing question mark: if Fallows had lived would he have completed and published an unexpurgated biography based on all the information he had researched and received? In one of Robertson's diaries there are a number of entries in code. Fallows sent them to his friend John Bowker, Professor of Religious Studies at Lancaster University, who wrote to this biographer:

> Gordon passed on to me the diary in the hope that I would be able to decode it – which indeed I did. Having read the contents, Gordon decided not to bring it to public attention. In my view it was relatively mild (relative at least to our own times), but it would have affected the usual estimate of him.

The entries refer to a romantically passionate infatuation with another woman.

Fallows' personal library was large and extensive. A morning with his books was time well spent. It is there that his mind was nourished and stretched, his vocabulary and style enhanced and formed. It is regrettable that there is only one published book carrying his name: *Mandell Creighton and the English Church* (1964). There is, however, another literary legacy where the lucidity of his mind and fluency of his pen are accompanied by a cogent critical appraisal of issues, and expressed with an unexpected boldness, passion and wit. In an earlier age his contributions to *The Modern Churchman* – papers, sermons, reviews – would have found a more permanent place between hard covers. If anyone wishes to examine and appreciate Fallows' progress they will find his forthright views expressed in this journal. In particular there are the papers read at Modern Churchmen's Union Conferences:

1943, 26–29 July, Somerville College, Oxford. Overall theme – The National Church and National Life. Fallows: 'National Christian Reunion.'

1947, 22–27 September, Westfield College, London. Overall theme – Problems of Christian Faith and Practice. Fallows: 'Church Administration.'

1951, 13–17 August, Somerville College, Oxford. Overall theme – The Church: Past, Present and Future. Fallows: 'Authority and Discipline in the Church.'

1954, 6–10 September, Westfield College, London. Overall theme - Christian Living in Modern Society. Fallows: 'Christian Life in the Modern World.'

1960, 2–6 August, Newnham College, Cambridge. Overall theme – Jesus Christ, His World and Ours. Fallows: 'The Anglican Tradition of Sound Learning.'

Also published in the journal was a Conference sermon preached by Fallows on 'Contemporary Christianity,' and the Annual Sermon of the M.C.U. preached at St Margaret's, Lothbury, London with the title 'The Aunt Sally of Christendom.' Substantial articles in the journal are likewise worthy of mention: 'The Jubilee of Phillips Brooks (1835–1893),' 'The Blinkered Saint of the Oxford Movement – John Keble,' 'Thomas Arnold: A Prophet for Today; Reflections on the Paul Report.' Any collection should also include Fallows' Thomas More annual sermon at Chelsea Old Church 1978 (separately published); 'The Church of England and the Free Churches', an Address delivered to the Society for the Study of Religions (published in *Religions* July 1945); and 'The Wesleys and Methodism,' his sermon preached during the Methodist Annual Conference in 1952.

On 'National Christian Union' (*The Modern Churchman* September, 1943) this is what Fallows had to say:

> Centuries of isolation and divergent development have created a marked difference in the ethos of the Anglican and Free Church world. The chasuble and the frock coat may belong to the same sartorial family, but there are deep-seated psychological repulsions on both sides. Mutual charity, increasing familiarity one with another and loyalty to the Spirit of Jesus Christ will break down the barriers. The greatest enemy of national reunion is the narrow and exclusive sacerdotalism of a section of our own Church. For practical reasons the Church must draw a line somewhere, but when she forgets the line is arbitrarily

drawn disastrous results follow. A wise maxim would be, it is right sometimes to exclude but when in doubt include. 'He that cometh unto me I will in no wise cast out.' In every period of Church history, however, and not least in our own, the cry has gone up in one form or another, 'Except ye be circumcised after the custom of Moses, ye cannot be saved.' Montanists and Novationists in the early Church, and Puritans in the sixteenth century, have stood for this rigidly exclusive principle. In the early period the Roman Church, in the sixteenth century the Anglican Church, stood for the more liberal interpretation of the principle exclusion. Today the parties have changed sides. Exclusion has become the war cry of the Ultra-Montane Roman and the extreme Anglo-Catholic section of the Church of England, while the sons of the Puritan stand for the catholic principle of inclusion. The struggle is the age-long one between prophet and priest. Their functions should be mutually complementary and not exclusive. They can be combined when the liberal and inclusive spirit prevails. National Christian reunion today can only be achieved as the liberal and inclusive spirit prevails over the exclusive and rigorist interpretation of Church order. We believe that the true spirit of the Church of England is liberal and inclusive, and we have never doubted that in being so she is loyal to the Spirit of Jesus Christ.

A crucial question and one most fruitful of dissension in the problem of reunion is the question of the ministry. Anglicans are wise in advocating the acceptance of the historic episcopacy in any United Church of the future. We make reunion impossible, however, when we assert the Apostolic Succession in the form in which it is taught by Anglo-Catholics. To assert that one form of church order is of divine appointment and necessary to the nature of the Church is to draw a conclusion which neither the Scriptures, nor history, nor experience will justify. Genevan, Roman and Anglo-Roman spectacles fog rather than clarify and should not be used in the reading of the New Testament and early Church history.

The recognition of non-episcopal ministries has never been withdrawn. The Church of England has its own rules for ordination but has never condemned non-episcopal orders. A necessary step in the direction of home reunion would be the mutual and unequivocal recognition of orders. Reunion can only proceed between equals and not between disparate partners ... We liberal Churchmen hold that the objective of Christian union will be reached the more quickly if there is a sharing of a common Christian experience in the ministry of the word and a fellowship in the sacrament of the Holy Communion. We plead for a free pulpit and an open altar, not in the spirit of licence or anarchy, but because the claims of Christian fellowship make such a policy for us imperative ... Hazlitt in one of his essays writes of a discriminating friend: 'It always struck me as a singular proof of good taste, good sense, and liberal thinking in an old friend who had Paine's Rights of Man and Burke's Reflections on the French Revolution bound up in one volume, and who said that, both together, they made a very good book.' So might it be with the Churches if the treasuries of their thought and history and devotion could be bound up in one volume. We for our part could bring among other things that delicate blending of law and liberty, of order and freedom, which is one of our most priceless treasures. There is a real danger of passing into an ecclesiastical ice-age if some of the forces now impeding Christian union should gain control. Twenty-three years have passed since the bishops of the Anglican Communion addressed their appeal (in 1920) to 'All Christian people.' The time is now surely ripe for action, for a scheme of Christian union at home, bold and large, commensurate both with the peril and the opportunity of these days.

In his 1945 Address to the Society for the Study of Religions, Fallows concluded:

The Anglican and Free Church traditions have made important contributions to English society, the one established, episcopal, and with its ordered liturgy in the Book of Common Prayer; the other with its free worship, freedom from state control, and its contribution to the development of democratic institutions. The recovery of unity can only be found in a synthesis which does full justice to the truth represented in every tradition; which achieves an ordered liberty, a nice balance between adventurous freedom and unifying order, a fusion of Catholic and Protestant principles for the achievement of a true Catholicity.

Fallows would lament and despair that more than sixty years on his plea for a moderate, liberal and inclusive spirit has not prevailed.

At the Thirtieth Annual Conference of Modern Churchmen in 1947 Fallows' two main submissions of his paper were (1) that Church Administration, following the prevailing fashion, is becoming over-centralized, uniform and bureaucratic and (2) that it is slowly but surely transforming the character of the Church of England from being the focus of the religious life of the nation to becoming an exclusive denomination. Centralization, uniformity and bureaucracy were the watchwords of modern secular organization.

The State's interest in and control of new and ever-expanding fields of social activity and human welfare necessitate an enlarging of the machinery of government. This may be inevitable to achieve a more equitable and better-planned society though there may well come a time when the loss outweighs the gain. One clear indication of this silent transformation of English society is the manner in which Whitehall is gradually ousting local government authorities as the real centre of administration. Local Government is gradually being reduced to a rubber-stamp status for the detailed application of a policy created, planned, and directed from above. The infinite variety and diversity which characterized the older system is giving place to a more uniform pattern. It cannot be denied that there are great potential benefits inherent in this change, and it is our hope and belief that the body politic will find its own characteristically English solution to this dilemma. Meanwhile there is a similar development taking place in the Administration of the Church of England. Increasingly its life is being controlled on a national, provincial and diocesan basis. Rules and regulations are made from above – with the very best intentions – and imposed on the parishes as a uniform pattern. Local parochial responsibility and the independence and status of the pastoral office are being openly assailed. The recent Diocesan Education Committee's Measure which prevents a body of parochial school managers determining the future of the parish school without the approval of the Diocesan Education Committee is a clear instance of this tendency. The attempt of the Houses of Convocation to abolish the independence and pastoral responsibility of the parochial clergy in the administration of the Marriage Law of the Church of England is a further straw which indicates the direction of the prevailing wind. Furthermore, there is a constant succession of national and diocesan appeals for larger and larger sums of money which an over-burdened and harassed vicar is expected to lay before an impecunious parochial church council, and he and they are regarded as ruffians, rascals and traitors, lacking in a corporate sense of the Church if they do not mutely and obediently respond.

'One of the most serious consequences of this development in the machinery and organisation of the Church is the tremendous burden which it imposes on the bishops as the chief officers of the Church.'

Fallows recognised the achievements of the Church Assembly, with over sixty measures having received the Royal Assent since its inception. However:

The disquiet which is felt about it arises from the unrepresentative character of the House of Clergy and still more of the House of Laity. 'Its membership' said Dick Sheppard, 'resembles nothing so much as the House of Commons before the passing of the Reform Bill'. The House of Clergy is over-weighted with dignitaries and the House of Laity with those whom we dub, in charitable moments, the ecclesiastically-minded laity. The significance of this for our present purpose is that the Assembly has failed to arrest the growth of bureaucracy and officialdom but has on the contrary promoted this expensive and authoritarian system of administration. In a notable sermon on the Church Assembly, preached before the University of Cambridge in 1931, Professor Ratcliff uttered words which are worth recalling: 'Beneath the cover of an apparently democratic institution the ecclesiastical authorities are pursuing a policy the reverse of democratic. Under the aegis of liberty liberties are being suppressed. What was to have been the megaphone of the church has become the microphone of its officials. What at the beginning was said to be only a change in the machinery of government is proving to be a change in the method of government. Whether or not the Assembly accepts the extreme interpretation of the bishop's function and office, the trend of its legislative effort is set in that direction, and its measures give effective expression to the theory. By means of its measures the Church Assembly is transforming the Church of England into a federation of petty monarchies.'

The Church Assembly as it is at present established is quite inadequate to sustain the Church of England as a national Church. Many of its members, no doubt, are not concerned to maintain the national character of the Church. As matters stand today the Church is governed to all intents and purposes by clerics. It has failed to find an adequate role for the layman such as has been wisely afforded to him in the Free Churches. The balance of power in the administration of the Church of England will not be adjusted until this failure is remedied.

If the evils of centralisation and bureaucracy form one of the greatest administrative problems confronting the Church of England to-day, an equally grave sign of the times is the tendency and openly advocated policy of narrowing the bounds of the Church so that it may be more clearly divided from the nation. It is a policy of exclusiveness rather than of inclusiveness, of rigidity and uniformity rather than of charity and comprehensiveness. The advocates of such a policy seek, wittingly or unwittingly, what the late Canon Streeter once called 'a nice tidy smooth running little church' whose privileges and pastoral ministrations would be confined to those who fulfilled certain obligations.

As a broad and liberal churchman Fallows had what appeared to be almost revolutionary thoughts! He would take up the cudgels to keep the Church of England, in Creighton's words 'a humane institution.' As we discern the tendencies at work in the life of the Church of England today it is not, we believe, too alarming to say that her charity no less than her liberalism is at stake. 'Prepare for conflict' was on his banner. It had the flavour of the Life and Liberty Movement which led to the 1920 Enabling Act which in turn led to the formation of the National Assembly of the Church of England. But his motives were different:

In the last resort we engage in it not because we are led thereto by considerations of history. Not because our estimate of the national character dictates such a course, not because by nature we are liberal in temper and tolerant in judgement, but because we believe we are impelled by obedience to the mind and spirit of Jesus Christ. 'And He came forth and saw a great multitude and He had compassion on them because they were as sheep not having a shepherd.' It is only as we learn His compassion that we shall do His will.

This chapter has delineated some of the internal affairs of the Church of England which deeply concerned Fallows. As a broad churchman he desired that liberalism should triumph. If it did, surely reasonableness would commend the Church to the English people. He was too sensible and wise to prophesy such a triumph. But there was always the historian in him who could not forget that Christianity arose in a decaying civilization and flourished as the decay grew worse.

CHAPTER 8

Pomfret

CONSPIRACY, INFAMY, TREACHERY and execution litter the history of Pontefract. To Shakespeare it was 'bloody Pomfret'. Its late twelfth-century castle housed Richard II (1367–1400) in his latter days – a cold, dank, miserable waiting room for death for a monarch who had put down the Peasants' Revolt in 1381. James I of Scotland (1394–1437), a strong but unpopular king was imprisoned in the castle as was Charles, Duc d'Orléans (1391–1465) after he was taken prisoner at Agincourt (1415) until ransomed. Ownership of the castle was no guarantee of safety. One owner, Thomas Earl of Lancaster was brought home in chains after the Battle of Boroughbridge in 1322, found guilty of treason and beheaded. It was a familar place for executions in the Wars of the Roses.

In the second Civil War the castle was a Royalist stronghold. When the 'New' Model Army defeated the Scots and the Royalists, Pontefract surrendered in 1648 and the townspeople petitioned that the castle be pulled down. With no planning laws to be navigated or circumvented the castle was in ruin within ten weeks, as it remains today. Yet there remains a smattering of history and a melancholic atmosphere on the site.

There are two churches in Pontefract. All Saints stood immediately below the castle. Badly damaged in the Civil War it was left as it foundered until its partial restoration in 1838 and further enhancement in the twentieth century, notably by George Pace in 1967. The fourteenth-century St Giles Church became the parish church of Pontefract in 1789. The town has many eighteenth- and nineteenth-century buildings of note including a 1734 butter cross, a round-arched, hipped-roof arcaded stone shelter; town hall of 1785, and the Red Lion Hotel remodelled in 1776 by Robert Adam.

However, it is not for its historic interest and importance that Pontefract is widely known. Liquorice is inseparable from the town's name. The famous Pontefract Cakes date from 1760. They were not the product of a money-grubbing entrepreneur. George Dunhill was a local chemist who was aware of the medicinal properties of liquorice. The Romans chewed the sweet root and cakes of liquorice made for medicinal purposes. George Dunhill added sugar and production of today's Pomfret or Pontefract cakes began and thenceforward flourished.

These few facts are given as flavour of the town of 25,000 people which also gave its name to the Suffragan Bishopric of Pontefract in 1933. The

Diocese of Wakefield was founded in 1888 and by 1968 had a population of one million people. It is divided into two archdeaconries, Halifax and Pontefract with 221 benefices and approximately 300 parochial clergy. The archdeaconry of Halifax includes the towns of Huddersfield, Brighouse and Elland; and Pontefract includes Wakefield, Dewsbury, Batley and Barnsley.

History is not a straight line. Fallows knew from his own researches that people are interconnected and intertwined. There are those who do not appear to have any obvious relationship that are crucial in the fortunes and misfortunes of one's life. We trace Fallows' indirect connection with Pontefract, and thus Sheffield, from 1949 with the surprise appointment of forty-four year old Roger Plumpton Wilson, Archdeacon of Nottingham and Vicar of Radcliffe-on-Trent, as Bishop of Wakefield. It represented Prime Minister Clement Attlee's preference for young and non-specialist bishops.

The immediate impression of Roger Wilson was of a 6ft. 1ins. athletic person whose gaitered countenance emphasised his height. And – keen eyes, youthful face, quick speech, active. No partisan, he made impressions rather than impact or ripples when he arrived. Although Yorkshire folk appreciated his friendliness and a young family was refreshing – children aged two, six and eleven – it cannot be said that there developed any widespread natural rapport between bishop and clergy particularly in the Anglo-Catholic mining parishes in the Pontefract archdeaconry where he was respected rather than admired or loved. He had two immediate appointments to make. The Bishop of Pontefract, Tom Longworth, was translated to Hereford. In his place Wilson appointed the safe, steady and pastoral Arthur Harold Morris, Archdeacon of Halifax, a man with an uncomplicated temperament, a capacity for listening and friendship and for whom hard work was welcome.

This left a vacancy for an Archdeacon of Halifax, the consequences of which will affect Fallows. It is important to appreciate the reasons for what seemed Roger Wilson's reckless initiative in approaching his close friend Eric Treacy, then Rector of Keighley in the Bradford diocese. There are some similarities of tasks and wide discrepancies of character between Treacy at Halifax and Fallows at Preston. Wilson's own reflections, provided to this episcopographer, are pertinent:

> In my first year as a bishop, the prospect of having Eric's companionship was almost more than I dared hope for. But there were difficulties. The Archdeaconry consisted of two large deaneries Halifax and Huddersfield, each comprising some 45 parishes, and the previous archdeacon had held the post with a Cathedral Canonry and no parochial commitment. This left him rather in the air. For the intense local patriotism of West Riding towns meant that nobody, yes, nobody counted for much ecclesiastically in Halifax and Huddersfield but their own vicars. This kind of situation would not have suited Eric,

who was accustomed to his own area of command and already had a big responsibility at Keighley. However a vacancy at Halifax Parish Church which the Crown was prepared to offer him, altered the scene.

It meant a colossal threefold task, when the archdeaconry was attached. Apart from his own commitments in Halifax, the Vicar of Halifax was inevitably in charge of an immense deanery, in churchmanship ranging from one end of the spectrum to the other. At this time the Church still suffered grievously from sectarian loyalties, while ecumenism was in its infancy; the rural dean found himself at the centre of much crossfire. Moreover out of this large deanery some 27 parishes were in the gift of the Vicar of Halifax. This gave him special links; but it also exacted long labours over the problem of patronage. In the aftermath of war the Church was suffering from an almost total dearth of curates, and therefore of potential incumbents, and the outward appearance of West Riding parishes (how different within!) deterred many who were unfamiliar with this part of industrial England.

The Vicar of Halifax was a persona in the best tradition of the Church of England, a trusted friend and figure-head in that active community. Eric supremely so. Halifax gave him a pulpit. Eric had a real gift of communication, alike in the spoken and the written word. He was never an academic unwinding a long skein of argument; he was a sharpshooter, quick on the draw. When he spoke he was forthright in manner, uncomplicated in substance, and contemporary in language. No doubt this meant that he was often not deep, but his punches got home. Speaking or preaching he made an impression.

As an archdeacon he had to turn his head to anything in the diocese, and represent an authority not his own. A good deal of this was a heavy addition to an already heavy programme. Sometimes he did fall asleep in the committee room or on the platform as he did in his arm chair at home, and with the same lack of inhibition. But the sheer routine of Boards and Committees, dilapidations, schools, finance, readers and the like was cheerfully discharged. He was too human to like much of this. Can't you spare me from . . . he would exclaim, he never stops talking! He could not be spared, but I am bound to say that however critical he was of colleagues who were pompous or cheap or voluble or slovenly, he always stood by his men when they said they were in need. Of course his real contribution to the diocese, as Archdeacon, lay in the originality and drive which he brought to its counsels and not least its Bishop.

In 1954 Harold Morris was appointed Bishop of St Edmundsbury and Ipswich so Roger Wilson was faced with a vital appointment at a moment of increasing advance in the diocese. In five years Treacy's impact had been massive and already he felt the pull towards some further responsibility and exercise of power. Was he disappointed when Wilson did not ask him to succeed Morris as Bishop Suffragan of Pontefract? The answer is in the affirmative and this is what Wilson says:

There were good reasons for not asking Eric to succeed Harold Morris, in no way derogatory of him. He had a full scale job, to which he had come recently and as Pontefract he would be giving up that part of his ministry which touched him most closely, Halifax. Besides, I hoped he would be called somewhere in due course and didn't want this step to get in the way. For in any case (as in fact became evident) he wasn't really cut out to be a No 2, dependent for his authority and his tasks on a No 1 with no specific episcope of his own. In fact he wasn't happy as a suffragan.

Wilson chose George William Clarkson, Vicar of Newark-on-Trent for Pontefract. He was a Yorkshireman, educated at Mexborough Grammar School, leaving for employment as a railway cleric. In 1915, aged seventeen, he enlisted with the Grenadier Guards. On demobilisation he went to test his vocation for holy orders at Knutsford Test School under Frank Russell Barry, later Bishop of Southwell, who was responsible for the appointment of Wilson and Clarkson to Radcliffe/Nottingham and Newark respectively. After Knutsford Clarkson went to New College, Oxford where he gained a second in modern history and did his theological training at Lincoln. Following ordination he served in several parishes and was also Sub-Dean of St Albans Cathedral.

What could Wakefield expect? Clarkson was shrewd, witty and wise. His shrewdness was as penetrating as his wit. Fools were hardly suffered at all, and never gladly, yet pastoral counsel and care were given indiscriminately to all who needed it. Competence was part of his nature, he did not have to acquire it. He could sum up a problem in five minutes, and a person in less. Giving him a knotty problem to solve was like providing a child a treat of candyfloss at the seaside. He was anchored in the traditional aspects of the faith and practice of the Church of England, with little patience for disloyal extremities which were met with robust Yorkshire common sense. There was a rotund stateliness about him. He was unmarried and lived with his sister. Some clergy found him reserved, stubborn and sober but he was a hidden gem in the Church.

In 1958 one of the greatest names of the twentieth-century church died – George Bell, Bishop of Chichester – and Roger Wilson succeeded him. Thoughtfulness was Wilson's abiding virtue. He was not given to effervescence or glibness. He made decisions after careful thought, weighing alternative ways forward before making a reasoned decision. His sympathies were liberal and tolerant. He survived many brickbats at Wakefield, once saying, 'Every dead cat thrown over a wall comes into the bishop's garden sooner or later.' With the strengths of Clarkson and Treacy it was advisable, even essential, that Wakefield's new bishop should already be in episcopal orders. There was renewed clamour that he should come with acknowledged and recognisable catholic credentials. John Alexander Ramsbotham, aged fifty-two, Bishop Suffragan of Jarrow, Archdeacon of Durham and Canon Residentiary of Durham Cathedral was appointed in 1958.

Ramsbotham was a son of the vicarage, born in County Durham, and educated at Haileybury College, Corpus Christi College, Cambridge, and theologically trained at Wells. Following a London curacy he joined the staff of Wells Theological College, leaving to be Warden of the College of the Ascension, Selly Oak, Birmingham. He was Vicar of St George's, Jesmond, Newcastle-upon-Tyne for eight years from 1942. That is the outline. What of the substance? He was one of Sir Edwyn Hoskyn's brilliant group of theological pupils at Cambridge. As a young priest he travelled widely to India and Africa, to the Orthodox Church in the Balkans, and to all Western European countries, some of it under the auspices of the Student Christian Movement, for which he was for a short period its missionary secretary. He savoured the interaction of Barthian and Anglo-Catholic theological thinking. He began to say unpopular things in a muted manner that saved him from reactionary attacks. It was a good way to be radical. As a parish priest in Jesmond he introduced liturgical and other changes, reflecting his support for the Parish and People Movement at whose conferences he was a frequent speaker. There was nothing of the sacristy mentality about him so changes were not imposed unless they provoked insight and action in the community and beyond. He represented the high ideal of good order in Anglican worship.

Why Wakefield? Ramsbotham was in an increasingly difficult position in Durham. He was appointed by Alwyn Williams who was translated to Winchester, served throughout Michael Ramsey's short episcopate, and continued under Maurice Harland. It was not conducive working with Harland who politically and socially was reactionary – hunting, shooting and fishing – the only bishop to vote for the retention of hanging, yet Harland had been a good and progressive thinking Bishop of Lincoln and cared deeply for his clergy though he expected them to 'stand on their own feet'. During two vacancies in the Durham See, Ramsbotham was relieved at being offered Wakefield.

In 1961 there was a *cause célèbre* at Guildford. The diocese had a new bishop, George Reindorp, and a new cathedral awaiting consecration. It was anticipated that the Provost, Walter Boulton, would be the cathedral's first Dean. That did not happen. It remained a live and sour scandal for more than a decade. One of Geoffrey Fisher's last acts before his resignation as Archbishop of Canterbury was to recommend to the Crown the appointment of a dean. It required a man of consummate skill who would have to endure and survive the flames which were everywhere ready to consume him, although he himself would have no part in the Guildford debacle. George

Clarkson of Pontefract was appointed Dean. It was an excellent choice as he was not a person to be pushed about by anyone, archbishop and bishop included. He was regarded as Tennyson's 'Tower of strength who stood four-square to all the winds that blow'.

In a brave move Ramsbotham asked Treacy to move to Pontefract as suffragan bishop. A mitre at last! But was it wise and would it work? Their personalities and interests were incompatible and Wakefield is so compact a diocese that they could not operate in different and specific areas. Nonetheless to Ramsbotham's credit he recognized Treacy's quality though without understanding his underlying frustration. Treacy was also Archdeacon but was relieved, in every sense of the word, of a canonry at Wakefield Cathedral. He was consecrated bishop on 18 October 1961. Eric and May Treacy lived in Dewsbury.

This left the archdeaconry of Halifax to be filled. Ramsbotham turned to John Field Lister who had served in the diocese since 1945 and been Vicar of Brighouse from 1954. Brighouse was a hothouse training parish and Lister, a priest of ability produced a long stream of curates. He was distinctly 'high church', a big man in almost every way, and unmarried. All the clergy of the diocese knew Lister and he knew everything there was to know about them. Outwardly there was little antipathy between Treacy and Lister (although there was between Lister and May Treacy) but neither was there warmth and their respective views on current issues confronting the Church were usually at variance. But one thing they had in common, they were both outstanding parish priests.

Ramsbotham's episcopate was a cascading disappointment as a result of illness and other pressures. He was liked by most, but by no means all, clergy and as father-in-God had a shrewd appreciation of their difficulties and problems. The administrative burden was crippling and made him indecisive. He had two strong men, Treacy and Lister, at his side but he failed to delegate much to them. He was involved in central church affairs – the Children's Council; the Deployment and Payment Commission – Partners in Ministry; the Guild of St Raphael; and was dutiful in his attendance at the House of Lords. This was too much for a sensitive man who cared for everything that was committed to his charge and which he accepted as a duty. He was diligent in pastoral visits to the parishes. Ramsbotham was never in robust health and in 1965 it deteriorated and thereafter was a constant worry and battle for him, until, in 1967 he suffered from arterial spasms which led to his resignation on 30 November at the age of sixty-one. The diocese was not in good heart and much had slipped for lack of episcopal leadership.

Who would follow? The diocese had been in the capable hands of Eric Treacy, by now a prominent figure not only in Wakefield but in the councils of the Church of England. But in 1967 he was already aged sixty. The question may be asked why he had not already been chosen for a diocesan bishopric? His friend and patron, Roger Wilson, reflects:

> There are a number of reasons. Pre-eminently I think it was due to his lack of a degree or whatever that was held to signify. It sounds surprising now, but the image of the theologian or the High Administrator, elevated from his professorial chair or the headmaster's dais to the Bench, died hard. University, moreover, for a long time meant Oxbridge. It's all different now but in the 50's this was still prevalent. Eric also gave the impression of being primarily a pragmatic individualist, critical of the Establishment or at least unpredictable in his judgements and actions. He couldn't be labelled – and therefore was difficult to 'place'. Perhaps too for all his gifts, he matured late, acquired gravitas slowly, with a suggestion always of the rogue elephant about him.

There is another psychological trait. Treacy suffered from a sense of inferiority, which he assuaged by action. This stemmed in part, though only in part, from his lack of educational fulfilment. He was right in 'divining' (Treacy's own word) that he got round this by quickness of wit and natural dynamism, until there came a time when he realised he could hold his own with those whom he imagined better circumstanced than himself. However, it was never simply a matter of 'getting away with it'. As a Forces chaplain he had shown courage and decisiveness and a great capacity for friendship which prevented him from feeling empty or shut out.

In Wakefield there was a popular move for Pontefract to become Wakefield but there were equally strong arguments against such a move. In practical terms it is difficult to see Treacy working in complementary harness with any new bishop. At his age it would be difficult to imagine him moving elsewhere, providing fresh impetus, starting from scratch. Ultimately there was an inevitability about the outcome when in January 1968, it was announced that Eric Treacy was the eighth Bishop of Wakefield. He was enthroned on 27 March 1968. Treacy's first task was to find a new Bishop of Pontefract. It was his choice but, as he should have known, and discovered to his considerable discomfort, not his alone. One of Treacy's supporters for Wakefield was the Archbishop of York, Donald Coggan, who wrote to Treacy (28 December 1967):

> I want you to know how profoundly thankful I am that things are turning out as they are. This has long been my hope, & for this I have worked.
>
> For your encouragement – & in confidence – I may tell you that there has been a quite wonderful unanimity of desire – one could almost say determination – on the part of people of all kinds & shades, clerical & lay that you should succeed John (Ramsbotham). This, I am sure, will be of great strength to you if

& when, as I most firmly hope, you send an affirmative reply to the Prime Minister . . . The task ahead of you is not an easy one, but God will give you grace in the bringing of order and sanity of Churchmanship & newness of life where it is greatly needed. The bigger the job, the greater the resource of grace, thank God!

Perhaps sometime we can talk further about this &, when the time comes about a Bp. of Pontefract . . .

Treacy would have been spared personal anguish and embarrassment had he talked with the Archbishop about the Pontefract succession before taking precipitate action. Treacy was blinkered when he sought a new bishop from within the diocese. He ignored the view that the diocese needed an injection from outside. We know from his journal that he thought it vital to appoint someone who would be sympathetic to the Anglo-Catholic constituency which was prevalent in the southern part of the diocese. He looked no further than John Lister, Archdeacon of Halifax. It is fortunate that he had the sense not to approach Lister direct before writing to the Archbishop informing him of his choice. He envisaged no query, simply the archiepiscopal seal on his choice. The Archbishop replied with a resolute 'No' to Lister! This made Treacy more determined in pressing his candidate but the Archbishop made it clear 'not in any circumstances'. It should not have escaped Treacy that any new bishop relied on the Archbishop for Consecration. In any event the appointment of Lister would have led to a great deal of friction in the diocese and for Treacy too. Treacy and Lister were not friends and trust between them was superficial. Lister had supported Treacy for Wakefield but afterwards considered it was not the right or best choice.

Following conversations with the Archbishop, Treacy was made aware that he should cast his net widely and that he should not focus on churchmanship to complement his own strengths and deficiences but on someone with known and distinctive gifts of his own. The first name he had before him was William Gordon Fallows, Principal of Ripon Hall. In February 1968 Treacy approached Frederick William Dillistone of Oriel College, Oxford, and a former Dean of Liverpool, for a view on Fallows. Dillistone replied on 19 February:

How greatly I appreciate your taking me into your confidence about this key appointment. Let me say at once that I regard Gordon as one of my closest friends. I have been in constant contact with him & his family over the past 12–13 years & in the light of it all I have no reservation that I can think of at all in commending him as an able administrator, a good scholar, an admirable colleague, a man with a great sense of humour, a leader and yet not a dominator, of wide experience in northern industry & also in training of clergy – in short one of the most all-round men that I know in the C of E to-day. I too cannot understand why he has not been chosen for a Diocese & it is my great hope that he still will be. I think he would like that & I am sure he would do it with the utmost grace and competence. I would like to think of him at Birmingham to follow Leonard (Wilson) but I do not know what the authorities have in mind. In any case if he became Bishop of Pontefract he could still become a Diocesan in 4–5 years time. I can't think of anyone whom I would prefer to see as your colleague. I have turned to him again & again for advice & know of no one with whom it is easier to talk things over. The only question mark that I can readily think of concerns the Diocese which I know has a strong Anglo-Catholic tradition. Gordon like yourself is not in the least a narrow Evangelical but he also has little place for extreme ritual or rigid doctrine. You alone know whether he is 'Catholic' enough to be your colleague in the particular diocese of Wakefield. But if this is clear in your mind & if there is nothing else in view for him I think it would be wonderful.

He has been nearly ten years at Ripon Hall & I think is ready to consider a move. I find it hard to think what would be the next move except for either a Bishopric or a Deanery. And my own judgment is that Gordon's training & experience fit him more for the former than the latter. One last word. I happened to be speaking to Ian Dunelm (Bishop Ian Ramsey of Durham) about him a week ago. Ian said that he thought something was in the wind for him. Could he have been referring to your own suggestion? Or could he have heard of it? If not, there may be something else in mind by the authorities in London but of it I know nothing. I would love to think of you & Gordon working together in Wakefield. And he knows the Archdeacon of Halifax also.

Treacy wasted no time in inviting Fallows to Pontefract but was not deluded that he may not have him for long. The appointment was made in March 1968 but for over one month Fallows had to continue his normal duties, carrying his secret in silence as the Queen's approval of the appointment did not come until 22 April and the public announcement followed two days later.

It can be no more than speculation, though not without foundation, that Fallows may have missed a diocese by a whisker. Two diocesan bishops retired in 1969 each of whom was a member of the Modern Churchmen's Union. They were Geoffrey Francis Allen of Derby and John Leonard Wilson of Birmingham. Fallows would be suited to either See but been a perfect 'fit' for Birmingham.

CHAPTER 9

Pontifex

WITH THE HONOUR and gratification of episcopacy there is a financial cost. There are numerous legal and other fees most noticeably for the adornments and appurtenances and not least the haberdashery of episcopacy. These are not usually mentioned in biographies but as we have details and accounts from Fallows it is of interest to list them. Fortunately, in most instances many of these are gifts from a college, a former parish, family and friends. Little has changed over the years except to increase in volume and price when some bishops see the necessity for an array of mitres and other vestments. Fallows' requirements were modest by comparison. He never forgot that he was a bishop of the Reformation which is reflected in the traditional robes of a Church of England bishop. For Fallows there were as follows:

1. A pastoral staff (crook) made for him by Robert Porter of Glenridding, Cumbria.
2. 9 ct Gold Amethyst Episcopal Ring (Payne & Son Goldsmiths Ltd. of Oxford.)
3. Anglican purple double breasted cassock with purple cincture, a pair of black bands and one pair of scarlet bands. Scarlet superfine chimere and black chimere. Nine-inch black ottoman scarf. Anglican purple waist stock and purple square stock. One pair linen preachers bands (all from McDonald's Clerical Tailors of Oxford.)
4. Fallows always had a keen eye for artistic design and excellence. Following a consultation with the Wardens of the Company of Goldsmiths he invited Robert Welch, a leading modern designer, to design and make his pectoral cross. The result was a cross of compelling beauty and striking simplicity.
5. There were other vestments which fill a bishop's wardrobe. Fallows never forgot the first time he wore a cope. In his Preston days he was invited to preach at the well-known Anglo-Catholic Church of St Stephen-on-the-Cliffs, Blackpool which was also known as the Actors Church. At the end of the service there was a procession and Fallows stood dutifully to attention and was enfolded in a cope. Now he required a cope and mitre. It was always his preference to wear Convocation robes (chimere and rochet) but by the 1960s there was fewer than a handful of bishops who refused to wear a mitre. And in the southern end of the Wakefield Diocese not only cope and mitre but chasuble and mitre were essential. Fallows was

careful to ensure that the cope and mitre would suit his personal appearance and add dignity not show to ceremonial. This was achieved in white and gold brocade with decorated mitre. There was also a white brocade preaching stole with fleury embroidery. In addition there was clothing for regular wear and for special occasions, including a dignitary's frock coat, breeches and gaiters in Venetian cloth; apron and band in Persian cord; buckle shoes in fine calf; and a purple silk stock. One item, always important to Fallows and frequently carried and worn, was a purple velvet Canterbury cap.

The Consecration was fixed for the Feast of St Barnabas, 11 June 1968. In view of extensive building operations at York Minster, the Archbishop agreed that the Consecration should take place at Wakefield Cathedral. In accordance with custom all bishops of the Northern Province were invited. In addition Fallows asked for some special episcopal friends to be invited from the Province of Canterbury. These were Leonard Wilson of Birmingham, Geoffrey Allen of Derby, David Loveday of Dorchester, and Warren Hunt of Repton.

During the service Fallows was presented to the Archbishop by the Bishops of Durham (Ian Ramsey) and Wakefield (Treacy). By custom the preacher is the choice of the consecrand, Fallows asked Canon F.W. Dillistone. A few extracts are quoted as they provide a perceptive portrait of Fallows' unrehearsed future in an unusual way:

> In the year 1803 a certain Mr Edward Dayes of London undertook what was called a picturesque tour through the principal parts of Yorkshire and Derbyshire. In the narrative of his journey he tells us that after leaving Robin Hood's Well he proceeded to Pontefract, Broken-bridge ... Pontefract – the very name reminds us of the earliest civilisation to leave its mark on Britain. The Romans were an extraordinary people in many ways; perhaps none of their technical achievements was finer than the building of bridges. Whether or not they constructed a bridge of Pontefract I have not attempted to discover. What is certain is that from somewhere in the remote past there lingers a memory of a broken bridge, a breakdown of communication.
>
> But in contrast to Pontefract another word leaps to the mind – it is the word pontifex, bridge maker. It has long been an intriguing fact that a leading religious official in ancient Rome was called Pontifex, and although we cannot be sure that the office was originally regarded as concerned with building bridges between earth and heaven it is not surprising that pontifex has often been interpreted in this way. As Christianity became an established religion the title pontifex was applied to the bishop and the words pontiff and pontifical have found their way into the English language. A 17th century writing has the succession 'pontifical, stately, bishoplike' while Milton speaks of bridge-building

as the wondrous art pontifical. So Pontefract – Pontifex, Broken Bridge, Bridge builder, this is the connection that has fascinated me as I have looked forward to this great day.

But of course another connection with the day is still more compelling. It is the connection with St Barnabas, that so attractive figure of the New Testament, the man of immense generosity and sheer goodness, the man full of the Holy Spirit, the man of courage and consolation. No one is certain of the origin or exact interpretation of the name Barnabas but in the New Testament it is linked with the great word Paraclete: he was a man altogether characterised by a spirit of encouragement, of sympathy, of conciliation . . . Barnabas was a man of conciliation, a man who built bridges, a pontifex who tried to repair the pontefracts which even the Apostolic Age experienced.

Think of the records. The new convert Saul wants to join himself to the assembly of disciples in Jerusalem. But they are suspicious of his motives, afraid of his record. It is Barnabas who takes the risk, who throws out the reconciling bridges and brings them into the fellowship. The tension between converts of Jewish and Gentile backgrounds becomes acute. It is Barnabas who is sent with Paul to convey the word of reconciliation. Most poignantly – because a bridge in one direction may sometimes lead to a breach in another – when young John Mark is under a cloud and in danger of being excluded from the Christian mission it is Barnabas who sets up the bridge which can enable him to regain his confidence and his identity. All this he did in the power of that Holy Spirit who is the creator of conciliation and the coordinator of the common life.

We have gathered together here today for the consecration to new office of one who has already proved himself a friend to many, a minister of conciliation in many contexts. Today he becomes bishop, pontifex. In the course of Christian history this office has taken on varying emphases: in St Augustine's day, the teacher, in the Middle Ages, the ruler; in the English Reformation the banisher of false doctrine; in the 19th and 20th centuries increasingly the administrator. I am persuaded that in our present situation no quality or characteristic is more urgently needed than that of bridge-builder. In the words of Marshall McLuhan the world has become a global village. Yet the rivers of separation which flow between East and West, European and African, the affluent and the poverty-stricken, the older and the younger generation, the radical and the conservative seem to grow wider and deeper every day. A professor from California called on me a few hours after the shooting of Robert Kennedy. He said, 'There is no longer any middle ground, any mediating position. If you are on one side you are the enemy of the other.' Since then a distinguished playwright speaking on *Late Night Line Up* said exactly the same thing about his art. High brow or low brow, box office triumph or improvised happening, nothing in between. And the man who tries to bridge these gulfs to leave the safety and solidity of one side and stretch out towards the other, exposes himself to risk, to danger, to being shot down, even to be killed. The opening paragraph of the leading article in one of the great Sunday newspapers contained these words: 'Bobby Kennedy was seeking for an approach to politics which was essentially one of reconciliation . . .

And then I turn back to the fine words of our Authorised Version about Barnabas and Saul, men who hazarded their lives for the name of the Lord Jesus Christ – hazarded them by trying to bridge the gulfs between Jew and Gentile, between conservative and radical, between the Church and the world.

The ancient ceremonies moved with dignified and solemn ritual towards the moment when the Archbishop with all the other bishops present laid their hands upon the head of William Gordon Fallows to be Consecrated with these words, 'Receive the Holy Ghost, for the Office and Work of a Bishop in the Church of God.'

There were two conditions of the move. When Fallows and his wife, Edna, visited 4 Oxford Road, Dewsbury where Treacy had lived, it was clear that it was unsuitable for them. They did not feel it was the right house in the right place. And something important was missing. No one who knew Edna Fallows can imagine her living in a house without a garden. Treacy responded to this need and a house was found in Wakefield ('Highfield', 306 Barnsley Road, Sandal, Wakefield). The Church Commissioners were reluctant and Treacy had to fight for the change of domicile. Fallows was grateful as conveyed in a letter to Treacy:

> Both Edna & I would like you to know how deeply we appreciate your courage and, as we believe, your wisdom in pursuing this project. It is a great morale booster to us (not that one was needed) and in the long term one that could be of inestimable benefit to the diocese. The immediate problems it raises are as nothing compared with the joy we experience as the weary but elated tenants of this lovely home. It has been a master-stroke on your part & I trust it will redound to the advantage of our joint episcopal enterprise.

The second condition was the separation of the suffragan bishopric from the position of archdeacon. Fallows was a Canon Stipendiary of Wakefield Cathedral. As Archdeacon of Pontefract Treacy appointed Edward Chance Henderson, aged fifty-two, who had served in the diocese for eighteen years. He was a sound and broad, rather than narrow, Evangelical with considerable parochial experience. He was cautious, not a man to be rushed into making a decision, and trusted. His effect on the archdeaconry was considerable, particularly behind the scenes. He solved many tricky situations by a combination of friendliness, firmness and stealth.

Fallows had been used to working in communities: Styvechale, Preston, Ripon Hall. He was to learn that a diocese is not a parish or theological college writ large. A bishop suffragan – even, to an extent, a diocesan bishop – may be treated as possessing inordinate authority whereas in fact he has very little. Whatever realized authority comes from and with his office will emerge because people see in their bishop the servant leader and a worthy channel of Apostolic tradition and they will join with him in a ministry of care and compassion. If he acts otherwise, they will probably ignore him. Some of the paradoxes are unsettling for a new bishop. He may be central to people's religious lives but not very much part of any one community. As he looks for some living stability for his wife, his family and himself, he will discover how itinerant his ministry is.

What were the hopes of people for their new bishop? Granted, any inflated expectations could never be met or satisfied. But what may be realisable? What was evident as Fallows began his episcopal ministry? And how would he be contrasted with Eric Treacy? Fallows called Treacy an 'Advent Christian' ('Stir up we beseech thee . . .') Outwardly all was concord and light between them. It cannot have been easy for any suffragan to work with Treacy, whose 'larger than life' presence in the diocese appeared massive and everywhere. Parishioners asked Fallows 'How's the Bishop?' or 'How's Dr Treacy?' In lengthy, frank and relaxed conversation between this biographer and Fallows (5 March 1979) the latter said, 'I go around the Diocese with a shadow on my back.' There were few common characteristics between the two men beyond that of friendship. Treacy had a capacity for intelligence, common sense but little intellectual equipment. Fallows had all three, and he reflected 'Eric had all his goods in the shop window.' On the negative side Treacy was too greatly influenced by his wife, May, who had a dangerous and unhealthy effect with her rigorous puritanism and rigid teetotalism. She led and caused Treacy to act unwisely in condemning books he had not read and a show – *Oh! Calcutta* – he had not seen.

Treacy followed his wife's intent leadership on alcoholic beverage in public but was happy to have an 'unofficial' glass of very good cider with Fallows and when in the Diocesan Office a bottle of sherry would occasionally emerge from a locked drawer of the diocesan secretary. Fallows never forgot one slip of the tongue when May said, 'When we were ordained' instead of 'married!'

Fallows learned that Treacy was a much more complex person than the rather bluff exterior allowed. 'He ran with the hare and hunted with the hounds. I was not always sure where he really stood on issues.' Treacy's mouth could be as wide as the Grand Canyon and his pen could be that of a journalist. He loved the applause of the crowd which was an ever present foible for there was a demagogic trait in him. Equally, when he realised that he had spoken rashly or written hastily or otherwise erred and strayed he was quick to repent. Fallows thought, correctly, that Treacy was out of his depth over questions of homosexuality and the Charismatic Movement. 'Although Eric was generally and genuinely left of centre he was not a liberal.'

Fallows disliked Treacy's indulgence in 'Church hennery.' 'He would talk for hours about church personalities' and, more indictable, 'Although he pontificated on national and world affairs he was not really gripped by the iniquities in the world.' However:

> Eric's biggest quality was courage. Being a bishop was his whole life. He cared for his clergy particularly those who were in trouble or had breakdowns, and they were not few. Night and day he was at their side. I learned so much from him. It was marvellous working with him because of, not despite, his vulnerabilities. He was happy that I should continue with my national appointments, for example, Deputy Chairman of the Church of England Pensions Board and membership of the Central Board of Finance. Of course there was nothing in me which posed any kind of threat to Eric for my interests and gifts were quite different. At Eric's funeral I wept as never before.

There may have been mutual antipathy between Treacy and Archdeacon Lister of Halifax. Fortunately Fallows' temperament accommodated Lister and his blemishes whilst not pandering to his intrigues and conceits. His duties as Canon Stipendiary at the cathedral were neither regular nor taxing. The worship with a whiff of incense was not Fallows' natural milieu but he was a much-needed member of staff in an environment of friction notably between the Provost, Philip Pare and Vice-Provost, John Montague. Each had been at the cathedral since 1962. Pare was variously gifted, unhappy and psychologically afflicted. As a pastor on a personal level he could be penetrating and perceptive. He was Provost in name but was totally unsuited to the position. Bishop John Ramsbotham hoped to persuade the 'powers that be' to find another post for Pare, perhaps even a bishopric! Without success. Montague was also unhappy and frustrated as Number Two at the cathedral. Unfortunately Treacy was impulsive which led him to make offers to clergy, for example, Montague to have an archdeaconry, which were either not technically vacant or were subsequently withdrawn! Fallows had an effect on Treacy by gently but firmly restraining Treacy's rashness and impulsiveness. There was little atmospheric change for the better at the cathedral until 1972 when John Lister was appointed Provost.

Fallows' strength in the diocese was evident in two directions. First and foremost were his welcome visits to parishes. The visit of a bishop is seldom a normal occasion. He comes for a centenary, a dedication, an institution, a confirmation and everything, including the size of the congregation, is abnormal. Just because it is a special occasion the bishop is expected to instruct a mass of people whose ages range from toddlers to ninety-year olds. Fallows attempted to stretch his arms wide and embrace a mingled multitude of people in his preaching. His archidiaconal years were a help. A bishop preaches in a different church each Sunday and on several occasions during the week. As he faced a congregation from the pulpit he saw a multitude of expectant faces. Respecting his congregation or audience he took great care in the preparation and presentation of his sermons. An apposite text was chosen, a pertinent story or nugget was used to illustrate it – perfected at Sheffield – with a clear beginning and ending. He never wandered from the path knowing only too well the perils of so doing from his mountain climbs. There was something deceptively substantial about his preaching. He did not parade himself although he shared facets of his own continuing journey of faith, never claiming that it was easy to believe. He stayed after a service for the proverbial 'bun fight', always thanking those who had worked so hard behind the scenes to provide such an appetizing 'spread'. After all this was Yorkshire and there was something inextricably linked between the service and the after 'do', in a sense sacramental. He did not sprinkle a benign benediction as he floated among the people, or glance to see if there was someone important to meet, but had real conversations with everyone he met showing a genuine interest in them. And he remembered the people. His presence remained with the people.

Some of the biggest tributes from his short time at Pontefract came from unexpected sources. Even some rather prickly Conservative Evangelicals acknowledged that he had 'the heart of the matter' in him. If he had a 'fan club' its headquarters and staff were the Sisters of the Community of St Peter's, Horbury. From the moment he first visited the Convent there was deep empathy between him and the Sisters. They greatly appreciated his guidance in spiritual matters, he was helpful in practical ways, and there was much fun and laughter as he relaxed with them. In 1968 the Community undertook teaching work with maladjusted children, in addition to retreats and mission work. The Mother Superior appreciated Fallows' personal as well as episcopal interest. 'Oh dear, oh dear, OH DEAR!' was her reaction when he went to Sheffield. 'At the present moment I hate the appointments board or whatever it is that has done this to us.' She added 'and there will be a garden for Mrs Fallows' who was also popular with the Community.

The second direction in which Fallows was a valuable asset to Wakefield was as chairman of committees. He had been a member of the Christian Stewardship Committee of the Central Board of Finance for some years. It was natural that he should chair the 'Bishop of Wakefield's Advisory Council' on this subject. Christian Stewardship has always been something of a 'Cinderella' in the Church of England. Wakefield was known as a weak stewardship diocese. Congregations gave their pittance and expected the bulk of income to come from elsewhere. On this subject Fallows was a 'no nonsense' chairman, refusing to have the wool pulled over his eyes by those who claimed nothing could be done. In this and similar settings one can imagine Fallows as chief executive of a large company. Faced with excuses and inaction his approach to why so little was done to promote stewardship, he was clear and brutal. Such a state of affairs could not exist in industry. A board of directors with executive power would have been unceremoniously swept out several times over if company returns over a lengthy period had shown such a catastrophic drop at a time when the general public's need was unprecedented and competition negligible. Had any branch of the company shown signs of growth in such a period of adversity? The reasons would have been carefully investigated and the methods more widely adopted. There were exceptions in Wakefield but they were very few. Fallows knew that the most effective campaigns started with the question 'What is it worth?' and continued by explaining Christian Stewardship in terms of time (in worship and witness); abilities (talents and skills – in God's service); and money. In committee and parishes Fallows stressed that Stewardship should be seen as a relationship involving trusteeship and not as a money-raising gimmick. Proper trusteeship of the self, time, possessions, opportunity and influence was vital. He endeavoured to strip schemes to bare essentials for, as with some aspects of Church of England life, there was too much to read, too little time to digest and no time to think. Even with enthusiasms here and there the figures in the Church of England for all types of campaigns were lamentable and diminishing. In 1961 there were 686; in 1964, 210.

Wakefield was fortunate in having a former theological college principal as Warden of its Fellowship of Vocation. Many dioceses have annual get-togethers for ordinands at the bishop's house. Fallows thought this a welcome but inadequate focus for ordinands. He sought ways of binding ordinands together. In one of his informative Newsletters he reminded them that:

we have a wide range of professions, occupations, trades and callings. A casual glance through the records reveals that there are at present in training a Local Government Officer, a Grocer, a Mental Hospital Nurse, a Driver-Salesman, a Journalist, an Office Clerk, a Royal Air Force Sergeant, a Builder, and, of course, a number of 'Straight Students' who have proceeded from School to University and Theological College. Quite a number of these 'Straight Students' take some secular occupation for a year or so before being Ordained ... One of the interesting features of the call to ordination in the last decade or two has been the high proportion of candidates who have sought ordination from some secure and often well-established and well-paid appointment in some other work. As I know from the testimony of many such ordinands, they have only realised their true fulfilment and found their deepest satisfaction in the work of the ordained ministry. Often this involves considerable personal sacrifice and that may well be the test of the reality of their calling. Doubtless in some cases, perhaps unconsciously, ordination is sought as a way of escape from frustration and failure in another sphere and Selectors must always be on the look-out for such unconscious motives. But I am thankful to know many men in the ordained ministry today who were formerly able and successful in some other work. So if you are a good and successful butcher, baker or candlestick-maker, watch out. God may be calling you.

Fallows contributed a 'Message' to each issue of the Newsletter and an occasional article. Ordinands' own experiences were recorded, including from a former journalist on a high income training at Salisbury Theological College; another training at Lichfield describing an out-of-college project with the Social Services on drug dependency; another on the theological, pastoral and liturgical ingredients of his training at Lincoln. Fallows enabled more meetings of the Fellowship to take place with the pleasing benefit of ordinands making and maintaining friendships with each other. He was always on the look out for ordinands and could usually spot a good prospect. He eagerly accepted invitations to speak at grammar school speech days or prize-givings in the diocese. Although ordination was not mentioned in his addresses his youthful audiences were impressed by 'the bishop' and God knows what seeds may have been planted.

Fallows was also Diocesan Director of Post-Ordination Training, not an easy task. Here he could be rigorous, albeit usually in a non-confrontational way. Once ordained and in a parish many clergy do not appear to appreciate the need for further and continuous study. This is a mistake which affects their future ministry. As an archdeacon Fallows was able to gauge when a clergyman ceased studying and stopped thinking. He always examined vicarage bookcases and bemoaned the lack of books on history, politics, travel, novels and poetry, anything that reflected a parson had a rich hinterland.

He prepared a balanced and wholesome, never bland, diet of study and reading for post-ordination work. He wanted men to learn from each other as from their seniors. At all costs they must not be isolated in their parishes. He was ever watchful and wary lest a curate should become an extra pair of hands because the incumbent was getting old, or in poor health, or so hard working that he was in danger of a breakdown. He carefully monitored a first curacy which he held should be closely supervised by someone other than the incumbent of the parish, and there should be no hesitation in making a change where the job for one reason or another was not suiting the curate in the opinion of his supervisor. This was too radical for Eric Treacy. Fallows was in the process of drawing up an important reappraisal of the complete way in which the Church looked after its junior clergy, when he was translated to Sheffield.

Wakefield could not contain the knowledge and energies of Fallows. He was increasingly in demand for outside work as he emerged as a diocesan bishop in embryo! Many of these commitments were inherited and new ones are mentioned elsewhere. A thoroughly congenial one came when Fallows was appointed Chairman of the Committee for Religious Drama in the Northern Province. The committee's adviser was the unsung heroine of religious drama, Miss Pamela Keilly, who wrote to Fallows (7 December 1968):

> It is splendid to hear that you feel able to undertake the chairmanship. I am wondering if there will be any chance of having a talk about the work. It's an extremely lonely job, & I can't tell you how glad I shall be to know there is someone in the background to whom I can turn. Bishop Ram (John Ramsbotham) shouldered the whole thing when the last Bishop of Sheffield (Leslie Hunter) retired. I really came to live in Wakefield because of him.

An early meeting was arranged at Chateau Fallows (her description) followed by an immediate rapport between Chairman and Adviser. Pamela Keilly felt supported which regular meetings and correspondence confirmed. Fallows quickly discerned that the words 'Northern Province' in the committee's title were misleading, almost an aberration. Only the dioceses of Manchester, Sheffield, Wakefield and Ripon gave moral, practical, active and financial support. Sheffield was the original force for religious drama but by 1968 was no longer the scene of action. The other three were haphazardly flourishing. No one travelled and spoke to groups and rural decanal conferences more than Pamela Keilly but the clergy, in particular, were an ungrateful lot. Eric Treacy wrote to Fallows (2 June 1970), 'I know how depressing it must be to Pamela that all the work she puts in to Religious Drama seems to be so little appreciated. I am afraid that this is the fate of anyone concerned with the Arts in the Industrial North.'

Yet with a mixture of courage, inspiration and perspiration Keilly was responsible for producing and directing some wonderful productions during Fallows' short sojourn in Pontefract. He was quick to arrange for a £100 increase in her salary and for her use of taxis wherever it was expedient and helpful.

On 9 May 1969, an excellent lunchtime talk on T.S. Eliot's plays was given by E. Martin Browne, President of RADIUS (the Religious Drama Society of Great Britain), friend of Bishop George Bell of Chichester, and a notable producer of all the plays of T.S. Eliot and many of Christopher Fry in London and New York, and responsible for the revival of the York Cycle of Mystery Plays. His talk led to *The Family Reunion* in Manchester Cathedral in 1970, also at Whitcliffe Mount Grammar School, Cleckheaton, in Yorkshire's West Riding. The cathedral setting was a mistake for this play and attendances were thin. At Cleckheaton, Eliot's presentation of sin and expiation was achieved and appreciated.

In November 1969 *Go Down Moses* by Philip J. Lamb was produced in Wakefield Cathedral, for the first time in a church building. There was little support from the parishes. Perhaps mentioning Moses in the title was a deterrent. Someone suggested an alternative, 'Sin in the Wilderness'. In 1970 Philip Turner's *Madonna in Concrete* was presented in Stanley Parish Church, Wakefield. It was an American commission, never previously seen in England. The disturbing play about abortion and responsibility was movingly and clearly interpreted by Keilly. It caused powerful reactions both for and against the play. A professional actor and ex-producer of the Sheffield Playhouse wrote to Keilly after seeing the play:

> this piece rests as a sharp, pungent, witty, scathing comment on our modern society, immensely worth doing. You lifted my spirits enormously, gave me one of the most stimulating evenings in a theatre I've had in ages . . . Anyone who finds nothing in it simply has no ears to hear, and such folk are very difficult to talk to. Don't let them shout too loud.

Keilly directed a memorable and moving performance of Eliot's *Murder in the Cathedral* at Ripon Cathedral. The Dean of Ripon, Edwin Le Grice, wrote to Fallows:

> The 'rapport' between Beckett and the four tempters was illuminating – instead of remaining passive and inert, it was as though his whole face and being reflected his instinctive reaction to temptation and the struggle it produced within him. I had always regarded the women of Canterbury as one of the least satisfactory features of the play: but here they were transfigured; both by their acting and their speaking they were the antithesis of the 'wailing women' one had previously encountered.

Gheon's *Way of the Cross* was a Holy Week production by the Spenborough Council of Churches, and also at St Paul's Church, Mirfield, at Askrigg, near Leyburn, in Ripon and Wakefield Cathedrals, and in Wakefield Prison. Audiences were transparently affected, and so were the actors, as one of them wrote her impressions, sent to Fallows after Wakefield Prison, 'This particular performance, and above all the conversation afterwards, was so moving and cut us down to size so much, that we felt that if we had only done the preparation for this particular evening alone, it would have been worthwhile.'

After Christopher Fry's *The Boy with a Cart* at Askrigg a prospective professional actor in the parish played the leading part. Bishop Leonard Wilson lived in retirement in the parish and undertook to play Tawm in the play, but died before its production. Other productions directed by Keilly and supported by Fallows were R.H. Ward's *Holy Family*; John Hunter's play about hospitals *Take My Life;* and Kay Baxter's new play *Hermit and Hooligan*.

Fallows wanted to stir the wider Church to a realisation of the value of drama. If the Church is truly the servant of God in the world, the consequences of its decisions go rippling out into society, and decisions are taken every time a play is produced or not produced. History recalls the medieval synthesis and the post-restoration antithesis between Church and drama. The twentieth century knew a more adult Church and an independent drama. Potentially this could make for a deeper and more mutually profitable relationship between them than had hitherto existed, or it could mean that the Church and the drama would go their separate ways, self-sufficient and self contained. Not if Fallows had his way, but the signs are that he didn't.

Wakefield was enjoying the combination and contrast of Treacy as Captain of the Diocesan ship but with Fallows' trusted hand on the tiller. He was a calm and reassuring presence and clergy and laity alike looked forward to a lengthy and productive time of these two bishops in harness. Then, on 1 March 1971 Prime Minister Edward Heath wrote to Fallows asking if he would be agreeable to be nominated to the Queen as Bishop of Sheffield. It is the subject of Fallows' views on Episcopal ministry that are now considered.

CHAPTER 10

Episcope

FALLOWS CLEARED A MENTAL PATH for himself through the overgrown nettle and bramble-ridden surroundings of any examination of episcopacy. His Ripon Hall training – or was it a subtle kind of indoctrination! – made him wary of the phrase 'the historic episcopate' which was used to bolster a particular conviction on the episcopate. He never lost that wariness. The phrase, borrowed from the resolutions of the 1888 Lambeth Conference was properly absurd when used to indicate the Anglican variety of episcopacy. Was it the presbyter bishop of the pastoral epistles and St Clement of Rome? Or the monarchical bishop of St Ignatius and St Cyprian? Or the tribal bishop of the Celtic Church? Or the feudal bishop of mediaeval Europe? Or the Erastian bishop of Tudor England? Or the 'tulchan bishop' of seventeenth-century Scotland? Or the political bishop of the Hanoverians? Or the 'Apostolic' bishop of the Tractarians? Or the episcopal presbyter of the Presbyterian 'High' Churchmen? Or the delegate bishop of modern Rome? Or the superintendent bishop of the Lutherans and Episcopal Methodists? All are historic, if not equally, and so are many other forms of ecclesiastical system. History is never a partisan and the tradition which it delivers from the past to the present is too vast and various to serve any particular theory.

Fallows was concerned with attribution and practice, and the former tested the latter when he became a bishop. He differed from some liberal churchmen over the subject of authority. He accepted that authority in any sphere must be constantly watched to keep it within reasonable bounds, whereas many of his modernist friends were suspicious of anything that had the odour of an authoritarian church. Granted that in the church there should be vigilant scrutiny but Fallows was in no doubt that authority there must be. What did he mean? At the Modern Churchmen's Union Conference in 1951, Fallows gave a paper on 'Authority and Discipline in the Church':

> There are two types of authority represented by the Latin words *auctoritas* and *imperium*. Authority of the former kind implies no power of coercion; it is the capacity to impart knowledge and guidance; it is concerned with matters of fact and truth. Its rule is moral rather than legal, its method is persuasive rather than coercive. True authority has the right to command respect, assent and loyalty. Authority in this sense belongs to every department of knowledge, and we are dependent on it every day of our lives. When Dean Inge was asked whether he

was interested in liturgiology and he replied, 'No, neither do I collect postage stamps' he was disclaiming authority in the sphere of liturgy and philately. On the other hand it would be right to call Dean Inge an authority on Plotinus and Mysticism, or to describe G.W. Russell as an authority on lupins and Mrs Beeton as an authority on cooking. Authority commands respect, therefore, only when it is exercised within the sphere of its own competence. Authority in religion is akin to authority in anything else. When we speak of the authority of the Church, we mean its claim to command assent and loyalty that derives from its capacity to impart knowledge and guidance about God and his will for man. The Church speaks with authority as the guardian of the revelation of God more adequately than can be found elsewhere. The second type of authority (corresponding to the Latin *imperium*) is of a different kind. This is the authority of command and control. Whereas *auctoritas* commands assent, *imperium* implies the power to enforce it. The coercive authority of the Church is largely a thing of the past, though the Roman Church has never officially repudiated its right to coerce in the interests of the human soul and what it regards as religious truth. Where then is the seat of authority in the Christian religion? It is not to be found in a corporation, or an infallible pontiff, or in the General Councils of the undivided Church, or in those Churches that have maintained an episcopal succession. The only seat of authority is a Person, Jesus Christ, Whose work is continued by His Spirit. Jesus Christ then is our primary Authority. Because our Authority is a person, it is developing and growing, not static. Our appeal is not only to the records of His life and teaching, but to His Spirit dwelling within us. It is not primarily an external authority, but essentially an internal authority. Our appeal to this authority is not to isolate sayings consulted as an oracle, but to the teaching as a whole interpreted in the light of reason and common sense.

Thus far it appears that Fallows did not lay too great a store on the authority of tradition. He acknowledged the sacredness of ancient tradition, though not to the extent of it being final or absolute. How much of an Anglican was he? Did he accept with approval the words of the American Quaker poet, John Greenleaf Whittier (1807–1892) whom he quoted on several occasions:

'I know how well the fathers taught'
What work the latter schoolmen wrought;
I reverence old time faith and men
But God is near us now and then;
His force of love is still unspent
His hate of sin as imminent.
And still the measure of our needs
Outgrows the cramping bounds of creeds;
The manna gathered yesterday
Already savours of decay;
Doubts to the world's child heart unknown
Question us now from star and stone.

How did Fallows reconcile such freelancing thoughts with his ordination in the Church of England? Was he a member of a take-as-you-please Church? Where indeed did he stand on authority and discipline in the church?

> Its purpose is to preserve order and unity. An authority that preserves order at the price of unity, or order at the price of liberty, is deficient because it is grounded on a doctrine of Church authority too narrow and too rigid to comprehend the largeness of truth. This is the chief stumbling block in the sphere of Church relations. So, too, in the sphere of worship and sacraments. The tendency of the English Church has been to identify order and unity with uniformity. History has exposed the falsity of this ideal and the impossibility of achieving it. A comprehensiveness is needed if unity and order are to be maintained.

Fallows was always on guard whenever he saw signs of authority choking freedom. That is why there was always in him, only slightly submerged below the surface, a forthright radicalism to uphold, even fight for a great and indispensable liberalism in the Church of England. He said, 'Though our cause may have its setbacks and the vision be not for today, we can but be faithful to the light as we see it and strive for the future we may never see. "Though it tarry wait for it, because it will surely come."'

Where does this leave Fallows as a bishop? Here is some perspective. The Church of England embarked at the Reformation on a great venture to accommodate old to new, tradition to reform; to maintain Church authority, while allowing freedom to private judgement; to continue the ministry of bishops, priests and deacons, while asserting complete independence of the Papacy. The great experiment has had its shortcomings but the value of the ideal should not be disparaged or minimized. Of all the Christian bodies, it alone tries to fuse both Catholic and Protestant together into a unity which shall comprehend both.

Gordon Fallows studied, used and commended the argument for episcopacy found in *Doctrine in the Church of England* (1938). In that report the nature of the office of bishop depends upon the unity of the elements, summarised as follows:

1. Historically the Episcopate is the organ of the mission and authority of the Church.
2. One of the functions of the Episcopate is to guard the Church against erroneous teaching.
3. The Bishop represents the whole Church in and to his diocese, and his diocese in and to the Councils of the Church.
4. The Bishop in his diocese represents the Good Shepherd; the ideal of pastoral care is inherent in his office. Both clergy and laity look to him as Chief

Pastor, and he represents in a special degree the paternal quality of pastoral care.

5. Inasmuch as the unity of the Church is part secured by an orderly method of making new ministers and the Bishop is the proper organ of unity and universality, he is the appropriate agent for carrying on through ordination the authority of the apostolic mission of the Church.

The activity neurosis and lust for reform of the 1960s kept the office and work of bishops under constant discussion and pressure. Fallows followed this movement with care and his critical antennae picked up nuances. Here are a few examples. In his 1960 Bampton Lectures 'Counsel and Consent' Eric Kemp advocated the multiplication of dioceses from forty-three to something like eighty-five. The dioceses would be arranged in new regional groupings, taking account of proposals by geographers and sociologists for the provincial division of England for secular purposes. Fallows' reaction was immediate and succinct, 'Perhaps the expense of implementing these proposals will save us from them.'

In 1964, Leslie Paul, a sociologist, produced a report commissioned by the Central Advisory Council of Training for the Ministry (CACTM), *The Deployment and Payment of the Clergy*, which proposed a coherent plan for redistributing the clergy to match shifts in population. The report recommended utilising the whole force of the clergy to best advantage within a coherent plan, in the belief that this would revitalise the Church and improve clergy morale. The parson's freehold should be abolished and become a leasehold; the distinction between beneficed and unbeneficed clergy should come to an end, patronage should be replaced by regional appointment bodies, together with a Central Clergy Staff Board, and there should be a new form of parochial unit – the 'major parish' – staffed by a college of clergy, all of incumbent status for high density urban areas and widely-scattered rural parishes. There would be a national salary structure and a common stipends fund. In the furore which greeted the 'Paul Report' one proposal was drowned. The report referred to the need for laity to exercise ministry, by the formation of a parochial lay apostolate and street organisations based on house communions.

The Bishop of Chester, Gerald Ellison, led a phalanx of bishops opposing the Paul Report, claiming that implementation would change the character of the Church of England for ever and for ill. Fallows was wary of proposals which would bear directly, and most vitally, upon the relations of the incumbents and their parishioners, because the characteristic figure of the Church of England was the parson in his parish. His independence, his pastoral freedom, and his security of tenure, were the great circumstances which made the profession of an English clergyman, in spite of many disadvantages, an

attractive calling to men of independent character. He accepted the need for
change, even of a radical nature, but 'Paul' enacted completely may change
not simply the face but the innards of the Established Church beyond
recognition. Fallows dissected the proposals in 'Reflections on the Paul
Report' in *The Modern Churchman*. Whilst he accepted the need for reform of
the freehold, the deployment of clergy and the patronage system he was
severely critical of the way in which this would be achieved. He was in favour
of major parishes, group and team ministries but experimentation should
precede wholesale implementation. The freehold could be modified not
abolished. Regional boards might have as many as 2,000 benefices in their gift:

> This would involve an enormous amount of administrative work, and would
> almost necessarily have to be done by a paid secretariat, while the members of
> the board would become little more than a rubber-stamping machine. There is
> in fact a danger of creating a civil service to run a civil service.

He feared the creation of a super-bureaucracy. When he reviewed the report
he could not know that he will become a central figure in some of the
controversial proposals. The 'Sheffield Report' will become as enlightened or
as notorious as the 'Paul Report'. But of the latter his chief criticism and deep
anxiety was 'the planner's desire to create a tidy organisation' which:

> is sometimes blind to the important question of human freedom, and in the last
> resort good organisation is dependent upon our respect for human freedom . . .
> Mr Paul stated at the Press conference at which the Report was launched, that
> one of the underlying reasons for the proposals contained in his report was that
> the Church should have a 'grip' on its clerical man-power. For my part I do not
> wish to live in a Church that has a grip on its clergy so much as I want to live
> in a Church in which the clergy have a grip on themselves.

There was another report in 1964 by a group of five diocesan bishops, headed
by the Bishop of London, Robert Stopford, who were in favour of a large
number of dioceses – over one hundred – grouped into a number of
provinces. In 1965 a CACTM working party on the nature of the pastoral
ministry, chaired by the Bishop of Southwell, Gordon Savage, proposed that
the number of clergy in a diocese should be in the range of 120 to 150.

In 1966 the Archbishop of Canterbury, Michael Ramsey, wrote a
memorandum on Anglican episcopacy for the guidance of the Deployment
and Payment Commission in which he said:

> The authority of a diocesan bishop cannot be delegated either to his suffragans
> or to his brother diocesans. It can, however, be shared with both in a collegiate
> manner. If and how it is practicable to share authority in a group of dioceses

needs closer and more detailed consideration than appears yet to have been given.

In 1967 the report *'Diocesan Boundaries', being the Report of the Archbishop of Canterbury's Commission on the Organisation of the Church by the Dioceses in London and the South-east of England* was published.

A short report in 1967 on 'The Nature and the Function of the Episcopate' from the Faith and Advisory Group of the Missionary and Ecumenical Council was of particular interest on three counts – first, for the theological questions it raised; secondly, by reason of its membership: credibility and integrity were assured by the inclusion of respected names from every tradition including Percy Coleman, Bob Edwards, James Packer, John Lawrence, Donald Allchin, Lionel du Toit, Geoffrey Lampe and Bernard Pawley. Only one bishop, W.Q. Lash, formerly of Bombay, was a member although three would become bishops, Eric Kemp (the group's chairman), Robin Woods, and David Jenkins to Chichester, Worcester and Durham respectively; and thirdly, for its importance and implications for Fallows himself. The group studied schemes for reunion among and with non-episcopal churches and by developments within episcopal churches themselves, including the Roman Catholic Church under Pope John XXIII who consecrated to the episcopate all the cardinals in the curia who were not already bishops. This 'appears to be based on the theory that persons who are doing certain kinds of work in the Church ought to have the status of being bishops, their work being a form of episcope comparable to that of a diocesan bishop.' The group asked the Church of England to give urgent theological consideration to four questions:

1. There is raised the question of the tightness of viewing episcopacy in terms of status.
2. There is raised the question of the relationship of the episcopate to the Church at large. In the Church of England we have at present two classes of bishop, both in full-time employment as bishops of the Church. The members of one of these classes, suffragans and assistants, have no place by right in the conciliar government of the Church. Their exercise of episcopacy is deprived of its collegiate aspect. They have no share in corporate guardianship of the faith and discipline of the Church which the bishops of the province should exercise together.
3. There is raised the question of the relationship of the bishop to his flock. The performance of episcopal duties by deputy in so many English dioceses calls in question the rightness of the argument of the Australian Scheme and the Doctrine Report, as well as what some Anglicans are accustomed to say in support of the practice of episcopal confirmation, e.g., the emphasis upon a person being brought to the head of the local church before being admitted

to communion. Both the determination of the proper size for dioceses and the decision as to the rightness of consecrating to the episcopate men who are not going to have the responsibilities of diocesan bishops depend upon a theology of the right relationship between a bishop and his clergy and people.

4. There is raised the question of the function of the bishop as a centre of unity, as one who draws together the various groups in the Church, having a responsibility for all of them. The more the episcopate is itself fragmented into those having responsibility for particular classes or groups of men the more difficult it will be for the bishop to be seen as a centre of unity.

In 1967 a report was published which, again, will have major repercussions for Fallows when he is at Sheffield. *Partners in Ministry*, under the chairmanship of Canon W. Fenton Morley, Vicar of Leeds was definitely slanted in a radically bold direction. Its starting point was that the way the Church handled the care, deployment, and payment of the clergy was inadequate and wasteful. Its recommendations followed closely those of the 'Paul' Report and included the merging of all patronage; the disappearance of the benefice as then known, and the replacement of the parson's freehold by two alternative forms of tenure: either for a term of years with the possibility of renewal by mutual consent, or without term of years with a greater degree of uniformity of clerical stipends; and the development of overall coordination both of manpower and of financial resources by the establishment of two central bodies with executive as well as advisory powers. It was proposed that all patronage should be vested in a Diocesan Ministry Commission which would have an executive committee presided over by the Diocesan Bishop. This was a reversal of history and it was inevitable that there would be a volcanic eruption which came from a range of bishops, not all predictable names including Chester (Gerald Ellison), Ely (Edward Roberts), Peterborough (Cyril Eastaugh), Exeter (Robert Mortimer), Winchester (Falkner Allison), Lichfield (Stretton Reeve), Bath and Wells (Edward Henderson), and Hereford (Mark Hodson). It also included two bishops whom Fallows will succeed – Pontefract (Eric Treacy), and Sheffield (John Taylor). Equally, there was vocal episcopal support for the proposals, notably from Bristol (Oliver Tomkins), Blackburn (Charles Claxton), Guildford (George Reindorp), St Edmundsbury and Ipswich (Leslie Brown), Salisbury (Joseph Fison), and Southwell (Gordon Savage). As Bishop of Pontefract, Fallows attended the 1968 Lambeth Conference which recommended that bishops should have opportunities of training for their office; that all coadjutor, suffragan and full-time assistant bishops should exercise every kind of episcopal function and have their place as bishops in the councils of the Church; and that as leaders and representatives of a servant Church should radically examine the honours paid to them in the course of divine worship, in titles and customary address, and in style of living, while having the necessary facilities for the efficient carrying on of their work, The temptations and pitfalls for Church of England bishops were greater than anywhere else in the Anglican Communion on some of these issues.

The overarching theme of the Conference was the Renewal of the Church, divided into three sections – in Faith, in Ministry, in Unity. Fallows was a member of Renewal in Unity and belonged to a sub-section of the Wider Episcopal Fellowship, namely, 'The Role of the Anglican Communion in the Families of Christendom.' There were eleven members from England, United States of America, the Phillipines, New Zealand, West Africa, and Brazil. Its chairman was the Bishop of Sodor and Man, George Eric Gordon, a former Principal of the defunct Bishop Wilson Theological College, Isle of Man (the oldest in the Church of England, founded in 1700 and re-founded in 1870). Gordon was a liberal evangelical, and a leading member of the Anglican Evangelical Group Movement. The Vice-Chairman was the Bishop of Gambia and the Rio Pongas, T.O. Olufosoye – a future Archbishop of West Africa, and the Bishop of Nelson, New Zealand, P.E. Sutton was Secretary. Fallows enjoyed being a member of this group and his influence was not negligible. Although 'The Aims of Anglicanism' were described in officialese blandness there is no mistaking what Fallows had always advocated and practised so far as opportunities arose:

1. To welcome, encourage, and be ready to give counsel in the merging of Anglican Churches in united national or regional Churches.
2. To enter into full communion with all such united Churches, even while anomalies remain.
3. To maintain support of such united Churches, as well as to support one another, Church and Church in the Anglican Communion, as need and opportunity arise, with spiritual, intellectual, and material assistance: and to take common counsel.
4. To preserve and enrich our special insights and to contribute them to the whole Christian Church and to the world.

    We believe that the Anglican witness and the Anglican role will continue; but the process of church union will mean that the frontiers of Anglicanism become less defined. Our Anglican contribution to Christendom will be made partly through a closely-knit communion and partly through co-operation and fellowship with others. We believe that the concept of 'communion with the See of Canterbury' affords a sacramental link of abiding value. We believe that it would be premature to define now the future relations between the Anglican Churches and the united Churches which will be a fruitful sharing and interpenetration of many traditions, as the Anglican Communion affirms and merges its own insights of faith and order in each new expression of the one, holy, catholic, and apostolic Church.

We also regard full participation of the various provinces and regions of the Anglican Communion in the consultations and work of the World Council of Churches and in their promotion of joint action for mission as of vital importance. Every opportunity of dialogue and co-operation with other communions should be welcomed. Concern with specific Anglican structures or with the concept of wider episcopal fellowships must not exclude the widest possible ecumenical involvement.

In July 1969 Fallows attended a Senior Diocesan Officers Course at St George's House, Windsor Castle. Of the eighteen people present seven were recently appointed suffragan bishops. In addition there were archdeacons, a diocesan secretary, two lay members of the Church Assembly staff, the head of a theological college, a priest from the staff of the Bishop of New York, and a lecturer in management. The theme was 'The Modern Diocese in our Plural and Changing Society.' Although Fallows found the course congenial he was less enamoured with its focus on bishops as chief executives requiring chief staff officers and selected persons to provide day-to-day advice, and to execute the bishops' policies and decisions. For him these were aspects of episcopacy to be avoided rather than to be absorbed. He had no intention of being a purple-bibbed bureaucrat.

During this period other reports were decanted into the already overflowing glass of the Church including *Crown Appointment and the Church* (The Howick Commission) 1964; and *The Church's Needs and Resources* 1965, not to mention the frequent reports on new forms of services, and church unity. Perhaps more important, were reports on medical ethics and marriage and divorce, which affected, and occasionally changed the law of the land.

One subject had deep interest for Fallows. Between 1870 and 1970 ten commissions and committees met to review the relations between the Church of England and the State. In 1970 *Church and State* was the result of an Archbishops' Commission chaired by Professor Owen Chadwick. It was skilfully Anglican in showing how to remove a number of bricks without disturbing the structure. Recommendations included changes in the manner of choosing bishops; leading members of other Churches should sit in the House of Lords; clergy should not be excluded from standing for Parliament; a programme of legislation should be inaugurated making the intervention of Parliament unnecessary in matters affecting the Church – in short, the Church, through its General Synod should become the final authority on all matters affecting worship and doctrine. Yet there was no agreement on how this should or could be effected. There is a revealing paragraph in the report:

The people of England still want to feel that religion has a place in the land to which they can turn on the too rare occasions when they think that they need it; and they are not likely to be pleased by legislation which might suggest that the English people as a whole were going unChristian.

The last portion of the report headed *A Memorandum of Dissent* was contributed by Miss Valerie Pitt, Head of School of Humanities, Thames Polytechnic, supported by two other members of the commission – Rev. Peter Cornwell, a young vicar from the Durham diocese and Mr D.W. Coe, Labour MP for Middleton and Prestwich. But the impressive and persuasive writing – Fallows called it 'rumbustious eloquence' – was Pitt's alone. She was one of the most colourful characters of the old Church Assembly and capable there – and in the Commission too – of making provocative statements with conviction, and unleashed them at the lethargy, humbug and vested interest surrounding her, as she saw it. In style and effect the *Memorandum* was a polemic, wanting the Acts of Uniformity and other Acts which make up the backbone of the church-state constitutional relationship, to be repealed. In short, she advocated disestablishment. The report talked much of the 'folk religion' held by English people but Miss Pitt wrote: 'Christianity is not a folk or a tribal religion, it is not bred into us by the traditions of our ancestors. It is a gospel, a revealed religion, demanding an active and personal assent.' That is why she wanted the church-state link to be 'modified, broken, before the church can in any way begin to release, or to feel within its structures, the energies of its "ordinary" congregations . . . it is not fair to build the nostalgias, still more our father's nostalgias, into our grandchildren's lives.'

Fallows considered the report in the *Wakefield Diocesan News* (February 1971) not knowing that within a month he would be nominated for the See of Sheffield:

> In our pluralist and increasingly secular society the Establishment of the Church of England looks strangely anachronistic and anomalous. That is not to say it is harmful and undesirable. The inarticulate mass of English people value the recognition of religion which the establishment symbolises. No doubt there is genuine disquiet in certain quarters. Some people regard the establishment in the present state of society as illogical and inappropriate. Some find it positively offensive (particularly in relation to the appointment of bishops!) Some believe the protective veneer of the establishment is a positive hindrance in the Church's witness and mission.

Fallows examined the pros and cons in the establishment versus the disestablishment debate and accepted the pragmatic approach 'of making adjustments to the existing system.' The commission was divided over the proposals for the appointment of bishops. Fallows observes:

> In Proposal A, supported by eight members of the Commission it is stated that there are formidable arguments against the election of bishops. They recommend

the setting up of a Church Advisory Committee consisting of the Archbishop of the Province (where the vacancy occurs) as Chairman, with the other Archbishop (or his nominee), six members appointed by the Vacancy-in-See Committee of the diocese concerned and the Dean or Provost of the Cathedral. This committee would propose two or more names for submission to the Prime Minister who, it is suggested, might adopt the custom of submitting the first name on the list to the Crown. Proposal B, supported by five members of the Commission (but the three who did not sign the report would have opted for this proposal) recommends that a new bishop should be chosen by a small electoral board (very similar in composition to the Church Advisory Committee of Proposal A) having direct access to the Crown. Proposal B would therefore eliminate the Prime Minister from any part or function in the appointment of bishops. Both Proposal A and B go much further than the Howick report on Crown appointments and both, in effect, add up to an electoral college system. Whether they can avoid the pit-falls of an electoral procedure is doubtful and certainly those who believe the method of nomination by the Prime Minister (after careful enquiry and consultations) is the best of all systems will find little to cheer in this section of the Chadwick Commission report.

Fallows was in favour of bishops continuing to be well represented in the House of Lords. Overall he wanted an establishment that spells not status or privilege but responsibility and opportunity.

There was one friend and bishop on the Commission, Ronald Williams of Leicester, who wrote to Fallows on his appointment to Sheffield, 'When men become Suffragan Bishops we rightly say that they are real Bishops, but this does not prevent us from rejoicing with them when they get the chance to exercise their episcopacy at the head of a full family grouping of the Church in a Diocese.' When Fallows was consecrated Williams was near retirement. If they had served on the bench of bishops together they would have shared many convictions from a common base, although Williams, unlike Fallows, was a liberal evangelical with traditionalist traits with an equal emphasis on each word. He was a critic of modernism. The commission's chairman, Owen Chadwick, has some sparkling inside impressions which illuminate Williams and, in a real sense, indicate where Fallows might have stood! He would have loved to have been a member of that Commission:

> At the first meeting, which was held at Number One, Millbank, on 2 December 1966, they all bubbled and spluttered and muttered and bored each other and bashed about. But the Chairman noted on his agenda paper this sentence: Bishop of Leicester splendid – calm humorous sense.
>
> He gave the impression of being a descendant of Dr Arnold, without possessing the wildness of that divine. Arnold had wanted to save the establishment of the Church of England by uniting with all the leading denominations of the nonconformists and establishing them. Like Dr Arnold,

Ronald Williams deeply valued the historic connection between Church and State in England. Any plan to sunder the connection, or 'disestablish' would never have his vote. But he took a large and liberal view of Christian communion, and hoped that in time the ecumenical charities would progress far enough to enable the State, to establish, not only the Church of England, but Christianity.

On the Commission were several radicals. He was as kind to them as possible but their viewpoint somehow offended him, as though it knocked away at part of his reverence for a historic heritage. Not that he sounded ultra-conservative. No man who thought even partly like Dr Arnold could be regarded as a blimp. On the Commission he was never, on any point, the most conservative man in the room. But he valued history dearly, and loved the Church of England that he had known all his life, and disliked radical questions while he liked radicals.

In the interviewing of witnesses he was a courteous but penetrating questioner, Lord Reith with his immense personality and burling brows, a deep-dyed presbyterian with a love of John Keble; the New Testament professors (Moule, Nineham, Lampe) who declared with one voice that you can extract from the New Testament nothing that would give any guidance to a Commission on Church and State – and the Bishop of Leicester, who had taught the New Testament, did not believe a word that they said; and, amusingly but wisely, the Commission trusted the opinion of the Bishop of Leicester more than it believed what the professors said; Trevor Huddleston, angry with the traditionalism of the Church, yet not willing to jettison it altogether; the leaders of Old Nonconformity, who were no longer out to disestablish, but still thought the Church of England 'superior' in its attitudes, and who were not disinclined to Williams' Arnoldian doctrine that they could be included within a future established Church; Eric Fletcher, M.P., who said that the relation of Church and State was excellent and needed no change but you had to have a Church and State Commission every so often to keep people happy. Occasionally a witness would appear with a rigid closed little mind, and then one or two members of the Commission could not help boiling at their bigotry; but if Ronald Williams boiled internally, the others never knew, for at such times he would sit silent and patient, waiting with hopefulness for the interview to end. The Archbishop of Canterbury, Michael Ramsey, came to a meeting at Blackheath to give evidence; and his evidence was so brilliant, setting all the problems in the long perspective of European history, that the Commission sat spell-bound.

At one point in the debate with the Archbishop, the Bishop of Leicester said, 'Parliament needs to be educated out of the idea of uniformity'. That shows how little the man was the mere conservative that some people fancied.

In 1969 the Ministry Committee of the Advisory Council for the Church's Ministry (ACCM) formed a Working Party to consider *Bishops and Dioceses*, the title of its report published in October 1971. Its purpose was to examine the issues raised about the reorganization of dioceses which the Church would have to undertake if, as an episcopal church, it attempted to meet the changing situation. Most of the reports mentioned in this chapter came under scrutiny and the 1967 Missionary and Ecumenical Report was an Appendix. Fallows was a member of the working party during the course of which he metamorphosed from Pontefract to Sheffield. The complete list of members in alphabetical order was:

The Bishop of Derby, C.W.J. Bowles (Chairman)
The Bishop of Barking, W.F.P. Chadwick
The Archdeacon of Birmingham, V.S. Nicholls (later Bishop of Sodor and Man)
Mr G.E. Duffield, Church Assembly member, evangelical and author.
The Rev. A. Ecclestone, former Vicar of Holy Trinity, Darnall, Sheffield
The Rev. A.A.K. Graham of Worcester College, Oxford and from 1970 Warden of Lincoln Theological College (later Bishop of Newcastle)
Mrs B.E. Haworth, Church Assembly and General Synod member; and Member of the Council of ACCM
The Bishop of Liverpool, S.Y. Blanch (later Archbishop of York)
The Bishop of Middleton, E.R. Wickham
The Rev. J.L. Packer, Warden of Latimer House, Oxford
Dr L. Paul, of the 'Paul' Report, Author and Lecturer in Ethics and Social Studies, Queen's College, Birmingham
Canon G.J. Paul, Canon Residentiary of Bristol Cathedral (later Bishop of Bradford)
The Bishop of Sheffield, W.G. Fallows
Professor E.A.O.G. Wedell, Professor of Adult Education and Director of Extra-Mural Studies, Manchester University
The Rev. R.L. Coppin (Secretary)
Consultants: The Rev. J. Coventry, SJ
             The Rev. R. Davies of the Methodist Church
             The Rev. H.M. Springbett of the Presbyterian Church of England
             The Bishop of Monmouth, E.S. Thomas, attended as an observer for the Church in Wales

This chapter has followed the movement of episcopacy from the time of the 1938 Doctrine Report. One word had entered current theological studies on the ministry – 'episcope' – which was generally intended to convey the function of oversight or supervision, which is one of the roles attaching to the Christian ministry as it is to be seen in its embryonic state in the New Testament, and subsequently in the history of the Church.

The Working Party discussed the practice of episcope and the pressures on modern bishops. It was not a recent development. Pressures accelerated over one hundred years and bishops themselves were not free of blame. In the House of Commons' debate on the Bishopric Bill in 1878 – establishing the dioceses of Liverpool, Newcastle, Wakefield and Southwell – one member said that 'the present morbid activity among Bishops had created a degeneracy among the parsons, who were continually running to their bishops, like children running to a nurse!' This point was also made by Bishop Mandell Creighton of London who inwardly wailed at the tiresome people with trivial questions who demanded a hearing, and the time-consuming demands of incessant correspondence. Once asked how he was he replied, 'As well as can be expected when every ass in the diocese thinks that he has a right to come and bray in my study.' On 14 April 1890 Brooke Foss Westcott, Bishop-elect of Durham, wrote to the Archdeacons of Durham and Auckland:

> In the exercise of spiritual oversight, temptations to restless activity, to haste, to self-will must constantly imperil the maintenance of wise, just, and sympathetic government. That unceasing pressure of small cares upon the attention of a Bishop tends to thrust out of his sight those larger duties of the Episcopate which require calm and sustained thought and study. In no other position are the impulses of unreflecting benevolence more likely to disturb the action of that quiet and patient self-devotion through which all stable reforms are accomplished.

Fallows contributed his own thoughts on episcope for the Working Party which reflect his gathering experience of 'being a bishop'.

> Richard Watson was consecrated Bishop of Llandaff in 1782 and held the Bishopric until his death thirty-four years later. There was no official residence and Watson built himself a house on the wooded shores of Lake Windermere where he engaged in country pursuits including sheep-breeding and afforestation. He held an annual ordination and visited his diocese every three years for confirmations and a triennial Visitation Charge. The one in which he warned the clergy of the evils of absenteeism must have sounded incongruous in the ears of his Welsh subordinates. The job specification for Watson's 'episcope' must make the modern Bishop wonder whether he is in the same firm. Between Watson and the contemporary Anglican episcopate, with which the Working Party is concerned, came Samuel Wilberforce (of Oxford, and Winchester) who was largely responsible for the transformation in the conception of the role and function of present day episcopacy. In a letter marked 'Most Private' dated 12 March, 1888 Archbishop Benson wrote to the Dean of Windsor (Randall Davidson): 'S. Wilberforce will be the Execration of the Church of the Future for two things, (1) The Shortened Service, (2) The "New Type" of Bishop. But

he had far too much sense to be himself the 'new type'. His crime was the misleading of his weak little Brothers.' In one sense the Working Party may be said to be wrestling with the consequences of Samuel Wilberforce's crime – the emergence of a new type of Bishop with a 'role expectation' conditioned by the social and economic changes that divide Richard Watson's world from our own. At the same time we are also considering an historic ministry, an episcopacy that goes back (at least) to the second century, an episcopacy that the Church of England has been at pains to preserve.

Maintenance of the Ministry. A primary duty of the episcopate is to preserve the continuity of the ministry. The Bishop ordains. He has an ultimate responsibility for the selection and training of ordinands. Until recent times this was often a perfunctory business but it is now a serious and time-consuming matter. It is made practicable by delegation of part of the responsibility to ACCM, Theological Colleges, Diocesan Directors of Ordinands, Directors of Post-Ordination Training etc. Except perhaps in the very largest urban dioceses this all-important aspect of episcopacy can be discharged under the present arrangement of dioceses. The plea for smaller dioceses does not derive from the need for a bishop to be responsible for fewer ordinations. In any case ordinations have decreased in the last few years and are not likely to increase in the near future. The Bishop, however, being the minister of ordination, enjoys a close relationship to all the Clergy. Hence derives the Bishop's special pastoral care for the clergy. They are his men. The bond between the Minister of Ordination and the Presbyters is more clearly seen in the Roman Catholic Church where men stay in the same diocese, under the same bishop (or his successor) than in our own where movement across diocesan frontiers is frequent and not generally viewed with any particular disfavour or suspicion. But in the Anglican no less than the Roman conception of episcopacy there is built-in this special pastoral care and concern for the clergy.

The question arises how many clergy can one diocesan bishop truly shepherd. The plea for smaller dioceses largely derives from the desire of a Bishop to know his clergy better and the desire of the clergy to know their bishop better. 'The Bishop in his diocese represents the Good Shepherd; the idea of pastoral care is inherent in his office.' This is true but it raises the question how many clergy can one bishop know and care for in any depth. He can only be effectively Father of the Family when the family is a small group, varying in size according to geography (for distances as well as numbers have a bearing on the matter) but always very much smaller than any existing English diocese. The problem of the pastoral care of the clergy may be better resolved by delegation than by such wholesale multiplication of dioceses as would be necessary for the bishop wholly to discharge this function himself. At the present time the Parochial Clergy are up against it. They need a lot of inspiration and encouragement and they rightly look to the Bishop to provide it. But they ought not to become too dependent on their Father-in-God and there are some signs that this is happening. Let the Bishop be a true shepherd but let him keep his distance; let the parochial clergy look to their Father-in-God without forfeiting their rightful and healthy independence.

General Oversight. The diocesan bishop is the chief executive in the diocese. Again this function can only be made tolerable by delegation. There must be a management structure going all down the line and making full use of middle management. The prevalent idea that Bishops are over-burdened by administration is largely a myth. They have quite a measure of control over their diaries and more freedom than the Parish Priest, being less involved in the Sunday round and the pressure of such inescapable duties as funerals, weddings and the like. This isn't to say that Bishops aren't immensely busy people and that their deskwork isn't too heavy. But it is possible for most of them to accept overseas lectures and preaching tours (not excluding the Antipodes) and it is altogether good that this is so.

Discipline. The Bishop is the officer responsible for discipline. Much of his time (and not a little of his spiritual energy) will be expended dealing with the difficult Clergy and the moral breakdowns. There is no adequate substitute for this personal ministry. It is sometime immensely taxing.

Teacher of the Faith – Guardian of Doctrine. Prophet and Enabler of Mission. No analysis of episcope can omit these functions. An early draft of the report suggests that in different historical situations special emphasis in the understanding of the episcopal office will be made e.g. 'When it is on guard against heresy it will call for learned Bishops.' The Church of course is always on guard against heresy and is conspicuously so in these days. There has been a continuous tradition of learned Bishops not least in the English Church. But the supply does not always meet the need and there have been fewer appointments from high academic posts in recent years. Perhaps the prevailing understanding of episcope stresses the pastoral and administrative function at the expense of the intellectual and the prophetic. When so much importance is attached to the Church's supreme task of Mission in the contemporary world it is fatal to underestimate the place of intellectual leadership and the prophetic role of the Bishop.

Confirmation. In the Anglican Church the Bishop is the sole minister of confirmation and it is sometimes suggested that the pressure of his office might be relieved by removing this particular burden. A proposal was recently made that Rural Deans should be 'licensed' as Ministers for Confirmation. This would have the unfortunate result of removing the one personal link between the Bishop and the laity. Candidates for Confirmation (like ordinands) are fewer than they were and to that extent the burden (if burden it be) is already lessened. Most Bishops enjoy confirmations and would not wish to be relieved of them. Changes could be made which would relieve the pressure when necessary. More candidates could be presented at fewer centres. More use could be made of the Cathedral Church as a centre for Confirmations. In this way the demands on the Bishop could be reduced (when desirable) and there would be some consequent gain for the candidates to offset what might be lost by not being confirmed in their own Parish Church.

As each draft of the *Bishops and Dioceses* report was circulated Fallows went through them with a fine-toothed comb, paying attention to both substance and style, suggesting amendments, ever watchful that the conception of the bishop as *pastor pastorum* was not diluted. There were members of the Working Party who considered that the familiar image of the bishop as 'shepherd' or 'father' was outdated, a view strongly resisted by Fallows. Fallows was a Suffragan Bishop when he joined the Working Party and had learned of the difficulties involved when the various roles and functions of a bishop in a diocese are such that they only make sense in a single person. When he was moving to a diocese of his own he wrote a farewell article in the *Wakefield Diocesan News* (May 1971) accepting, 'A body can only have one head, a family one father, a flock one shepherd. And so the poor Suffragan Bishop has to play second fiddle in what is by definition a one-man band. Or so the argument runs.' Accordingly he asked, 'Well, is it a dog's life being a Suffragan Bishop?' and answered:

> Not really. It depends where you are and with whom you serve. Let me (an ecclesiastical anomaly and theological monstrosity, if you like) testify, as I prepare to pack my bags, that the two and three quarter years I have served in the Wakefield diocese have been wonderfully happy and satisfying. They have been years of unclouded joy in my ministry . . . There is one obvious reason for this. I have been treated with the utmost consideration and generosity. Discerning readers will know what I mean when I say that I have always been conscious of engaging in a shared episcopate, an episcopal partnership, an altogether precious experience for which I am profoundly grateful. I have been freely consulted; I have shared fully in all the episcopal work; I have taken a full part in ordinations both of deacons and priests (a rare experience for suffragans!).

This says a great deal about both Eric Treacy and Gordon Fallows but it depended on their friendship, Treacy realising that he had a gem of a suffragan and Fallows acting with reserve, not pushing himself forwards, always aware of 'no trespassing' signs.

When *Bishops and Dioceses* was published in October 1971 there were some forthright observations and recommendations. On suffragan bishops, 'Where it is necessary to have more than one bishop in a diocese it would be better to abolish the title "suffragan" so that it may be clear that each one is a bishop exercising the full episcopal office.' There were words which essentially represented Fallows' own approach to episcope, 'Episcopal work is essentially personal, both within the life of the Church and the world. This we believe is the most important element in the word "pastoral".' But 'we value the concept of the bishop as a "father-in-God" but the idea of a single bishop as the personal head of such a diocese imposes on one man responsibilities which

27. Preaching at Enthronement June 1971

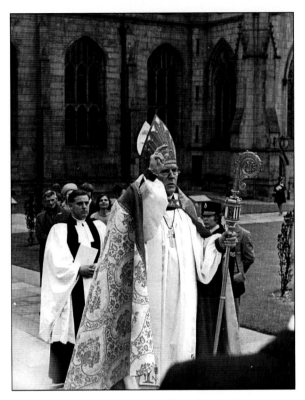

28. *Blessing the City of Sheffield after Enthronement*

29. *Drawing of F.W. Robertson*

30. Mandell Creighton

31. Dr Henry Major (from the archives of Ripon College, Cuddesdon)

32 & 33. Bishop Samuel Fallows, Gordon's American namesake; born at Pendleton 13 December 1835; died 5 September 1922 at Chicago; founded an Episcopalian Methodist denomination, described in posthumous biography by his daughter Alice, Everybody's Bishop. *(Sears 1927) Friend of President Theodore Roosevelt. Reputation in Chicago dented when his approved Bishop's Beer failed to meet demand during Prohibition*

34. *Introduction to the House of Lords; supported by John Phillips, Bishop of Portsmouth and Eric Treacy, Bishop of Wakefield*

35. Hetley Price, first Bishop of Doncaster; later Bishop of Ripon

36. Stewart Cross, second Bishop of Doncaster; later Bishop of Blackburn

37. Meeting the Queen with Edna at York, June 1972 (reproduced by permission of Newsquest York Ltd)

38. *With Edna in the study at Bishopscroft (reproduced by permission of Sheffield Newspapers Ltd)*

no single person can carry.' In a large diocese or those in metropolitan or urban areas a College of Bishops was recommended. Collegial episcopacy would provide a variety of episcopal ministry. What was the suggested practice and will it affect Fallows' own action as Bishop of Sheffield, a single bishop as the head of the diocese?

The focusing of episcopacy in a personal way is of fundamental importance. Yet it is impossible to provide 'coalescence in a single person' in the large urban areas except by ways which in practice deny the objective they are intended to achieve. The division of these areas into units small enough for an individual bishop to manage would produce units which had meaning only in terms of dormitory residence. Further, if these bishops were assisted by other bishops whose responsibilities were for functional areas such as industry, education, local government and community service, then people might reside in one diocese, but at work be the concern of another bishop.

A college of bishops would be able to hold together the Church's care for people in all these aspects of their lives, so that the Church could be active within the community and also care for its own members. The bishops would not be prevented from being representative persons in the larger civic community and there would be no separation of pastoral care from administration, for example in finance or deployment, which must be done in large units. By contrast, independent small dioceses would have to share common administrative services to such an extent that the reality of their independence would be severely limited. Worse still, such sharing would separate the diocese from its administration and make it less effective pastorally. This is why it seems to us that a province of small dioceses would be much less satisfactory than a single diocese with a collegial episcopate in an area which is already a social, cultural and administrative unit.

The precise structure and division of responsibilities in the college could only be worked out through experience but there are guiding principles necessary to establish the character of this collegial episcopate.

(a) All members of the College should be appointed by whatever method is used for appointing diocesan bishops.

(b) The college should have a head (the president) to enable it to function as a group.

(c) The president should be appointed in the same way as the other bishops and we would expect this to include consultation with the college by those making the appointment, in addition to the other and statutory consultations.

(d) The title of the president would normally be associated with a principal community in the area, for example in the West Midlands, the Bishop of Birmingham; or South East Lancashire, the Bishop of Manchester, on Merseyside, the Bishop of Liverpool.

(e) The method of making decisions used by the college would be crucial. A critical point would be whether the president would be willing that the college should accept and act on the corporate view of his colleagues when it was other than his own.

(f) The college as a team of bishops would need to accept that amongst themselves leadership is a function which would be exercised within the college by different members at different times according to the knowledge and experience of each other.

In the college each bishop would have a personal episcope involving, (a) a territorial area, where he would normally ordain, confirm, institute and license as the person who represents and relates the universal Church to the local Church; (b) a sphere of community life (e.g. education, industry, local government, hospitals, the mass media) in which he would bear the general responsibility of the Church in the diocese; (c) a personal knowledge of his clergy and lay readers in his territorial area; (d) his skill and knowledge being formally recognised within the college, and by the diocese; (e) contributing his specialised knowledge and gifts to the college of bishops and the Bishop's Council and integrating the work in his area and sphere of responsibility in the whole strategy and work of the Church in the entire diocese; (f) his representation as a bishop in the synods. All the bishops in a diocese should constitute the House of Bishops of the Diocesan Synod. And the diocese should be represented in the House of Bishops of the General Synod by the president of the episcopal college or one of the other members of the episcopal college. To secure parity with the smaller dioceses it might be advisable in the case of large metropolitan dioceses to appoint more than one bishop to the General Synod.

What could be done in smaller dioceses with urban and rural areas such as Wakefield, Bradford, Ripon and Sheffield? In 1971 Bradford and Sheffield had solo diocesan bishops and Wakefield and Ripon had one suffragan each. Would the traditional provincial structure – York – be necessarily disturbed if a college of bishops was introduced? How would the bishops work in harness?

It is difficult to imagine how this could be effective. There was merit in those dioceses which were sufficiently small for those who lived in them to feel they belonged together although there was a divide in both Ripon and Bradford between the cities of Leeds and Bradford respectively from the northern dales areas. The working party report recommended team episcopacy for large rural dioceses, for example, Norwich and Lincoln, or ones with varied components, for example, York, Oxford, Chichester and Lichfield. Here the solution would be a team episcopate of bishop-archdeacons on the lines of a team ministry under the Pastoral Measure.

We will now discover how Fallows develops episcopal ministry in Sheffield.

CHAPTER 11

Sheffield

IN 1971 THE City of Sheffield produced a lavish forty-four page publication advertising its wares and its future – 'City on the move':

Yorkshire's largest city and the finest shopping in the north;
Europe's cleanest industrial city, where the smoke of yesterday has been ruthlessly eliminated;
the city of quality, with an unrivalled reputation for skill and craftsmanship;
the friendly, trouble-free city, unfamiliar with industrial strife and student unrest;
the city dominated by trees and flowers and surrounded by countryside of exquisite beauty.

If a prospective bishop had been seduced by this enticing description he would have packed his bags for an Eldorado of a See. This brazen gloss on Sheffield would not have squeezed or squeaked through trades description legislation. At least the City was in better condition than the Diocese.

When Fallows received the Prime Minister's letter he consulted John Hewitt, the Prime Minister's Appointments Secretary, Eric Treacy, and a very few others, before accepting within a week and the appointment was soon made public. There was scratching of heads and some furrowed brows from people who did not know Fallows when *The Times* prematurely aged Gordon Fallows at sixty-seven years rather than the accurate fifty-seven years!

Wakefield felt bereft. Letters from the diocese to Fallows expressed grief at having their bishop snatched away from them. The letters from Sheffield were ones of expectancy and gladness. Extracts from a few letters are of interest as they came from people who were familiar with the extent of the problems he was inheriting. The Archbishop of Canterbury, Michael Ramsey, considered Fallows would bring 'loving care and wisdom to his new work.' The robust Bishop of Blackburn, Charles Claxton, intimated that Fallows 'had the ability and experience to carry out a tough job.' The Bishop of Rochester, David Say, wrote, 'I hope you can quickly gather about you a strong team. Loyal colleagues who are also friends are the essential requirement for the job.' Harry Carpenter, retired Bishop of Oxford, noted:

I am tempted to say how fortunate you are to have had an apprenticeship as a Suffragan Bishop and not to have been thrown into a diocese at the deep end, as some of us were. After John Taylor's long illness, there must be much to catch up with in Sheffield, but you have the steadiness and the patience which seems to be so much in demand if one is going to keep people working together in some kind of unity. Synodical Government will help in this no doubt, but the need to explain everything more and more times to more and more bodies is perhaps an extra tax on one's patience. I began to find it so before I left Oxford.

The Bishop of Carlisle, Cyril Bulley, conveyed a sense of what might have been:

I've told Eric (Treacy) that there's only one thing I regret about your move to Sheffield. That is that I had cherished the hope that you might have followed me here! (in 1972) But Sheffield's need is immediate and could not be better met. It's a tough assignment for any man but you have the gifts and the experience and you will be given the grace. Barrow will be proud that one of its sons is to undertake so responsible a task and you will take a place alongside Norman Birkett in the Barrow Grammar School's list of eminent Old Boys.

And one of the Church of England's wisest women, Mrs (later Dame) Betty Ridley, who knew and saw Fallows at work on national boards and committees observed, 'One gathers that the situation is such an unhappy one and I know that in you they will have a Father in God who is both firm and decisive, but also loving and understanding.' A friendly communication came from the Bishop of Repton, Warren Hunt:

There was a young fellow named Fallows
Whom the Tudors would have had on the gallows
He was summoned by Ted
To go to Sheffield instead
All Hail to the Fallows who hallows. (Poor but all my own work.)

Pre-eminent in the huge correspondence which follows the appointment of any bishop was the emotional exchange between Treacy and Fallows:

(Treacy to Fallows 14 March 1971)
When I was appointed to Wakefield, I received a pretty heavy mail, and I have no doubt that you and Edna are being engulfed in letters – and a very heart warming experience it is. It made me wonder how I had managed to deceive so many people for so long! . . . No letter will come to you from a fuller heart than mine. Full with sorrow and joy. I simply cannot find words to express what these last 3 years have meant to me. It has been all joy to be together. Taking over Wakefield has not been easy for a person of my limited resources (I mean that), and to have had you standing by my side has given such strength. Your wisdom, steadiness, and understanding, and above all, your marvellous loyalty, have given me a security that I am going to miss terribly. But more than any of those things – it has been our mutual affection that has been so precious. . . . Thank God we shall be neighbours – that makes it a bit easier.

(Fallows to Treacy 15 March 1971)

I am even more bowled over by your letter than I was by the P.M.'s letter. Having been in a whirl for a week & a half I was just recovering consciousness when you floored me again by the generosity of your sentiments.

I really don't know how to thank you for all you have meant to me & all you have done for me during these three ecstatically happy years. As you know Edna & I could have lived out our working days with complete joy & satisfaction & fulfilment. Such was our harmony – both diocesan and domestic. You & May were responsible for that blissful contentment we have experienced here.

Oh, how much I have learned to my profit at your side. And how much I have learned to admire – magnanimity, courage & compassion. I trust a little of your virtue has brushed off on me to strengthen me for what lies ahead. I believe I have been singularly fortunate in serving an episcopal apprenticeship in such favourable circumstances. No one could have been more blessed in his boss or less bossed by him. Our partnership has been infinitely precious to me & I am thrilled it has been to your satisfaction too.

You will realise that a mountain of mail arrives daily & brings much encouragement. But no letter has strengthened me like yours & none will be more treasured. I only wish I could reply adequately & express what is in my heart.

There is a mistaken notion that smaller dioceses are more easily shepherded, generate fewer administrative chores, and are less pressurised than larger dioceses. The following figures of the Northern Province of York apply to 1978:

Diocese	Area (sq. mls)	Population	Benefices/ Churches	Stip. Clergy
York	2,661	1,297,000	309/632	330
Durham	1,015	1,580,000	237/315	307
Blackburn	878	1,240,000	235/299	261
Bradford	920	630,000	122/180	138
Carlisle	2,475	477,000	189/357	187
Chester	1,017	1,543,000	247/394	310
Liverpool	389	1,643,000	207/265	303
Manchester	415	1,994,000	308/386	367
Newcastle	2,084	780,000	143/249	181
Ripon	1,359	765,000	140/227	173
Sheffield	571	1,198,000	163/238	219
Sodor and Man	221	65,000	27/43	19
Southwell	848	999,000	209/327	209
Wakefield	562	1,058,000	199/269	208

Including bishops suffragan in 1971 York had four bishops; Blackburn, Chester and Manchester – three; Durham, Carlisle, Liverpool, Ripon, Southwell and Wakefield – two; and Bradford, Newcastle, Sodor and Man, and Sheffield –

diocesan bishop only. There was additional assistance from retired bishops in some Sees.

The Diocese of Sheffield was created in 1914, covering South Yorkshire with major centres of population at Sheffield, Rotherham and Doncaster. Everywhere there were signs of a past influenced, if not wholly created, by the Industrial Revolution. Grime and grit were features in 1914 with notable manufacturing industry in heavy engineering; pride in its high quality steel; renowned for its cutlery; and coal mining. By 1971 the glory and the prosperity had receded into a gathering gloom. It was too early to predict any future for a depressed and depressing area. Yet there were many conspicuous buildings of architectural significance, including the Town Hall, City Hall and Cutlers Hall. There were other features of this mixed diocese. Mines may have closed but not the strong village communities which they represented. There were rich agricultural pastures together with ancient churches, ruined castles and abbeys, sentinels of a much distant historic past. The population of the diocese was one hundred thousand fewer than it was in 1935.

In order to understand the reception received by the fourth bishop of Sheffield, a few notes about his episcopal inheritance may be useful. Leonard Hedley Burrows did not have any of the obvious attributes of breathing life into a newly created diocese in the industrial North of England. To local people his first disqualification was that he had no Northern antecedents and was emphatically not a Yorkshireman. But Northerners should be aware that the bishops on whom they lavish praise are usually ones with foreign southern blood in their veins! Burrows owed his ecclesiastical ascendancy to the Archbishop of Canterbury, Randall Thomas Davidson. The Archbishop of York, Cosmo Gordon Lang, appears to have had little say in the appointment of Burrows, who, at the time of his appointment to Sheffield, was Bishop Suffragan of Lewes in the Chichester diocese. In 1914 he was an energetic fifty-seven year old. Chichester, then as now, was known for its Anglo-Catholicism. Was Burrows tainted? Sheffield did not have any particular colouring but it veered to 'low' away from 'high.' There was only a handful of churches where a whiff of incense could be regularly inhaled. As it happened Burrows was mainstream, of flexible churchmanship. On moving to Sheffield he consigned his Chichester cope and mitre to the wardrobe and never wore them in Sheffield.

Burrows, educated at Charterhouse and New College, Oxford, was tall, charming, confident, good humoured. He was respected for his hard work and the determined way in which he secured the foundations of the diocese and presided over the establishment of the considerable organisational aspects involved. His gifts were evident in the way he chaired meetings with dignity, without pomposity and a determination to reach and achieve conclusions leading to action. He knew how to lay foundations which would not be disturbed by seismic shifts after he left. But he stayed too long. When he retired in 1939, after twenty-five years, the world was a different place. The diocese was created at the outbreak of the First World War and he retired at the outbreak of the Second World War. How could an eighty-two year old bishop wholly comprehend or be sympathetic to the dramatic changes in society and of the industrial life of his diocese?

Such queries could not be raised or held against forty-nine year old Leslie Stannard Hunter, son of a noted Congregational minister in Scotland. He was educated at Kelvinside and New College, Oxford. He had many interests and gifts and could have been a professional pianist. Instead he joined the Student Christian Movement as a layman. The S.C.M. was at the pinnacle of its influence. Ordained during the First World War, Hunter served with the Y.M.C.A. in France and afterwards with the Army of Occupation. After a curacy at St Martin-in-the-Fields, he moved to Newcastle Cathedral as Canon Residentiary, where he was closely involved with education, social service initiatives and unemployment. He was meticulous with his research, not simply gathering facts but testing and authenticating them. From 1926 to 1930 he was vicar of the large parish of Barking on the fringes of London's East End. His book *A Parson's Job – Aspects of Work in the English Church* (1931) was a fruit of this period. In the year of publication Hunter returned to Tyneside as Archdeacon of Northumberland. He was the driving power of the diocese of Newcastle during the lacklustre episcopate of Harold Ernest Bilbrough (1927–1941). Hunter was also a power in the Tyneside Council of Social Service. Always a great promoter of causes and of public education, these complemented his archidiaconal duties. Yet if these facts convey an impression of a maverick figure, robust in appearance and powerful in speech, then they would be unrecognisable in Sheffield given the persona and presence of Leslie Hunter. But he was the right man for Sheffield.

Hunter was both thinker and doer, a reformer, a better judge than advocate. Strangely he was devoid of a distinctive personality. Did this matter? He was short, quiet and shy, given to long silences, not at social ease. He could appear arrogant. He was also very far-seeing and shrewd; censorious of laziness, both of the flesh and even more of the intellect and probably almost contemptuous of intellectual or spiritual cowardice. He was a tremendous admirer of Baron von Hugel. There was foresight and insight in abundance and Hunter appointed many people to key positions in the diocese who complemented his own limitations of personality. He valued, and planned for, lay ministry, even if lay people found him formidable and could not relax in his presence.

There is another, and more important, dimension which flowed from his transparent integrity. He was no ecclesiastical partisan but had a distinctive leaning towards the left in politics. He won the confidence of Labour, civic leaders and trade unionists. His shortcomings were ones of personality and were far outweighed by his considerable strengths. He had a gift for listening to people on both sides of industry, management and unions in the steel works and related industries, and they knew he was listening both attentively and with intent! He was more than aided and abetted by the work of the Sheffield Industrial Mission under the unusual, controversial and inspiring leadership of Ted Wickham, later Bishop of Middleton. Hunter pioneered many national initiatives. Behind his daunting looks and disconcerting silences, Sheffield was fortunate in having as its second bishop one of the most forward-looking bishops of his generation, regarded by many as a prophet. He retired in 1962.

Francis John Taylor, aged forty-nine, Principal of Wycliffe Hall Theological College, Oxford succeeded Hunter. Born in Lincolnshire, he strayed into Yorkshire for his schooling at Hymers' College, Hull, thence to Queen's College, Oxford. The twin peaks of his ministry were as Vicar of Christ Church, Claughton, Birkenhead from 1942–1954, and two bouts at Wycliffe Hall, as tutor and lecturer 1938–1942, returning as Principal in 1955 until his appointment to Sheffield. He came from the already diminishing school of Liberal Evangelicalism. He was a Proctor in Convocation for the Oxford diocese and his close association with the ever-growing Parish and People Movement (he edited their periodical) brought him to the attention of a wide circle of acquaintances. Prior to Sheffield he had a reputation of being a matter-of-fact, down-to-earth person, quick to spot a hollow claim. In his youth he had a devastating wit and although maturity helped to guard his tongue the wit remained. He was quick to expose expediency disguised as principle because he placed a high value upon expediency. Surely a match for Sheffield.

Taylor was consecrated bishop on 25 July 1962 and his Enthronement was fixed for 15 September. And then . . . tragedy! On 4 September, the last day of a holiday, Taylor suffered a cerebral thrombosis causing weakness of his left leg and arm. The Enthronement was postponed. In an interview with a *Sheffield Telegraph* reporter (30 October) the bishop said, 'What does it feel like to be struck down, suddenly and quite unexpectedly, by a serious and disabling illness, just on the eve of the beginning of the biggest job of your life? Crushing, bewildering, frustrating, these are the words that naturally suggest themselves to describe your state of mind at such a moment.' Although Taylor made some recovery he could never use his left hand again. His speech was not affected. The Enthronement took place on 21 March 1963.

It was not the first time that a bishop had been 'struck down' at the beginning of his episcopate. The question may be asked – it was certainly asked in Sheffield – if the stroke after his consecration should have debarred Taylor from taking up his post?

In one sense Taylor showed great courage in continuing. His speeches and writings were learned. His lengthy articles in the *Sheffield Diocesan Review* were masterly, forensic in their arguments, always thought-provoking, causing as much dissension as discussion. One priest used to describe him as so right, so trite, so erudite, but many lay people preferred him to Leslie Hunter. The paralysis had not affected his voice and they could hear him – Hunter mumbled – and admired his speaking without notes. But he had only a little more capacity for small talk than his predecessor. His overall style was cold, withdrawn and remote, partly because of his stroke. His approach to industrial mission was wholly negative. His strident and 'unbudgeable' stance caused the British Iron and Steel and Kindred Trades Association to break its links with the Sheffield Industrial Mission. He brought death to one of the most imaginative initiatives of the Church which was admired in Europe and beyond.

Taylor gathered round him as his senior staff, men of identical views whose respect for his learning led them to accept his unequivocal leadership, largely without question. His main supporters in the parishes were therefore those who tended to be blinkered or blind to any theological and doctrinal positions but their own. Thus there emerged in the diocese clergy and laity who felt outcasts for whom their bishop had neither sympathy nor time. They perceived him as stiff and formal, brooking no deviation from his own policy and views. Was the diocese in danger of losing much that it had become and achieved during Leslie Hunter's episcopate? For many, Taylor's vote against Anglican Methodist Unity was the last straw. Nonetheless he was a very gifted man and it was a tragedy that his stroke prevented him from being the bishop he might and should have been.

In 1970 Taylor suffered a recurrence of his illness and although he battled heroically in striving towards recovery, medical advice and pressure compelled him to retire in April 1971. He was most generous to his successor as Gordon Fallows acknowledged 'even from his hospital bed, he has shown me the utmost consideration and kindness.'

The diocese was fortunate to have an assistant bishop, George Vincent Gerard from 1947 to 1971. For part of the period he was also Vicar and Rural Dean of Rotherham, and later Canon Residentiary of Sheffield Cathedral. Gerard had made his name as Bishop of Waiapu, New Zealand (1938–1944) and Senior Chaplain to the New Zealand Forces. He had an MC and a CBE from the First and Second World Wars respectively. He was a robust chairman, not a man to trifle with, but respected, trusted and loved by clergy, proven by his appointment as Vice-Chairman of the House of Clergy of Church Assembly. Although clearly a man of and under authority he was unassuming as a person. By conviction he was High Church and insisted on dignity in worship. Everyone who knew him appreciated that the daily rhythm of worship was both anchor and spur to his work. After forty-nine years of ordained ministry he retired as Fallows arrived.

There is often a chasm between the bishop a diocese wants and the bishop a diocese needs. In Sheffield there were clergy working in desperately discouraging conditions in the industrial and struggling centres of the diocese and a feeling of isolation in some of the rural parishes. The diocese required more than pastoring – that is taken for granted – it needed warmth, cheering up and encouraging, even a bit of celebration and whoopee, before new challenges and inspiration would have any effect.

The upheaval of moving from one house to another was another change as the Church Commissioners had decided that Ranmoor Grange, Sheffield, the house occupied by Hunter and Taylor, was unsuitable to continue as the See house. It was in need of extensive and expensive repairs, before it could be brought up to anywhere near standard. In 1969 the Commissioners purchased a modern home 'Molescroft' in Snaithing Lane, Sheffield for adaptation as the See house, to be renamed 'Bishopscroft'. It comprised 'office' and 'domestic' portions, ample room for hospitality and entertainment, a chapel for the bishop's use. There was also the alluring prospect of one and a quarter acres of grounds and garden which was sufficient to whet the appetite of 'Mrs Bishop'.

Fallows was as eager as was the diocese for his episcopate to commence. There were legal formalities and farewells in Wakefield and Pontefract with much dabbing of eyes. It was a little under three months following the announcement of his appointment before Fallows presented himself for Enthronement in his Cathedral Church of St Peter and St Paul on 4 June 1971. In common with all such occasions it was a mixture of prayer and pageantry, fanfares and processions, music and blessings. Fallows looked more pontifical than pontifex in a new cope and mitre. In the service there were also quiet moments for him to kneel and pray under the Lantern, before being enveloped in an act of worship which was both simple and profound, as only the Church of England is capable of doing. In his sermon he used as a text words which are usually used to precede a sermon: 'Let the words of my mouth and the meditation of my heart be now and always acceptable in Thy sight, O Lord, my strength and my redeemer.' (Psalm 19, 14–15).

These words are singularly appropriate for this occasion especially when we understand them in their original sense. The Hebrew poet meant something more by 'words' than we do in the ordinary usage of language. To the Psalmist, words stood for deeds, for action, for life itself. Again, when he speaks of meditations he means not just inner thoughts, but inward character and true being. So as I make this prayer, and as you make it with me, we make our self-offering and dedication to the task which we are called together. What then as we look to the future, are the 'words' that is to say the life, what are the 'meditations' that is to say the inner character that are acceptable to God in our time and well pleasing in His sight today. 'Jesus Christ is the same, yesterday, today and for ever.' Though we must present the gospel in modern dress, we must remember it is the everlasting gospel. We are not called to be 'with it.' Our concern is truth, not fashion. Dean Inge, in a characteristic sentiment, reminded us that 'he who marries the spirit of the age will be a widower tomorrow.' And the seventeenth-century Bishop Joseph Hall, when chided for not preaching to the times, defended himself by saying that 'when everyone is preaching to the times, may not one preach to eternity.' Here I believe is a pointer to the vocation of the church. It is to lead men to know and experience the eternal, to remind men of the beyond in our midst and that there is more to life than consumer goods. 'The Kingdom of God is not eating and drinking but in righteousness and peace and joy in the Holy Spirit.' Lose this dimension and we perish. When the clergy lose faith in our calling, when we are perplexed and puzzled about our role, we need to see that calling and that role at its highest and best. When our spirits droop, then is the time to:

Lift up your hearts
Let us lift them up to the Lord
It is meet and right so to do.

But if Heaven is God's throne, we must also remember that the earth is His footstool. For the Christian there is only one Kingdom. Josef Hromodka, in his Thoughts of a Czech Pastor, is intensely critical of the thesis of the two kingdoms whereby 'a deeply religious inner life and a total lack of interest in the situation of the world go together. The worship which it is our joy and privilege to offer must issue in life.' This is what Hromodka bore witness to in a Marxist regime. Profoundly honest he was deeply committed to a theology and a Christianity that sees the struggle for a 'genuine humanity in its dignity and freedom, in its weakness, but also in its creative capabilities . . . as . . . not only a difficult task but a joyous privilege.' Such is our call today – to promote the mission of the Church to a hungry generation; a difficult task, but a joyous privilege. This diocese is well equipped for such a task. In its conference centre at Whirlow Grange, in its Industrial Mission, in Hollowford Training Centre, in its educational chaplaincies as well as in the steady, undramatic but all important work of the parish clergy and the devotion of the laity – here are the tools and the craftsmen for the task. I come to share the task with you. I bring no manifesto, but many concerns. I mention only one today. It is the concern to win the younger generation for Christ and his Church. If we fail at that point the future is bleak indeed. In a recent Sunday Colour Supplement article, the theologian Charles Davis described his impressions of the American scene in such a way as to suggest that it had close similarities to our own. 'The overt crisis in the church is the noisy rootlessness of the disillusioned middle-aged; the hidden crisis, which is more serious for the Church, is the quiet ignoring of the Church by the young.' There is too much truth in that impression for any of us to be comfortable. I see in the forefront of our task our mission to the rapidly expanding student world and our need to proclaim Christ to all our young people, so that their idealism and zeal may be harnessed in the cause of the Kingdom and that they may find their own freedom in his service. As we survey the task ahead, however, St Paul's question strikes home. 'Who is sufficient for these things?' It is encouraging to have present today leading members of other Christian Churches and to know that their support and co-operation is available for a shared Christian enterprise. But all of us in this exacting and challenging time are called to tasks beyond our strength.

It is just here that the Whitsuntide message speaks its own encouraging and heartening word. The Holy Spirit is our guide, our strengthener, and by His light we walk, and by His power we work . . .

For all its grandeur, there is at the heart of this service the call: 'Be to the flock of Christ a Shepherd, feed them.' . . . Every other quality and adornment of the human mind – learning, skill, diplomacy, executive ability – can indeed complete and enrich the pastoral office but can in no way substitute for it . . . the most important qualities are the zeal and solicitude of the Good Shepherd.

Clergy and laity walked out of the cathedral in a thoughtful way but also with a spring in their step. One priest used a colloquial and effective expression, 'He gave us a break. Some of us were so uptight under the unequivocal leadership of his predecessor, that when Gordon Fallows came it felt as if we could breathe again and think for ourselves.' Desmond Carnelly, Vicar of Balby with Hexthorpe was sure that 'Gordon Fallows brought to the diocese a very necessary era of peace and unity of purpose. Into a situation of unease and friction, he brought his own talents of warmth, geniality, humour and trust in those around him.'

In area, population, number of benefices and churches, and stipendiary clergy Sheffield was near identical to Wakefield. From the moment of his appointment to Sheffield Gordon Fallows knew he could not lead, administer and pastor a diocese on his own. He had learned valuable lessons from his short time as a suffragan bishop. He knew what he had enjoyed and also what he had had to endure. Theologically and doctrinally bishops, whether diocesan, suffragan or assistant, are all bishops together. It was too early for any recommendations of the *Bishops and Dioceses* report to be considered and we now know that the majority of them remained in the folds of the report. When faced with practical proposals for collegiality the Church was divided. There were a few conspicuous developments by the end of the century, for example in York, London, Oxford, Chichester, Chelmsford, Norwich, Lincoln, Manchester, but little or no progress in smaller dioceses of sharing administrative or other resources with neighbouring dioceses.

If Fallows wanted episcopal assistance the only way to proceed was to ask the authorities for a new suffragan see. He was convinced by his own experience that a suffragan bishop has an important ministry in his own right, not least as an encourager, a pastor and befriender of the clergy. There never was a time when they were more in need of care, understanding and inspiration. And not only the clergy but also their wives and families. The place of women was already changing in society. A bishop's wife could no longer be expected to be an unpaid secretary, unpaid catering manager and unpaid diocesan social worker. She may wish to serve in this way and usually, not always, both bishop and diocese were fortunate if she so chose. But wives were being set free to live their own lives and many wished to follow careers for which they had been trained. Alternatively they may put their skills and energies into being wives and mothers. Edna Fallows was a wonderful example of loving care: care for Gordon who never knew what it was like to return to an empty home after a busy, sometimes gruelling, day. He was always able to shed the burden of the day, which may not end until late, following an evening meeting or Institution, and enjoy his time with his wife, or with friends. He kept his personal life fresh and renewed, even when dire illness struck.

Fallows proceeded with alacrity to prepare his case for a suffragan by assembling all relevant facts, cognisant of the heavy financial implications involved. Bishops do not come cheap! With thorough preparation, presentation and persuasiveness he achieved his objective in record time. There was a sense of relaxed assurance in his manner that belied his determination which was not to be underrated. There was a silver lining to a core of steel. He was able to announce the creation of a Suffragan See of Doncaster in February 1972, making it clear that there would be no territorial sphere for the Bishop of Doncaster, each bishop operating throughout the diocese. He was clear that he was not looking for someone whose theology and churchmanship was different from his own.

In March the appointment of fifty-year old Stuart Hetley Price, Archdeacon of Manchester and Canon Residentiary of Manchester Cathedral, was made. If Price had learned 'how to be a bishop' it was from watching one at work, namely William Derrick Lindsay Greer, one time Bishop of Manchester, to whom he was Domestic Chaplain. Greer was a very good bishop and one independent in his convictions. Hetley Price had established a reputation with students (he had worked with the Student Christian Movement); was active in ecumenical relations; and was known for his sensitivity in pastoral care. He was consecrated Bishop, together with Ralph Emmerson as Bishop Suffragan of Knaresborough, on 1 May 1972 in York Minster. Fallows had learned from his experience in Wakefield, both positively and negatively, so there was no question that it would be a shared episcope, a collegial relationship and an excellent one too! In the *Sheffield Diocesan News* (April 1976) Price confirmed that his 'job' depended primarily for its fulfilment 'on personal relationships and especially on personal relationships with the episcopal team.' Was the promise matched by experience? Later Price reflected:

> The job itself is ill-defined. For my part that has seemed to me a particularly worrying fact. Indeed I would go further and say that it seems to me to present it in very much the same terms as being a Christian in the world. Discipleship and obedience in my understanding demand a continued attempt to buy up the opportunities which God puts in front of us. You can buy up opportunities only if you have a certain freedom. So often our generation, in society at large as well as in the Church, seems to deny itself that freedom. We are so uncertain of ourselves and sometimes so uncertain of lasting verities on which we may stand that we have a passion for trying to reduce everything to rule. Good sense and tacit understanding of gentlemen's agreements may not be adequate when we are protecting other people's interests; in many cases they should be the mark of mature Christian discipleship when we are considering our own. I rejoice to have done a job (as Bishop of Doncaster) where the boundaries were not clearly defined – indeed looking back I think this has been true in different ways of all the jobs I have done since I was ordained. The freedom is one of the great privileges of the Christian ministry. Of course its abuse is obvious and part of the clergyman's great occupational hazard. This sort of freedom may breed idleness, or if not an inclination to put off doing the things you do not particularly enjoy and concentrating on the things in which (perhaps mistakenly) you imagine you excel. The freedom and its use has constantly to be monitored and it is just one of the functions of the Christian fellowship to do just that.

Throughout the diocese Hetley Doncaster had an episcopal ministry of constant activity and of personal contact, warm, shrewd, humorous, unfussy and effective. He was an administrator par excellence, with a remarkably clear head and astonishing grasp of business of many kinds. Being neither stiff nor bureaucratic he was able to explain situations sympathetically and communicate decisions in a way that could be understood and followed. Fallows let his suffragan share the 'Bishop's Letter' in the *Diocesan News*.

Hetley Price had the stature for a diocesan bishopric and in his heart Fallows knew that he would not be able to keep his suffragan for long. In 1975 he was nominated to succeed John Moorman as Bishop of Ripon and was enthroned in April 1976. There is an interesting passage in his enthronement sermon:

> One of my secret heroes has long been the Duke of Plaza Toro, whom you will recall was prudent enough to lead his regiment from behind. In a real sense I believe the same to be true of the bishop. Not that there will never be an

occasion when he is out in front: perhaps in a highly exposed position. Not that there will never be occasions when he has to speak a public, and perhaps unpopular, word. But he will avoid the temptation of imagining that anything worthwhile is achieved by the empty gesture or the easy pronouncement. He will avoid, with God's help, the characteristic episcopal disease – a folie de grandeur – the assumption that because he occupies his office he automatically counts for a great deal both in the Church and the community.

The truth is a good deal more complicated and, as I would believe, a good deal healthier. The bishop has to prove himself; thinking a little, by reading a little, by speaking a very little, by praying a lot, by friendship, sensitivity to what is happening in church and world, by alertness to the signs of the times, by the blessed ability to put himself in other people's shoes, it is in ways like these that he may be able to lead the people of God another short way along their pilgrimage. But note the nature of the leadership: it will be primarily a leadership without stress – which frees other people, clergy and laity alike, to do their Christian 'thing' in the place where God has put them.

Very soon after his enthronement Price suffered a stroke and a second one in September. At the beginning of March 1977 his resignation was announced. Within a week, on 15 March 1977 he was dead. The dioceses of Manchester, Sheffield and Ripon were in mourning. In common with Fallows Price appreciated the writings of Richard Baxter. When Price left Doncaster for Ripon he used some lines of Baxter which 'represent most faithfully my feelings in taking affectionate leave of this Diocese – and viewed in another sense they reflect all the joy and hope and certainty of the good news of Easter, at about which time this will be appearing in print:

He wants not friends that hath thy love,
And may converse and walk with thee.
And with thy saints here and above,
With whom for ever I must be.

As for my friends, they are not lost;
The several vessels of thy fleet
Though parted now, by tempests tost,
Shall safely in the haven meet.

Still we are centred all in thee,
Members, though distant of one Head;
In the same family we be,
By the same faith and spirit led.'

Fallows' choice as the second Bishop of Doncaster was David Stewart Cross, Religious Programmes Producer for the BBC Northern Region. He was forty-eight, Lancashire born, educated at Trinity College Dublin, and trained for the ordained ministry at Westcott House, Cambridge. After serving at Hexham Abbey and St Alban's Cathedral, he moved in 1963 to Manchester University as a member of the chaplaincy team which he combined with parish work in Chorlton-on-Medlock. But it was his work in religious broadcasting from 1968 to 1976 which brought him to the attention of a wide audience. He was an imaginative and discriminating producer – quiet and modest too – who was able to bring the best out of inexperienced broadcasters, and his liberal, tolerant outlook was well suited to the times. It was inevitable that he would be hired onto committees and organisations concerned with the general issues of broadcasting. During this period he made a heap of friends for life. These years gave him professional skills denied to most clergy, in communication, high standards in the presentation of worship and a working acquaintance with people of different religious traditions and diverse social and ethnic origins. And, as Fallows might enquire, what else? Music was paramount; photography was the craft that absorbed him in periods of leisure; and he was a notable punster. Stewart Cross' heroes were William Temple, man of faith; Julian of Norwich, woman of hope; and Jesus of Nazareth, the Christ the Son of the living God, man of sorrows, crucified and risen, the Saviour, the Good Shepherd, the Prince of Peace for love!

Cross had a different kind of vitality to that of Hetley Price or of Gordon Fallows. He thought deeply using poetry to stimulate both mind and senses. His presence in the diocese was always noticeable even if there was a reticence about him. It could have been said of him:

> He never stood on his dignity, but he never lost it. That dignity rested on a vision of God whose love enfolded the entire gamut of human experience and touched even the most desperate form of suffering. He was not an authoritarian figure. He seemed to have taken to heart the ancient prayer to the Holy Spirit, What is rigid, gently bend; what is frozen, warmly tend.

Once again, almost from the start, Fallows felt he would not keep Cross. He was translated to Blackburn in 1982, a few years after Fallows' death. It was as if the tragedy of Fallows followed Cross to Blackburn for cancer was diagnosed and there were periods in hospital. In February 1988 he hoped he might be able to work again on 'half a liver' as he put it. He was open with his clergy and people about what was happening to him. However, on 6 June 1988 he addressed an *Ad Clerum* to 'My dear Sisters and Brothers' of the diocese, prefaced by words in *East Coker* by T.S. Eliot:

> I said to my soul, be still, and wait without hope
> For hope would be hope for the wrong thing; wait without love
> For love would be love of the wrong thing; there is yet faith
> But the faith and the love and the hope are all in the waiting.

During the past months the cancer had spread and taken its toll. Cross announced his retirement on 31 October. By this time he was a gaunt and emaciated figure. In September he went to the Blackburn Diocesan Clergy Conference and, as one participant wrote afterwards, 'The intensity of the spontaneous standing ovation (tears streaming down many clergy faces) which greeted his unexpected appearance was a most moving testimony to the love and esteem in which he came to be held.' Cross died on 6 April 1989. His chaplain, Paul Warren, wrote movingly in the *See of Blackburn* words which bear repetition here, bearing in mind that it was Fallows who was responsible for bringing him to the episcopate at Doncaster:

> At the heart of his ministry was the simple fact that he loved God and he loved other people. God was a reality to him, a dynamic God who revealed new aspects of His truth and called His people forward to face up to changes in the life of the Church. His spirituality was rooted in the offices and the Eucharist, and drew inspiration from poetry, music and the beauties of nature which he so skilfully photographed. Because he loved God he loved God's people . . . The clergy of the diocese experienced this love in his warm pastoral care, his concern for their families, the joyful hospitality which he and Mary provided at Bishop's House . . . (Also) I have been struck by the number of lay folk who during his illness have expressed real affection and concern for him. Pastoral care of individuals was the prime concern of his ministry, and being a sensitive man, that pastoral care cost him a lot of pain. St Paul wrote to the Galatians, 'The fruit of the Spirit is love, joy, peace, patience, kindness, goodness, faithfulness, gentleness, self-control. That's a pretty accurate pen-portrait of Bishop Stewart.'

Fallows was able to share episcope with Hetley Price and Stewart Cross in the service of the diocese of Sheffield. He was already looking forward to this 'fullness of life' in every sense of the phrase.

CHAPTER 12

Encouraging and strengthening

FALLOWS ADMITTED THAT his first two years in Sheffield were ones of 'hard slog'. It was sixty miles across and Bishopscroft was in a corner of the diocese. He travelled 20,000 miles a year and received twenty letters a day requiring his attention. Preparation of sermons and addresses was time consuming. They were usually typed in note form on small pieces of paper, more than prompters and easily extended to complete manuscripts if required for printing or publication. He allocated time for research, reading and study.

He was fortunate in having Mrs M. Salvin as a well-seasoned, adaptable and efficient secretary. She knew the diocese having worked for Bishops Hunter, Taylor, then Fallows, and then into David Lunn's episcopate. She writes of Fallows:

> With his arrival there seemed to be a welcome breath of fresh air. He was lively and enthusiastic, with a sense of humour, not over-used, but it gave a lightness to the atmosphere. He was approachable and made people feel at ease and at their best. He didn't speak down to you but listened to you and your point of view. But he was able to say what he wanted to say and make his point without giving offence. I do not know what was said in interviews but I always had the impression that even though some clergy were summoned for a reprimand, the meeting ended on a 'friendly' note. In his work he was meticulous; his desk was always tidy and papers were not lost. He admired tidiness in other people. Each morning at around 9.00 a.m. he would walk into the office. He would stand in the doorway, salute and bow and say 'Good-morning'. This was standard procedure, but I will remember for a long time one occasion when he was ill and struggling to work. He stood in the doorway, slowly bowed and saluted and said, 'Half a Bishop'. When at home he would spend the day dealing with correspondence, interviews and preparation, but he endeavoured around 4.00 p.m. to have a short brisk walk before signing letters. Then, of course, he would have a light meal before going off for a Confirmation or meeting.

Fallows inherited two archdeacons, Hayman Johnson, of Sheffield since 1963, also Canon Residentiary of the Cathedral, and Gwyn Rogers, of Doncaster since 1961, also Vicar of High Melton. With contrasting personalities – Johnson, a man of discipline and duty and RAF chaplain during the war and twenty-four years' parochial experience in various dioceses; Rogers, energetic and wide-ranging, a Liverpool Diocesan Missioner, and Director of Religious

150

Education in Bradford – they were equally trusted by clergy and loyal to their bishop. It was only at the end of his episcopate that Fallows was able to appoint his own archdeacons, Michael Paton, Vicar of St Mark's, Broomhill, to Sheffield and Canon Residentiary of the Cathedral, instituted on 10 November 1978; and Ian Harland, Vicar of Rotherham, to Doncaster, without parochial responsibilities, instituted on 1 May 1979. Paton retired in 1988 and Bishop Stewart Cross invited Harland to be Suffragan of Lancaster in 1985. Four years later he was Bishop of Carlisle.

Fallows relied on his archdeacons for background knowledge of clergy and foreground information on the ups and downs of parochial life. He was not a bishop who put his head on the pillow each night and forgot the travails of the day. He was a worrier and a worrier because he cared. And he cared because he was bidden to serve those who served the people in the parishes. Fallows admired Herbert Hensley Henson, Bishop of Durham, and quoted words of Henson as a guide for pastors and parish parsons!

> The pastor is not wholly unlike the artist, for he is, in a very real sense, under the control of the material with which he has to work. He may not seek to do with stone what he may fairly hope to do with wood, nor attempt to make with brick what he might well succeed in making with iron. Every material has potencies and limitations of its own, and unless these are understood, and allowed for, the ablest artist will effect nothing. The material with which the minister of Christ has to deal is far more delicate, difficult, and subtly conditioned than any with which the artist must reckon. We have to make our count with English folk, and before we can hope to influence them for good, we must understand and allow for their natural temperament, inherited prejudices, bias of place, class, employment, interest, inevitable points of view, probable reactions to our approaches. To ignore all these is to make misunderstanding certain and complete failure probable. I have recently directed attention to the ill consequences of the prevalent clerical practice of using religious terms and phrases which cannot but puzzle, alarm and exasperate ordinary English folk. If you provoke suspicion and resentment, be sure that you have destroyed the first condition of teaching.

Fallows' episcopal ministry amongst South Yorkshire people had commenced at Pontefract. He was no stranger to their ways, language and forthrightness. He was well prepared.

Archdeacon Michael Paton has recollections:

> Pastor. Kindly, approachable, shrewd, very experienced, probably the most general experience of any bishop. Hardworking. When he was asking me to be his archdeacon, his secretary came in with a call from the vicar of X, and Gordon remarked 'you can thank the Lord he isn't in your archdeaconry'. Also forgiving.

Leader. Accepted his responsibilities fully. I once, when an incumbent, told him about a wedding I proposed to take, despite one party being divorced: I took the view that legally the responsibility was mine, and tho' I was quite sure that the bishop would agree with me in the very distressing circumstances (which virtually gave grounds for technical 'nullity') I felt I must make it clear that I was informing him, not seeking his permission. He took the point instantly, commented that some others might have sought his advice first. And left me feeling that he truly respected both my decision and me. I realise now how encouraging and strengthening such an attitude is – and not all that common. His whole ministry was one of encouragement rather than rebuke.

Teacher. He attended the meetings of the theological society when he could, certainly more than most bishops. I recall him coming to attend an informal group of lay people for whose theological strugglings I was kind of 'anchor-man', at their request as a successor to Stephen Burnett (Education Secretary of the diocese) who had started it. Gordon came to us after a day's work at meetings in London, straight from the railway station, without going home first, and commented to me on 'a valuable piece of lay training'. It hadn't occurred to me that it was that – I just enjoyed it as friends. But he was right, and gave precious relaxation time to encourage us.

Administrator. Efficient: a good chairman (perhaps a little too kind to the long-winded). Good judgement: I recall his remarking of one person being considered for a particular post 'I think X has reached his ceiling' – surprised me at the time largely because I was newly archdeacon and quite unaccustomed to thinking of my fellow-clergy in 'career' terms. But later experience showed Gordon to have been dead right in that particular case, and I think was so usually.

Focus of unity. I found his liberal and moderately catholic stance congenial, and truly Anglican. I think he probably valued Establishment more than some (including me!) Probably those who Harry Williams dubs 'out-and-outers' whether of catholic or evangelical persuasion would have found Gordon 'unsound': but I personally heard no complaints. Gordon clearly 'thought it possible that he might be mistaken', and this humility, combined with personal likeableness and obvious faith in God probably disarmed those who might have criticised him.

Collegiality, Admirable: imaginative and sharing: most friendly – and of course any meal at Bishopscroft was always warmed by dear Edna's kindness, cordon bleu and competence!

The man. A thoroughly reassuring physical presence: friendly and approachable: quite free of pomposity and prelacy (he cheerfully accepted my declared wish to not wear gaiters). He suffered the sad loss of his daughter Angela most bravely and Christianity (I was at that time chaplain of the radiotherapy hospital, part time with St Mark's, and so got to know Gordon and Edna a bit more): and his own illness seemed to me a model: brave, thoughtful, uncomplaining, and I remember him saying to me once when in considerable pain 'If the Lord chastises those whom He loves . . . Boy, He certainly must love me'. He was a lovely man.

Restoring peace to the diocese was Fallows' primary task. Michael Paton thought:

> the adjuration to restore peace may have made him unduly reluctant to take steps which might have caused dissension: and I think it may have been that those in my view, few clergy who in fact need rebuke more than encouragement, continued in sloth, or at least the unimaginative humdrum style of living which can be a form of sublime confidence.

A few further recollections from a wide selection by clergy confirm or complement Paton's memories. There is understandable duplication of views but it is seemly to quote completely rather than edit the contributions, for there are words used to describe Fallows which merit repetition.

Canon Trevor Page served the whole of his ministry in the diocese, which included time as Diocesan Director of Ordinands and Post-Ordination Training, and Canon Residentiary of the Cathedral.

> At the time of Gordon Fallows' appointment I was Chaplain to the University of Sheffield and welcomed having a bishop who was so keenly interested in the world of higher education. He thought it was important, gave time to it, and enjoyed the conversation and wit of academics. 'Ah you lecture in politics then?' he said to a senior lecturer to whom I introduced him at a special chaplaincy Christmas party. 'That means you are much interested in the new discipline of sociology'. 'Oh no', replied the lecturer who was of conservative disposition, 'I avoid that; what matters is teaching the classical texts'. 'I do so agree', said the Bishop, 'that is exactly my conclusion from when I studied at Oxford and I did some politics there'. 'Oh yes, and boxing too judging by your conversational footwork' replied the lecturer, as the two men beamed at each other over their spectacles and foaming pints of beer.
>
> Bishop Fallows was prone to look at one by tilting his face downwards as he peered above his half-moon glasses. There was a special sense of attentiveness in his manner, a focused effort to listen and be helpful. Indeed, 'What can I do to help?' was one of his most characteristic sayings and likely to be the preface or climax to an interview. This was very much his way of living out the reality of being a servant to the servants of God. He was assiduous in accepting invitations to receptions for staff and students, even when this often involved a late night stop on his way back from some other engagement. But the engagement with the world of higher education was robust, down to earth so that he was interested in practical matters or organisation and welfare. His love of history was one point of affinity with this world and showed too in the care with which he approached his preaching in the parishes. His words often proved that he had read available sources of local history and worked hard to craft a piece that had

biblical study, historical content and well placed words about the direction which the incumbent of a parish might now take. So it was when he preached my own service of collation as Vicar of All Saints', Intake, a large area of council housing near Doncaster Racecourse. There he made much of the story of Nehemiah rebuilding the walls of Jerusalem. I wondered if this might not have been a very precisely intended sermon since I spent my first two years literally rebuilding the walls and fences of the church and its grounds. During my years in the parish I saw the Bishop less frequently but our occasional meetings gave evidence of three characteristics. The first was his continual enjoyment of humour so that at diocesan synods he would be quick to spot a pun or inject sparkle into dull debates. The second characteristic was his wish to support others however inconvenient to himself. He would travel miles to attend meetings of sub-committees held in Doncaster in order to let Doncaster people feel they were not neglected by a diocesan administration whose offices were in Sheffield. There is no doubt that it was, administratively speaking, an entire waste of episcopal time but it mattered much to him not to cause possible offence. The third characteristic was his tendency to work himself right up to the limits of his stamina. Quite early in his time here my wife and I were invited with another clergy couple to have dinner with the Bishop and his wife one Sunday evening at Bishopscroft. This followed a preaching engagement for the Bishop and so the meal didn't begin until after half past eight. It was a splendid meal with excellent wine followed by coffee in the lounge. The sight of the Bishop's head slumping forward as he finished his coffee and his eyes closing was not a sign of rudeness. But it was a rather alarming sign that Bishop Fallows tended to live each day with and for others right up to the point of exhaustion. This tendency was illustrated much more dramatically as I watched him chair diocesan synods in his later years whilst showing all the signs of a fatal illness, weight loss, thinness of voice and unsteady hands. In the coffee break of one conference I overheard one priest saying to him, 'Are you sure you are well?' 'Oh yes', said Gordon Fallows 'It's just that I can't manage five sets of tennis any more but have to make do with the best of three.'

My own conclusions that our Bishop was actually terribly ill then became overshadowed by the discovery in 1979 that I myself had cancer. There was surgery and eventually I was pronounced 'clear' but with a need to absorb a very large dosage of preventative radiotherapy. Like so many, I found that this treatment was more dramatic in its symptoms than had been the disease. I spent my days lying on my hospital bed with intense nausea and without the energy to negotiate expeditions further than the washbasin. On one day I was amazed at the door of my hospital room being opened by the Bishop. The amazement wasn't that a bishop should visit but that any man so ill as he looked could possibly find the energy to visit. He was pale, seemed very weak and his voice was thin to the point of quavering. The fact that we shared the same disease made honesty easy and in response to the news that my long-term prospects were good he was frank that his were not and that he would die very soon. 'You have youth on your side but I don't', I remember him saying. He then asked me whether there was anything particular to which I looked forward beyond recovery. I replied that there was, in that for reasons that were not entirely clear to me, I would rather like to take my wife to London, and walk down the Strand with her. Quite what we would then do I wasn't sure though a restaurant seemed likely. What would have been a healthy laugh but could not but be a dry cackle now broke from the Bishop's lips and he wished me well with that ambition. After a few more minutes he made to leave. I recall a moment of real anxiety. I felt too weak to rise and let him out yet he seemed so weak I could not imagine how he would make it to the ground floor without assistance and worried lest his visit to me should be the cause of some awful and final collapse. A week later I was returned home for a weekend in the vicarage before resuming treatment. There I found a letter from the Bishop wishing me well for my future ministry and enclosing a cheque for £100 towards a stay in London as soon as I should feel strong enough. The sum, of course, was then of very considerable value. I recall those few minutes in the hospital room as being one of the few, indeed possibly the only occasion, that I have experienced being in the presence of someone showing heroism since his own ghastly weakness made what for others would have been a routine visit into nothing less than an act of heroism.

Canon George Tolley, thrice doctored in philosophy and science, was Principal of Sheffield Polytechnic and Non Stipendiary Minister (N.S.M.) of an inner-city church:

I met Gordon Fallows and saw him at work in the company of industrial and business leaders, trades union officials and City Councillors and officers. When he came to Sheffield there were many things requiring nurturing after earlier upsets. Diocesan boundaries needed sorting out. Ecumenical affairs were at a low ebb. And parish clergy, for the most part, badly needed encouragement and inspiration from a bishop who would 'front up' the whole church in the Diocese. Gordon tackled these issues with speed and vigour. And it was necessary, also, to 'settle in' Synodical government. There were considerable tensions here. Some clergy in the Diocese wished to see a grass-roots democracy and a parliamentary type structure and operation which would have reduced the role of the Bishop to that of a chairman who executed the will of the majority. Others were seeking an episcopal authority responsive to the needs of the Diocese and providing discipline and stability. Gordon's combination of firmness in matters of principle, his evident real concern for clergy and people, his great capacity for listening and his vast experience, provided the Diocese with a leader who quickly gained the trust of others, a man trusted to build bridges and to mark out new paths.

During his episcopate, the economy of South Yorkshire was ravaged. In particular, the manufacturing base of Sheffield and Rotherham – special steels and engineering – suffered grievously. There were many closures, many redundancies, and the erosion of the very raison d'être of Sheffield – Sheffield steel – gave an almost tangible feeling of despair to the city. Gordon Fallows could not change the inevitabilities of trade and economics, but he was a notable force for encouragement and hope. Trusted by both sides of industry, and with a deep concern for the future of the people involved, he was indeed a comfort and a hope to many. This was not a time for eye-catching initiatives, but for reassurance for the banishment of despair, for strengthening courage and belief in the future. It was a time for pastoral support and guidance of clergy in parishes where the lives of so many were being devastated. Gordon the pastor, the friend, the man of prayer, provided a quiet reassuring leadership during these troubled times that was so greatly appreciated by so many. One has too many memories – his good humour; his wit; his ability to chair meetings, speedily and efficiently. And yet without hurry. And, of course, he did enjoy his Saturday afternoons in the Directors' box at Hillsborough.

Canon Ronald Thomson was ordained in 1954 by Leslie Hunter and served under John Taylor, Gordon Fallows and David Lunn. He was Vicar of St Hilda, Shiregreen 1957–1973, and Vicar of Worsborough 1973–1988.

Bishop Gordon was certainly my 'favourite bishop'. This no doubt has a good deal to do with the fact that he seemed to recognize me, but equally I felt drawn to his wise leadership in diocesan policy. I am by nature a follower rather than a leader, and I found in him a man I wanted to follow. A few minor incidents stayed with me as typical of his character.

A young lady clerk in the diocesan office was leaving (I think to get married). He was on the spot and made the small presentation himself. He did it off the cuff but with such graciousness and appositeness that what could have been a formality became for me what I considered a model for such an occasion.

He was very sensitive as to how others might view his actions. I had been made Rural Dean of Ecclesfield in 1972. Only one year later Bishop Gordon asked me if I would consider a move to Worsborough in the deanery of Tankersley. He recognised that I might feel that this was a 'judgement' on my performance as Rural Dean after such a short time. He asked me to see him and most generously and kindly reassured me that this was not so, that I needed a move (having been fifteen years at Shiregreen) and that Worsborough was just the place for me. How right he was! I had fifteen very good years there and he appointed me Rural Dean in the new Deanery two years later. At the institution of a new incumbent to the parish of Oughtibridge in 1977 there was a power cut just as the service was about to begin: Bishop Gordon carried on by candlelight with great aplomb and made it a memorable occasion.

Canon Geoffrey Mills was curate at Eccleshall 1965, Vicar of Endcliffe 1969, and Rector of Whiston 1978.

Bishop Fallows was first introduced to the clergy whilst we were at Conference at Swanwick (he was still Bishop of Pontefract at the time). I can picture him now moving about among the clergy laying a hand round the shoulder to each one to whom he spoke. At the time of his arrival there was growing awareness of the Ministry of Women, but much uncertainty about how to use it. There was also a move towards Lay Administration of the Chalice, but again difficulty in authorising it, particularly where women were concerned. My own request that a Licensed Woman Worker administer the Chalice had previously been refused. In 1971 our new Bishop Fallows gave approval in principle, but added: 'I think it most important to establish the principle that lay administration at the Holy Communion should only take place when there is real need for it arising out of large numbers of communicants at a particular service . . . If you can give me that assurance that you need lay assistance with the administration I am entirely happy for X to officiate in this way.' I replied that there were particular services, namely the Family Communion Services four times a year. There could be one hundred communicants, and another hundred coming forward for a blessing.

In the same year I sought the Bishop's approval for conducting a Service of Blessing for a couple who were to marry at the Register Office, also his approval for the lady to continue as a communicant. She had previously been divorced. The Bishop replied: 'I most gladly give you permission to take the Service of Blessing . . . and am equally glad to give permission for B to continue as a communicant.'

The Rev. Dennis Porter writes:

> My personal respect for and gratitude to Gordon Fallows was because under his vision and leadership I could at last be ordained to what was then called the 'auxiliary pastoral ministry' (now the non-stipendiary ministry). I obtained my theological qualifications in 1958, but neither in Birmingham (Leonard Wilson) nor in Sheffield (John Taylor) was there any movement towards the A.P.M. until Gordon Fallows arrived. I came to see him as a man with a strong sense of respect for the best traditions of the Church of England, but one who was forward thinking in a balanced way and not rigidly tied to the past. (I was on the University staff from 1961 to 1986). One anecdote to illustrate his humanity. There were just two of us at the ordination retreat at Advent 1972. We were reading in the Bishop's study before dinner on the first evening when there was a tap on the door and in walked the bishop with a decanter of sherry and two glasses! I cannot help having a warm impression of him!

Following proposed changes in local government with a suggested new Metropolitan County of South Yorkshire, a small commission was set up to consider its implications for the diocese. The Archdeacon of Pontefract, Edward Henderson, was its independent and outside chairman and Canon Heneage Ferraby acted as secretary. There were parishes in the City of Sheffield which were in the Diocese of Derby. The commission reported and 1 January 1974 became a significant date in the history of the diocese when ten parishes or conventional districts were transferred from Derby to Sheffield. The ease with which this transfer was achieved owed much to the cordial relations between Fallows and the Bishop of Derby, Cyril Bowles, and the Archdeacon of Derby, Robert Dell, former Principal and Vice-Principal of Ridley Hall Theological College, Cambridge respectively. In his imitable way Fallows acknowledged:

> It is easy, of course, for us at the receiving end to be considerate and helpful in arranging for the extension of our diocese by taking in an area which contains some vigorous and lively churches with clergy and lay readers of considerable calibre. The authorities of the Derby diocese deserve the credit for their willing co-operation in bringing this scheme to fruition ... I hope to visit all the incoming parishes at an early date. Meanwhile services of welcome are being arranged to mark this extension and increase in our diocesan family.

Archdeacon Desmond Carnelley served in Sheffield from 1960 to 1994 and was Archdeacon of Doncaster from 1985 to 1994. He was among the first batch of students at Ripon Hall when Fallows arrived as Principal:

> Gordon Fallows had no 'side'. I was privileged to be asked (perhaps because I was the only Ripon Hall man of his time in the diocese then) to act as one of the chaplains at his enthronement. I well remember him asking the Provost at the rehearsal for the occasion (and the subsequent reception in the Cutlers' Hall): 'Is this a gaiters occasion then?' He asked me to consider moving to Mosborough, one of the parishes which moved into the diocese from Derby, a post which turned out to be one the most important in that part of the diocese, as it was destined to grow in size from some 3,500 people when I went there to some 13,000 when I left, and one of the first Local Ecumenical Projects (then so called) in this part of the country. In inviting me to consider the post and knowing I was not at that time in a hurry to move he wrote, 'Sorry to land this on your plate, but you are the chosen chap and I know you will give it careful consideration,' illustrating his friendly approach and trust in one's judgement. When we were established in Mosborough he came out to spend a day with me, going over the plans for the future and making suggestions. Being 'ecumenical' was not easy in those days, but he gave us a free hand and did not interfere, trusting us to handle things with discretion – which we tried to do. I am sure he was aware of what we were doing however. He preached a fine sermon at my induction (though I was inducted by the Bishop of Derby, Mosborough being still in his diocese at that time). He was not a brilliant orator but preached with sincerity, fervour and occasionally with deep emotion. He brought to the diocese of Sheffield a very necessary era of peace and unity of purpose, after a troubled period in its history.

In 1974 a Commission was established to consider the 'Needs and Resources' of the diocese. Mr Douglas Knox, formerly Town Clerk of Doncaster, was chairman. The Bishop of Doncaster, Hetley Price, was secretary, of whom Fallows said, 'For Hetley organisation had a human heart – administration a human face.' The terms of reference were:

1. To review present and probable future forms of diocesan income and expenditure.
2. To scrutinize diocesan expenditure within the context of diocesan strategy, and, as possible, to consider ways of sharing work with neighbouring dioceses.
3. To review present and probable future forms of parochial income and expenditure in this and other dioceses and their relationship to diocesan income and expenditure, and the method by which individual parishes contribute to diocesan income.
4. To consider the demands likely to be made in the field of clergy stipends, including the provision of adequate expenses of office.
5. To consult as necessary with responsible diocesan bodies.
6. To review the contribution made to the work of the Church outside the borders of the diocese and especially overseas.
7. To examine the diocesan organisation, the means by which decisions are made and the relationship of that organisation to the deaneries and parishes.
8. And in any or all of these fields to make recommendations, including establishing the priorities, to the Bishop's Council.

The Commission met ten times, with smaller groups meeting on separate occasions, and the report was presented to the Diocesan Synod in July 1975. The work of such a commission was 'bread and butter' to Fallows. His competence was such that he could have chaired the commission himself! As one of the archbishops' nominees on the Central Board of Finance of the Church of England he was familiar with the financial implications involved. Professor David McClean was a member of the commission and thought the 'lay chairman was a little out his depth, and perhaps the report lacked bite. But Gordon Fallows regarded it as one of the good things he had set in hand, and it was a useful tool in the "settling" he faced.'

The diocese was not wholly at ease with the direction of synodical government. Was there a danger of multiplying rather than decreasing diocesan machinery? It was recognised that the organisational hub of the diocese at Church House, Sheffield, was unsuitable, even unworkable. Recommendations were made for its replacement, and the pay and conditions of the staff should be studied. The 'headquarters' are now Diocesan Church House, Rotherham, and, as with all dioceses of the Church of England, it is large, powerful and all-knowing but perhaps not all-seeing. But the 'new' has not liberated and set clergy free (in particular) and laity, but further enslaved them. Staffs have increased and salaries have grown fat. This is not the direction in which Fallows would have felt at home. He stressed that the deadliest danger of institutionalism was a chief concern with making the wheels go round, however well-oiled. The fatal character of this danger is in the fact that there is no essential creative life in machine-minding or computer subservience. Under the mechanistic or electronic obsession the life-changing aspect of religion is in danger of being forgotten.

The recommendations of the *Needs and Resources* report on education was that the Education Committee should concentrate on adult education and youth work; a full-time information officer should be appointed – 'Decisions made should be known to be made'; schools should continue to be of pre-eminent importance (nine new schools were opened during Fallows' episcopate); urgent repairs and increased staff for Whirlow Grange were essential so that it could continue as a residential training establishment; the old Boards and Committees needed replacing by synodical bodies. All these recommendations were implemented without delay to the diocese's benefit. Fallows' concern was that underlying everything must be mutual help and responsibility, and the growing unity of the diocese.

Fallows had witnessed the need for action in declaring churches redundant, closing some and building new ones in Preston with shifting populations. It needs a firm grip to tackle this always-painful subject with vigour and finality. A Pastoral Committee was formed in 1969 and during the next ten years eighteen churches were declared redundant; thirteen benefices were united, some of them into team ministries; two Anglican-Methodists shared buildings; two new parishes; and two new buildings.

Most priests valued their bishop. Canon Charles Richardson was Rector of Rawmarsh:

> I had been in the same large working-class parish for seventeen years and was considering a change. Bishop Gordon came and I stayed. He was a good encourager. You could trust him to back you up in the parish as he trusted you to do your job. It was good to know he was there; rather like mountains where we both liked to be.

Confirmations were a key ingredient of his ministry. The people of the parishes looked forward to the arrival of their bishop and he did not disappoint them. Canon Frank Ball, Vicar of St Leonard's, Norwood 1961–1987, remembers how he addressed himself to candidates in a most arresting way as he sang 'Happy Birthday to You' celebrating the beginning of a new and fuller life in the power of the Holy Spirit. There were repeated and favourite confirmation addresses – one emphasising 'joy in your worship; joy in your service; joy in your giving; and joy in your living.' And then there was the one when Fallows introduced congregations – and in particular young

candidates – to Christians with sweet-names, instead of toffee-noses. Canon
Ball remembers:

> First there are the Gobstoppers. They are not much use, because they are always
> dumbfounded. They do not speak up for Christ. Next, there are the Humbugs.
> They are not much use either, because their religion is a sham. They do not
> help the work for Christ. Those sweets reminded us of what Christians ought
> not to be. But then he told us about three sweet-names that are helpful. The
> first is Liquorice Allsorts. There are all kinds of people in the church and we
> have a variety of gifts to offer. Every kind of person is needed, all of us can be
> useful and helpful. And so we shall be, if we offer ourselves wholeheartedly to
> the Lord. Then there is Quality Street. This reminds us that our witness for
> Christ must always be the very best, it must have depth and quality. And finally
> there are Kendal's Mint Cakes. They give strength to the climber, and enable
> him to reach the summit. So the Sacraments give strength to us as we journey
> along the Pilgrim Way, and bring us safely to God.

Clear, simple, remembered and continuing to be a subject of conversation at
the 'bun fight'. Something to take away.

Fallows had the majority of patronage in the diocese. The Earl of
Fitzwilliam was the patron of twelve livings. The Sheffield Church Burgesses
held benefices, and party patronage and trustees held a number of livings, with
an assortment of others. There were sufficient varieties of churchmanship to
satisfy all tastes. Sheffield had adopted the Parish Communion which was the
normal eucharistic practice in many parishes. It was a time of the numerous
'Series' of Services which were widely adopted, but the 1662 *Book of Common
Prayer* rite remained central in many parishes.

The delight, relief and warmth with which Fallows was received in
Sheffield should not obscure another reality. It was more Gordon Fallows
rather than the Lord Bishop of Sheffield who was welcomed. The bishop as
bishop did not receive a fanfare from all the clergy of the diocese and laity
too. There were those for whom he carried the stigmata of Ripon Hall, a
modernist and liberal. We know that as a broad churchman he was not, as
such, concerned with the differences between Anglo-Catholic or Evangelical.
His own distinctive churchmanship was not given or accepted on account of
his views of the questions which divided the two. His characteristic opinions
related to other matters. But there were those who knew that broad
churchmen entertained doubts as to the miraculous clauses of the Apostles'
Creed; were concerned to adjust the teaching of the Church to the new truths
which science and learning brought to light. To clergy sceptics of Fallows'
position the characteristic function of broad churchmen was to consider the
measure of inconsistencies, and to re-state theological teaching in such a way
as to remove them. Such a conviction or approach was anathema to both

Catholics and Evangelicals, of which there were powerful groupings in Sheffield. With their admiration of Fallows the man went apprehension and distrust of their bishop's theology and doctrine. They resented and resisted any form of liberalism. Their mood was 'retrenchment' in the 1970s.

There was another movement, one of the Holy Spirit, which was seizing hold of some churches. There are many reasons why charismatics pushed at half open doors. When a church neglects its duty of teaching the faith and its consequences, minimises demands on its members, settles for a once weekly illusion of transitory well-being, the church's failure is the charismatic's opportunity. The word 'charismatic' used to be associated with Pentecostalism, existing outside the organised churches, more an hysterical harangue than a body of believers. The growth of this new tendency within the Church of England was swift, sweeping, suggestive – and permanent. It is more than 365 days of Hallelujahs. Teaching, evangelism and commitment are paramount. Alpha and other courses were as yet unknown, but the people behind them were already at work filling churches. Canon Trevor Page comments:

> A significant number of evangelical parishes in the diocese were beginning to experience an interest in the charismatic movement and in an informal approach to liturgy that would probably have baffled Bishop John Taylor as much as it was alien to Bishop Fallows. The 1970s were lean years for broad church traditional Anglicanism. For those who didn't see the future either Roman or renewed in a particular evangelical way, the prospect seemed to be the rather austere one of holding to the traditional faith amidst declining attendances. Many Catholics and evangelicals were looking for their own answers which were rather different from Bishop Fallows' experience or hopes.

There was something deeply incomprehensible and disturbing about charismatics to Fallows. As the movement developed and increased in numbers, strength and influence, Fallows contemplated a new uniformity which made him shudder. A charismatic congregation at worship follows an unwritten and unstated code of practice. Hand and body movements, even facial expressions, are monotonously identical. Even the smiling faces, like one of those television advertisements commending the latest toothpaste, seem ultra clean, surface deep, expressionless behind. Conformity begets uniformity. Spontaneity gives way to mechanical gestures. Another area of both meeting and disagreement concerned the inerrancy of Scripture and the lust for bible study so vital to most charismatics. A biblical code of conduct becomes law and governs the minutiae of faith and conduct. But does this diminish love and demean faith? Was there any longer room for the waverer, the seeker, the puzzled, and the doubter, for which Fallows leaves an ever-open door? Reason, charity and humility appear to be conspicuous by their absence when overweening certainty is matched by self-preening and an odour of arrogance. He admitted that people are saved by faith not by doubt, but he knew that fanaticism was lurking in the wings. And fanaticism is the disease of faith, not its fullest expression. It hungers ever for tokens and signs, and refuses to recognise God's Presence in what is normal, unexciting and commonplace. For Fallows it was the negation of the Divine Mind as disclosed in nature, in history, and supremely in the Incarnation.

There was a prophetic and characteristic greatness about Leslie Hunter with his pastoral outreach into the unchurched sections of the community. This was neglected under John Taylor, but in one way he should not be under-estimated. He recognised that the liberalism of theology in the 1960s had an ultimately corrosive effect on Christian orthodoxy, and that the fashions of the time needed to be resisted in order to defend the traditions of the faith. His stance was acclaimed, but did it come from those who, like drunkards leaning on a lamp post, did so for support rather than for enlightenment? But, it was far from a minority of Sheffield clergy who abandoned tradition for relevance and set aside dogma in favour of questions.

This is another perspective of the tasks facing Fallows throughout his Sheffield episcopate. In retrospect liberal Fallows was sandwiched between John Taylor, a conservative evangelical bishop, and David Lunn, a conserva-tive catholic bishop, each of them having a following of very loyal and articulate partisans.

But were they loved as Fallows was loved?

CHAPTER 13

The receding past or the increasing future?

ONE OF THE PRINCIPAL BURDENS on a modern bishop, and perhaps one of the main causes of the notable decline in episcopal authority which has so strangely gone along with an exaltation of episcopal theory, is the necessity of frequently making official or semi-official pronouncements. From the 1960s onwards no bishop was immune when faced with an avalanche of reports unleashed on the Church of England. The higher and more exacting the demand on a bishop's mind and time, the more imperative the need for some sanitation against the destructive force. Fallows was able to adopt Bishop J.B. Lightfoot's phrase, 'history is a cordial for drooping spirits' but it was no more a remedy than it had been for Mandell Creighton, 'When you begin to draw definite lessons and morals from history, you at once cease to be searchers after truth, because you have a bias which tends to take you to one side or another.' Ultimately, Creighton was right with his assertion, 'Life has no more to give than the opportunity of loving service.'

There were three subjects which Fallows could not circumvent. They were ones on which he had long had settled and irreversible views. Had they been to the forefront a decade earlier and he rather than John Taylor had been appointed Bishop of Sheffield in 1962, he would in some important respects have been the inheritor of much of Leslie Hunter's legacy. Hunter's footsteps remained visible of clergy who combined vision with clarity, who had theological depth and prophetic instincts for the future direction of the Church of England. Their ministry in the diocese became an example for others to follow. A few names prove the case including future Bishops: Stanley Booth-Clibborn, Ian Griggs, Richard Roseveare, William Stannard, Robin Woods, and Ted Wickham; Deans: Douglas Harrison, Alfred Jowett, and Alan Webster; Professors: James Atkinson and Ronald Preston; Revs: Alan Ecclestone, Hugh Kerklots, Keith Pound, and Roland Walls.

Time to wipe one's eyes for that glory had departed, and the diocese Fallows inherited had transmogrified. Partisans were more brittle, less open to other standpoints, erected barriers. Even Fallows' manners and methods could not budge their set ways and stubbornness. He enjoyed fulsome argument over a dinner table or with a pint of beer in his hand at a local inn, when shields were lowered and armour was temporarily discarded. Why could this not be sustained in diocesan organizations? It should not go without comment that in his major appointments of bishops of Doncaster and of archdeacons, he did not look for balances in churchmanship, theology or doctrine, but chose priests of similar, though not identical, views to his own. It was qualities of character and different experiences which attracted him to them.

The question of direction for Fallows was: backwards always to the receding past? Or forward to the increasing future? A creed of sterility, or a creed of growth? A religion of the letter, or of the spirit? That was the issue of the Reformation, and the 'Fathers' of the Church chose freedom, with all its shadows and risks. That was his position and he was loath lightly to cast aside the fruit of their hardly-won victory.

Fallows was an eager proponent for Anglican-Methodist unity. The Diocese of Sheffield had voted on 16 January 1969 that unity should be sought in two stages – Clergy 75%, Laity 83%. But when the detailed proposals were put to the Diocesan Conference the 'yes' results were decidedly mixed. Approving the proposed ordinal – Clergy 63%, Laity 64%; the proposed service of reconciliation – Clergy 51%, Laity 54%; should Convocations go ahead to Stage One? – Clergy 57% Laity 70%. When the moment of national decision came on 3 May 1971 at General Synod the scheme failed to get the two-thirds majority in either the House of Clergy or the House of Laity, and failed by 10% to reach 75% in the whole Synod. Six bishops voted against – Leicester, Ronald Williams; Norwich, Maurice Wood; Peterborough, Cyril Eastaugh; Carlisle, Cyril Bulley; Ripon, John Moorman; Sheffield, John Taylor.

The supporters of the original scheme made a second attempt to secure the approval at General Synod in May 1972. This time Fallows was Bishop of Sheffield. Unlike some bishops he was not a campaigner, not someone to tub-thump his way through the diocese. He thought – and was right to think – that perspiration would have changed few minds of those who would vote in the Diocesan Synod. Nevertheless, he made his earnest desire for a favourable outcome crystal clear. At the Diocesan Synod the percentage in favour was 64%, less than required at General Synod where it failed again with 65.81%. Fallows returned to Sheffield deeply saddened, but reflected, 'At least we are spared the possibility of division within our own Church and within the Methodist Church also. Now we must look for another way forward to unity.' He hoped 'a grass-roots movement from below may well gather momentum and show us a more excellent way.' In personal terms he continued to welcome all who presented themselves at the Lord's Table irrespective of denominational allegiance.

There was one subject on which Fallows consistently and persistently made his views known. It is tempting to use the word 'pronounce'! His letter in the *Sheffield Diocesan News* (September 1972) leaves no room for doubt:

No one in his senses wants to open the floodgates and use the solemn marriage service for those who do not genuinely and sincerely intend their union to be life-long. But there are many second marriages which bear a true witness to the Christian standard of marriage. Some man or woman who has been grievously wounded in a bitter experience of a first marriage may find joy and solace in being truly loved and cared for in a second marriage. Such has been my pastoral experience in preparing many such couples for marriage. I am not thinking of people who take their vows lightly. On the contrary, I am thinking of some devout regular communicants, some worthy parochial church councillors and some splendid churchwardens. Must we continue to send them to the register office in search of the bliss so many of them discover for the first time in second marriage? The time is ripe for a re-consideration of our Church's marriage discipline. Our Synods will soon be considering this question. It is one of the subjects on the agenda for our next Diocesan Synod. Perhaps I am declaring my vote too soon, but though I come down on the liberal side I would never want a marriage service without the phrase 'till death us do part.' Illogical it may be, but then life is larger than logic.

The rate of divorce was spiralling – 25,000 in 1970; 119,000 in 1972. An Archbishop of Canterbury's Commission on *Marriage, Divorce and the Church* reported in 1971. It was chaired by Canon Howard Root, Professor of Theology in the University of Southampton, and with a membership which included Hugh Montefiore, Bishop of Kingston-upon-Thames, and Rev. J.W. Bowker, Fellow of Corpus Christi College, Cambridge. Fallows had high liberal expectations of the report. He was not disappointed, for the Commission definitely advocated a reversal of traditional Church policy and recommended the remarriage of the divorced by the Church's marriage service. The 'Root' report provoked fury and uproar in the Church. Advocates and dissenters rushed to their wayside pulpits to praise or disclaim its findings. Bishop Hugh Montefiore provides an insider's comment:

Our report reached the conclusion that it should be in the discretion of the parish priest whether a person, with a previous spouse still alive, should be allowed to be re-married in Church; and if he does it should be with the full authorized service. I wrote the first draft of the 'Root' report at the Benedictine nuns at West Malling, and of course it was considerably knocked about later. I also wrote an appendix on Vows with Lady Oppenheimer and another on Jesus on Divorce and Remarriage. I think it was this that narked people who were opposed, although they could not actually fault it.

Fallows was pleased, perhaps surprised, when on 4 November 1972 the Sheffield Diocesan Synod by a substantial majority approved and endorsed the Commission's recommendations, and expressed the hope that the General Synod would change the regulations of the Church in accordance with the

Commission's conclusions. The usual procedure was for a report to be received by General Synod and referred to the dioceses for discussion. On this occasion after a confused debate, by a narrow margin it was decided not to require from the dioceses a specific opinion on the report.

That was not the end of the matter. Bishop Ronald Williams of Leicester was asked to chair a working party and to bring a report to Synod on the same subject; it was clear that it would need more weight than Synod could summon to change the existing law. The General Synod debated the 'Leicester' rather than the 'Root' report on 7 November 1973. Williams made the 'speech of his life' which both swayed waverers and made converts. He knew how to make a speech full of emotion – the more powerful because it was carefully controlled – with the result that there should be no remarriage of divorced parties in Church. The 'outside' world looked on and walked by. Fallows returned from General Synod somewhat depressed. In his December 1973 Letter in *Sheffield Diocesan News* he wrote:

> My depression stems partly from the procedural muddle in which the General Synod tied itself up in knots . . . I cannot believe that it settles the matter for very long. If it is out of accord with the mind and judgement of the Church at the grass roots then there must surely be a limit to the time during which the tail can wag the dog.

The Church of England's new experimental Marriage Service came into use on 1 November 1977. Fallows describes its advantages and limitations. (*Sheffield Diocesan News* November 1977):

> The revised service begins with the assertion that 'Marriage is given, that husband and wife may comfort and help each other, living faithfully together in need and in plenty, in sorrow and in joy.' The sexual element in marriage is refined in the statement: marriage 'is given that with delight and tenderness they may know each other in love, and through the joy of their bodily union, may strengthen the union of their hearts and lives.' Perhaps this is over-refined to the point of being squeamish. The procreation of children which figures first in the old service comes third in the revised one. Marriage 'is given, that they may have children and be blessed in caring for them and bringing them up in accordance with God's will, to His praise and glory.' The feudal element of 'giving away the bride' in the old service (as though the bride were a piece of property at the disposal of the father) becomes optional in the new service. The vexed problem in the vows of whether the bride should obey or not is dealt with by alternative sets of vows. Brides who still want 'to obey' may do so but there is a form of identical vows for bride and bridegroom for those who take a more equal view of their relationship. There is a concession to the modern and growing custom of each party giving and receiving a ring. The old exhortation to the bride to 'be a follower of holy and godly matrons' now becomes 'follow

the example of those holy women whose praises are sung in the scriptures,' but I question whether this is any more likely to appeal to the modern bride . . .

I do not quarrel with the Divorce Reform Act (1971) making irretrievable breakdown of marriage as the one reason for divorce. There is, however, a feature of the present divorce law which has been almost completely ignored. I mean the provision which was then made for attempts at reconciliation. Instead of making divorce procedure so simple as to take away any sense of its gravity and seriousness, we should be trying to carry out the reconciliation procedures which have become a dead letter of the present practice. It is to be hoped that the revised Marriage Service and the teaching that will go with it will play their part in inculcating a healthy and Christian view of marriage as a lifelong relationship of two persons to the exclusion of all others.

Here, to end, are three tips for those who are thinking of getting married: First, do not marry too young. There is incontrovertible evidence that the marriages at greatest risk are those where the partners are very young. Secondly, do not marry because you are pregnant, but only because you are deeply in love with your partner. Thirdly, do not be in a hurry. A broken engagement is better than a breakdown in marriage. Get to know each other well before the wedding bells ring and then there is much more likely to be the romantic ending 'they lived happily ever after'.

At the Diocesan Synod in October 1974 'The Ordination of Women to the Priesthood' was debated. Fallows led the debate. He had the ability of a judge, presenting or summing up, outlining the case for and the case against with equipoise, being scrupulously careful, leaving the 'jury' to make the decision. Any stranger listening to Fallows may not have been aware of his own strong convictions. The ensuing debate was fierce, emotional and opinionated at the same time as being highly principled and honest. The three sets of figures are probably an accurate reflection of the whole diocese. 'That the Synod considers that there are no fundamental objections to the Ordination of Women to the Priesthood':

For	Clergy	38	Laity	42
Against	Clergy	17	Laity	17
Abstentions	Clergy	5	Laity	0

'That this Synod believes that it would be inexpedient for the Church of England to take any action in this matter at the present time':

For	Clergy	23	Laity	21
Against	Clergy	28	Laity	33
Abstentions	Clergy	2	Laity	0

'That this Synod considers that the Church of England should now proceed to remove the legal and other barriers to the Ordination of Women'

| For | Clergy | 33 | Laity | 36 |
| Against | Clergy | 23 | Laity | 17 |

No abstentions recorded.

Of course, everyone knew that Fallows was in complete favour as he cast his votes in favour of the first and last motions.

The Bishop's Letter in the *Diocesan News* was 'predictable' Fallows. He did not use it for opinionated comment on contemporary national issues of the day, which does not mean that he dispensed comfort for his readers. He drew attention to the plight of severely handicapped children, and in particular thalidomide children, supporting the 1974 Government's decision to set up a trust fund to help children who suffer from severe congenital disability. In the first half of the twentieth century it was a feature of dioceses to have houses where unmarried mothers were trained as children's nannies and helped to find jobs. In 1942 St Agatha's Hostel in Sheffield provided residential care for twenty-four girls in their house and cottage. By 1973 numbers had dwindled to about half a dozen as more pregnant girls stayed at home, and there was a widespread use of contraceptives, and the law concerning abortion was relaxed. Since its opening 3,000 mothers and their babies had found shelter at St Agatha's and were given the courage to rebuild their lives and assisted to face their futures. The Hostel closed in 1973. For Fallows St Agatha's 'has been a notable case of the gospel in action, and we must be thankful for what has been achieved in the name of the Lord of Compassion.' In 1975 Sheffield was the only diocese in the country without a Board for Social Responsibility, yet it was one of the most socially responsible dioceses. Rather than producing reports and scratching around looking for ways to intervene, the diocese made funds available for local initiatives and projects. South Yorkshire had high levels of unemployment and Fallows was in constant touch with leaders in business and commerce and encouraged and supported any businesses attempting to provide job-training opportunities. Further afield he drew attention to the Women's Peace Movement in Northern Ireland.

On parish visits he was disappointed when he found a lack or absence of women churchwardens or occupying other Church offices. He commented:

The women's liberation movement does not seem to have reached Llandaff Cathedral for the Dean there was recently reported as saying: 'I have known women sidesmen in Church, but that surely is an admission of failure?' Let us also remember that whereas there is no discrimination of sex there is also no discrimination of colour and that our multi-racial society should be reflected in the election of our Church Officers as Christians from other races take their place in the rank and file of our integrated Church membership.

In May 1974 the diocese celebrated its Diamond Jubilee. There were diocesan and parochial celebrations, special services, folk festivals, exhibitions. Fallows arranged to mark the event with a Primary Visitation, visiting the four main centres of population – Sheffield, Doncaster, Rotherham and Goole – and delivering a message. One normal and attractive feature was having meetings of diocesan synod at different places and centres throughout the diocese.

Fallows was concerned with counselling services and was not wholly satisfied with their undirected and rapid advance. In the 'Bishop's Letter' (June 1973) he referred to this newcomer to the range of social services:

> It is already well established in the student world of the universities and polytechnics and is being introduced in some schools. As its name implies, it is an opportunity for persons to discuss matters of concern, not necessarily at times of crisis. Questions connected with choice of careers, family relationships, work, friendships and many other matters arise naturally in the course of counselling. There are some generally agreed qualities that the counsellor should possess. He must be a good listener, he must be a sensitive person. Confidentiality is essential, and the counsellor must therefore be able to keep other people's secrets. All this is familiar to the clergy in their pastoral work. Some advocates of the counselling service, however, depart from the well-established work of the clergy in pastoral care by insisting that the counsellor is amoral, that he must remain neutral in moral issues, that he does not express a moral opinion unless asked and not always then. The counsellor, in short, must never be judgemental. This is a highly questionable standpoint. There is a difference between condemning an act as wrong and condemning the person who is responsible for the act. Condemn the sin and always be ready to forgive and restore the sinner is surely the Christian way and a Counselling Service that dodges the issue of right and wrong is not what is needed in our morally bewildered world. Let him that is without sin throw the first stone is a warning we all need to heed. But the conclusion of the matter is 'Go thy way and sin no more.' All of us need counsel and advice but especially children and young people. They need firm, loving guidance. They will not be helped, nor will they thank us, for being morally neutral.

When Fallows was introduced into the House of Lords he was supported by the Bishops of Wakefield (Eric Treacy), and Portsmouth (John Phillips). The 'House' was the country's best club and Fallows was eminently and satisfyingly clubbable. It was a place for meeting people, airing views, having confidential conversations, and informal interviews. Although he appeared in the Chamber for debates he was not a regular contributor to them. It is worth recording one of his interventions on the experiments on animals for the purpose of the testing of cosmetics. It was a moral issue which disturbed his Christian conscience, but he did not take it out of context or from a wider perspective.

There are two principles on which I take my stand on the general question of experiments in animals. First, it is right to experiment on animals in the interest of medical research and human welfare generally. But, secondly, in the pursuit of these objectives man has a duty to restrict the infliction of suffering to an absolute minimum. I believe there are some animal experiments that do not fall within these twin principles. Tens of thousands of experiments take place each year in connection with the testing of cosmetic preparations and such experiments entail a considerable degree of pain and suffering. Bubble bath liquids, face creams, deodorants and other toiletries are all being tested on animals. While the object is the safety of the product, some of these experiments are extremely dubious and do not fall within the category of experiments for medical purposes to the relief of suffering and the conquest of disease. One of the difficulties stems from the fact that the line of demarcation between the strictly medical and cosmetic fields is not easy to draw. Some discoveries in cosmetic science may prove beneficial in the medical field, but we need to be vigilant so as to preclude the infliction of unnecessary suffering. The whole subject of animal welfare is, of course, bedevilled by sentiment. Emotionalism is all too easily aroused. I have no sympathy for those who care more for their cats than their cousins. There is, I believe, an underlying philosophy, to guide the Christian in his attitude to this sensitive subject. The teaching of the Bible makes clear that mankind has a trusteeship over the rest of the animal kingdom. Some enthusiasts speak of the rights of animals. I prefer to concentrate on the duties of man, and man's responsible dominion over nature includes acting responsibly towards animals. In the words of Alexander Pope: 'The more entirely the inferior creation is submitted to our power, the more answerable we should seem for our mismanagement of it.' Some experiments on animals constitute a grave mismanagement of our human dominion over the rest of the animal kingdom. In a cruel and violent age such as ours, marked as it is by an alarming increase in the use of torture on human beings, we need to be specially vigilant to outlaw any unnecessary cruelty.

Fallows was never a natural target for extremists of any kind. There was one issue where he was a target and people aimed their arrows at him by name. We turn to the 'Sheffield Report'

CHAPTER 14

Turbulence

Can the Church of England see its mission so clearly that of its own volition it will carry through the redistribution of its revenues, the alteration of the tenure of its clerical offices, and be converted to a more apostolic attitude towards wealth and the making of community? A Church so reconstructed by its own act would be able to face the future with confidence as today we cannot do. It would gain the moral respect of the nation and reassert the moral leadership which it no longer has to-day.

THIS IS NOT A SPIRITUAL CHALLENGE of the 1970s but one from 1937 in *Men, Money and the Ministry. A Plea for Economic Reform in the Church of England.* There was a sequel in 1941, *Putting Our House In Order*. So long as the Church's utterances were belied by its refusal to remove what were widely recognised as wasteful and indefensible anomalies in its administration of resources and manpower, how could the power of God flow freely into the body of the Church to make it a living instrument of redemption and reconstruction? Although these publications were written by bishops and clergy, their names were not disclosed. However, the chairman of the group was Bishop Leslie Hunter and when published there were named supporters led by Archbishop William Temple of York, twenty-six diocesan bishops (eleven from the Province of York), suffragan bishops, deans, archdeacons, clergy and a distinguished set of influential lay people. The latter included Lords Sankey, Birdwood and Wolmer; Knights of the Realm Richard Acland, Montague Barlow, Wyndham Deedes, Walter Moberly and Henry Willink. Distinctive names were there too, Ernest Barker, T.S.R. Boase, Margaret E. Bondfield, T.S. Eliot, Frank Fletcher, Eleonara Iredale, J. Middleton Murry, J.H. Oldham, Maude Royden and R.H. Tawney.

An Appendix to *Putting Our House In Order* described the remarkable ministry of the 'Kelham Fathers' (Society of the Sacred Mission) at St Cecilia, Parson Cross in Sheffield, with a population of 35,000, the largest parish of its kind in a northern industrial city, led by Richard Roseveare.

Fallows studied these publications and Leslie Hunter's *Let us Go Forward* was on his bookshelves. If Fallows had been a conspicuous cleric at the time and supported the two publications, he would have been in the company of people who have already appeared in this biography: H.H. Williams, Mervyn Haigh, W.M. Askwith, William Greer, Eric S. Loveday, W.R. Matthews and Charles E. Raven.

The war interrupted progress until the 1960s. In December 1972 the Clergy Deployment Working Group was appointed by the House of Bishops to assist them in the formulation of a scheme for the fairer distribution of clergy manpower. Perhaps Fallows' critical appraisal of the 'Paul' and 'Partners in Ministry' reports made him the perfect chairman of the Working Group to which he was appointed by the Archbishop of Canterbury, Michael Ramsey. Other members were:

The Ven. T.G.A. Baker, Archdeacon of Bath
The Rt. Rev. J.M. Bickersteth, Bishop of Warrington
The Rev. M. Bourke (Curate of Digswell, St Albans)
The Rev. A.G.K. Esdaile (Vicar of Hackbridge and North Boddington, Southwark)
Mrs B. Haworth (Member of Council, Advisory Council for the Church's Ministry, and Church Commissioner)
Air Vice-Marshall M.D. Lyne (Diocesan Secretary – Lincoln)
The Rt. Rev. J. Trillo, Bishop of Chelmsford.

The Group's work was set against the background of a fall in numbers of ordinands which was forecast to continue (a notion challenged by some), and the shadow of inflation which darkened and lengthened during the short duration of the Group's deliberations. Would economics bring the Church to its senses? Partly because of these factors many dioceses were already planning a run-down in their clerical manpower, and others were waiting for the conclusion of the 'Sheffield Report', and guidance from the House of Bishops.

The position of deployment was complex. A situation where, for example, eight dioceses had one clergyman in full-time pastoral employment for an average of under 2,000 people of the 1971 population was 'felt to be both intolerable and indefensible.' Yet 'at first glance, if all the 15,000 or so Church of England clergymen were evenly deployed there would be one to every 3,800 of the 1971 population of England.' But any solution could not be based on such simplistic facts.

The Group had to work out a system of deployment of the clergy in the forty-three dioceses and their first objective was to settle fair shares for each diocese. What is the right size of that allocation and what should be the criteria for settling it? Distance and natural community, as well as population numbers, were important considerations. The results of diocesan questionnaires were analysed and calculated by use of a computer. One of the Group's members, now Canon, Adrian Esdaile, has some memories:

I was a young incumbent at the time and a member of General Synod for Southwark, having been elected as a curate. Gordon Fallows was an excellent chairman allowing the discussion to develop and guiding us to our conclusions. As I was very inexperienced I was a little nervous, but he immediately put me at ease. I was a part-time industrial chaplain. We had been given the concept of trying to produce a fair distribution of clergy throughout the country, rural and urban, north and south. We established a series of criteria – electoral roll, Easter communicants, geographical area etc. – and I was able to draw in the help of an early computer at the Milliard factory where I was chaplain. With that help we were able to feed in the variables, giving them different weightings, until we were satisfied that the result was reasonable. This was the basis for our final allocations – though in due course the computer was no longer required.

One point from the diocesan replies was noted and rejected, namely 'A minority of dioceses argued persuasively for the proposition that the Church's strategy should be one of reinforcing success and that it would therefore be a mistake to adopt a policy of moving men out of rural into urban areas.' That would not cohere with the idea and resolve of fair shares for all the dioceses. The group was perhaps over-influenced by the *Chadwick Report on Church and State*, that two-thirds of the population still claimed nominal adherence to the Church of England; and the Church itself still broadly believed that it had a mission to the whole nation. Thus the Group's criteria related to the nation at large, as well as to the practising membership of the Church of England. Accordingly, a recommended formula with weightings was based on (1) population – 8 points; (2) the area of the diocese in square miles – 1 point; (3) the numbers on the electoral roll – 3 points; (4) the number of regular places of worship – 3 points. 'These four sets of figures are, therefore, the four basic criteria that we recommend.'

Turning to the key role of diocesan bishops the group was clear:

> The initiative and the executive responsibility for stimulating and channelling this flow of manpower must be with the Diocesan Bishops and their advisers. They have the key role at present in staffing their dioceses. They know, or have well-established means of getting to know, the clergy and the nature of the various posts in the diocese. Although deployment and staffing, as we have just emphasised, are not the same thing, they are closely linked, and we do not see how the responsibility for the one could be divorced from the responsibility for the other. We must stress that the formula which we are recommending is not automatic or self-fulfilling. This would be true of any formula. But it is essential for the Church, and for the House of Bishops in particular, to accept that the success of the formula now proposed will depend on a strong and continuing will to reorganise and on an acceptance of sacrifices by all dioceses, especially those which are at present better supplied with clergy.

On 16 May 1974 Fallows sent the completed Report to the Archbishop, who signed a prefatory note to it on 22 May and *Deployment of the Clergy, The*

Report of the House of Bishops' Working Group was published forthwith. Thereafter it was known as the 'Sheffield Report' so, when the furore and turbulence began, Fallows was on the receiving end of a battery of verbal and written assaults.

At a sweep the Report showed the uneven deployment between the dioceses, for example, one diocesan clergyman to over 5,000 people in Birmingham, Liverpool and Sheffield, while one to under 2,000 in Bath and Wells, Gloucester, Ely, Hereford, Norwich, Salisbury, and St Edmundsbury and Ipswich. But it was when dioceses turned to the various tables that real opposition entered the columns of newspapers, and diocesan synods gave vent to their opposition, sometimes led or supported by their bishops. The first table enumerated the effect of the application of the formula to the distribution of manpower in 1974. In the Province of Canterbury nineteen dioceses would have fewer clergy, for example Bath and Wells – 62, Norwich – 61, Exeter – 61, Oxford – 54, whereas there would be substantial gains, for Chelmsford – 76, Lichfield – 53. In the Province of York all dioceses except Carlisle and Sodor and Man gained; most substantially, Chester – 71, Liverpool – 65, Sheffield – 43.

The second table delineated the numbers of full-time diocesan clergymen, 1973 compared with the distribution of the predicted total number, 1980 according to the deployment formula. The following table by diocese has four columns (1) the actual numbers of full-time diocesan clergymen, 1973, (2) the 1973 distribution according to deployment formula, (3) the distribution of predicted total number of diocesan clergymen 1980 according to deployment formula, (4) the actual number of stipendiary parochial clergy in 2003.

Diocese	1973	D.P.	1980	2003
Canterbury	313	292	248	153
London	752	728	567	473
Winchester	299	302	259	224
Bath and Wells	374	312	265	226
Birmingham	258	305	246	176
Bristol	223	190	158	125
Chelmsford	517	593	499	383
Chichester	420	406	347	317
Coventry	201	205	174	134
Derby	246	271	224	171
Ely	232	190	160	141
Exeter	412	349	293	237
Gloucester	259	204	173	144
Guildford	221	232	199	186
Hereford	188	185	154	97
Leicester	238	229	195	146

Lichfield	491	544	462	317
Lincoln	341	334	280	200
Norwich	338	277	234	187
Oxford	557	503	437	402
Peterborough	249	210	179	147
Portsmouth	189	167	142	105
Rochester	279	285	241	209
St Albans	375	380	328	247
St Ed. & Ipswich	262	224	190	143
Salisbury	343	313	265	208
Southwark	464	468	368	341
Truro	183	165	139	115
Worcester	219	182	155	143
York	386	410	342	239
Durham	345	386	317	216
Blackburn	295	348	290	221
Bradford	153	167	138	107
Carlisle	254	233	193	133
Chester	327	398	340	260
Liverpool	316	381	311	235
Manchester	463	481	385	277
Newcastle	216	235	190	134
Ripon	207	233	193	129
Sheffield	220	263	218	169
Sodor and Man	31	25	21	19
Southwell	232	244	205	155
Wakefield	237	256	212	148

(The Diocese of Europe, founded in 1980, is not included.)

The Working Group concluded that the responsibility for the deployment and staffing of the Church's ministry should remain with the diocesan bishops; that there should be an annual central review of the working of the formula and the allocations under it, which should be entrusted to the Archbishops' Advisers on needs and resources. They also considered the deployment of money to be just as important as the deployment of manpower:

> As our investigations proceeded, it became increasingly clear to us that in practice the redeployment of the Church's ministers was in the last resort dependent on the redeployment also of finance. For the relatively higher allocations of manpower so clearly needed in some dioceses there must be money to pay stipends and to rent, buy or build houses for the men to live in.

The Church Commissioners, as Central Stipends Authority, should take account of the new manpower levels as they occur.

When the House of Bishops met in the autumn of 1974 discussion revealed dissent. The new Bishop of Truro, Graham Leonard, had care of a diocese which included among its wide range of parishes, some very large and scattered rural parishes. His vision was not restricted for, as Bishop of Willesden he was in charge of a densely populated urban area. His experience was shared by other bishops. And in that way he did not speak for himself alone. He objected to the phrase 'fairer distribution' saying, 'Had I been a member of the General Synod at the time of the debate, I should have pressed for some such phrase as "a distribution which more truly reflects the nature of the Church and the principles of the Kingdom".' He confessed to finding 'the Report superficial and in places unrealistic.' He perceived problems on the parochial level, and argued for a more radical approach:

> it assumes that the parochial basis of the Church of England must remain unchanged, without considering whether certain areas should not be designated 'missionary areas' to be treated differently with regard to staffing. It seems to me to overlook the fact, well recognised in other spheres of pastoral and personnel work, that a pastor could only sustain effective pastoral control with a limited number of people and that the reduction of the population of a parish from say 20,000 to 10,000 does not necessarily relieve the tensions of the pastor or improve the quality of pastoral care. It assumes that a larger number of the clergy are going to be willing to remain indefinitely as assistant clergy. It assumes that a majority of deacons will be men who are suitable for urban work. It does not take into account the fact that some men are temperamentally right in parishes where the Church is still the parish church of the community as a whole, whereas others are best with the gathered congregations which must inevitably be the basis of pastoral work in many very large urban and especially suburban parishes.

Fallows told his fellow bishops that this was a misreading of the Report. The demands of the rural ministry were insufficiently understood by bishops whose life and ministry was wholly urban, or, more likely, suburban. The rural parson cannot seek refuge in his vicarage. In a real sense he 'lives with' his parishioners. If a few fall out with the vicar in an urban parish they can slip up the road to another church or fall away. In a rural parish the vicar will still meet them constantly. In dioceses such as Norwich and Lincoln rural clergy were already driving distances every Sunday to officiate at five or more churches.

Fallows acknowledged several bishops' criticism of particular aspects of the Report. What he did not like was bishops referring 'for instance to the Parable of the Labourers in the Vineyard – illuminating as the parable is on the subject of the free boundless unmerited grace of God and when they use hortatory language it is not helpful in the deployment exercise with which we have wrestled.' When Graham Leonard questioned the proposed basis of fair share distribution as spiritually sound, 'If we make policy decisions on such a basis, have we any right to expect that God will endorse our policy?' Fallows retorted, 'Frankly I do not know. I do not know as much about God as perhaps I ought to do. Indeed I find Him a profoundly mysterious person.'

From within the Group, the Bishop of Warrington, John Bickersteth, thought more attention should have been given to the work of the Diocesan Directors of Ordinands:

> For years they have seen part of their role as encouraging young men to offer for the priesthood and so boosting the diocesan clergy strength. Many of them of course do have a wider vision in mind, but coping as they do with people who are fairly locally minded (particularly I find here in the north) they easily fall into the way of assuring a young man that he would be found a niche in the diocese when his actual time for ordination comes.

Reading newspaper columns the 'Sheffield Report' appeared the latest example of the death wish within the Church of England. It struck at the root of the established Church. The sky over Fallows was heavy with clouds and looming turbulence of dissent. His mail likewise! But he was able to speak with persuasive strength because he was convinced that the Report's conclusions represented the best way forward. The House of Bishops approved. At General Synod in July 1975 Fallows presented the findings with firmness amounting to aplomb. He subdued, when he did not swat, unreasoned opposition and listened to different points of view and accepted pleas for special cases where flexibility may have to be made in practice. Yet there was always a modesty, never ever arrogance, or pontifical certainty. He opened his speech by referring to Lord Randolph Churchill's description of Gladstone to the electors of South Paddington as 'an old man in a hurry' and closed it with these words, 'I believe some such work as is here proposed is part of our stewardship of our manpower resources. As such I believe it is the Lord's work, that we may claim at least that it is a first step in the right direction. The old man is still not in a hurry: But he is on the move.' The General Synod accepted the 'Sheffield' Report' in principle, and the House of Bishops was invited to report from time to time on further progress in implementing the proposals. The House of Bishops appointed 'Three Wise Men' (Fallows, Bickersteth, and the Bishop of Norwich, Maurice Wood) to do this. Their first task was to devise a scheme for sharing out deacons and to revise the 1980/1981 forecasts. This led to further turbulence, the details of which need not concern us here as they extended beyond Fallows' death. 'His' report had achieved a just balance and was a step into the future.

CHAPTER 15

Before the ending of the day

BISHOPS WHO FULFIL their ministry under the compulsion and direction of the Word of God carry heavy burdens. That they may be endued with apostolic wisdom, apostolic energy and at last see the fruit of their labours in apostolic achievements is, or should be, the prayer of all those who look to them as chief pastors in the Church of God.

Gordon Fallows did not live to see the maturation of all that he sowed. The fruitfulness of an episcopate cannot be measured by its length, and there is another and a worthier standard of judgement for human lives than the number of years. 'A righteous man, though he die before his time, shall be at rest. For honourable old age is not that which standeth in length of time, nor is its measure given by number of years: but understanding in grey hairs unto men, and an unspotted life is ripe old age.'

Any Christian knows that the teaching of the Gospel is quite plain. Those who seek to look after their life will lose it. True fulfilment is found through acceptance of whatever God puts in our way. The crosses and contradictions that are good for us are the ones He actually gives us. As de Caussade says, 'There is no moment at which God does not present Himself under the guise of some suffering, some conclusion or some duty. At every occurrence we should say *Dominus est,* It is the Lord: and in all circumstances we should find a gift from God.' Such words are easier said and quoted than accepted in practice. They will be an ever-present reality before the closing of Fallows' day. There continued to be a steadfastness about him that also embraced what St Benedict wrote of the pastor – 'let him always put mercy before judgement, let him not be jealous or suspicious, let him strive rather to be loved than feared.'

From whose lives did Fallows gain inner support, strength and illumination? Some nineteenth-century broad churchmen have already been enumerated and described. And others? It is an interesting mix. He preached the tenth 'Thomas More Sermon' at Chelsea Old Church in 1963. (Fifteen of these sermons were published in 1978 with a foreword by Lord Hailsham). What drew Fallows to Thomas More?

His zest for life, with its concomitant cheerfulness, that is the dominant impression he makes on me. He found life worth living and death worth dying. As H.A.L. Fisher says, 'his end was of a piece with his life, sweetened by

179

innocent mirth and unaffected piety.' He could say of his prison, the Tower of
London, 'Is not this house as nigh heaven as my own?' His zest and his
cheerfulness were rooted in his faith and trust in God. It has been well said, there
is no dull saint, and certainly Thomas More is an illustration of the saying. Few
men in our history are so attractive in all their cheerful acceptance of misfortune.
The zest of life was his, from his youth to the time when he was led from the
Tower to suffer the supreme penalty of fidelity to conscience. No misfortune
ever robbed him of it. When his house in Chelsea was burnt down he bade his
wife be of good cheer and thank God for what was still theirs. And he added
with a zest that comes from joy even in the day of misfortune, 'I pray you Alice
to be merry in God.' Surely such a man has learned the secret of zest in
companionship of the Lord of life. Here then is the message and the challenge
of this service today: to capture that sweet and cheerful spirit that breathed
through the life and character of Sir Thomas More; to be merry in God; to learn
in Christ that zest that gives life its savour. And whatsoever you do, do it heartily
as unto The Lord.

Fallows did not mention that More spent every Friday in seclusion, in order
to clear his mind, restore his spirit, and strengthen the resolve he brought to
the affairs of Church and State. All people need a desert in their lives and it
is crucial for modern people in their pilgrimages in a bustling and noisy world.
We know that Fallows received his spiritual sanity and refreshment through
fell-walking in the Lake District and by retreating to his study, in order to go
forward. He often quoted and lived words of Adlai Stevenson, the American
statesman, 'It's not the years in your life but the life in your years that counts.'
At Leamington Spa, Styvechale and Preston we followed Fallows as a
Christian minister or parson, words he used more often than 'priest'. As he
laboured honestly therein, he was justly entitled to the people's confidence,
their sympathy, and their support. His ordination did much for him. He had
received authority for his public ministry. He entered the door of opportunity
and advanced with enthusiasm and relish, leaving no task undone. In every
way, in thought and trouble and energy, he pushed himself just short of
breaking point. He served to the limits. Yet he must have been equally aware
that he had but prepared the altar. The fire which consumes the sacrifice
descends from above. Self-dependence is a sterilising blunder. It is the hardest
of all lessons which the Church of England parson or priest has to learn. God
deigns to use men as His instruments, but never accepts them as His
substitutes. 'There are diversities of workings, but the same God, who worketh
all things in all.' Spiritual power belongs to human ministries which might
seem strangely lacking in success. In the dioceses of Blackburn, Wakefield and
Sheffield Fallows encountered saintly priests, learned divines, missionary-
minded incumbents aflame with holy zeal, pastors who, if they did not lay

down their lives for their flocks, ran their health into the ground. Being a bishop is humbling when he visits and finds scenes of holy toil in cities and towns where a priest serves the wretched, poor, neglected, those well acquainted with the magistrates' court and the prison cell. Alternatively it may be serving in isolated villages year in and year out with unfailing and splendid devotion, pouring human love into a human ministry of pastoral labour.

When Fallows became Principal of Ripon Hall he had both call and duty to prepare those called to the ordained ministry for an already changed world and society in a reluctantly changing Church. This was not a pause in Fallows' personal development. It was a time of growth. He used his voice and pen to good effect. He had time to extend his reading of literature, novels and poetry, to enjoy art, music, theatre and dance. He was widely consulted. Had he been dean of an ancient cathedral he would have been able to harness all his interests and actual and latent gifts, in a way he would not do as a bishop. His memorial tablet may have contained a description used in Winchester Cathedral of Norman Sykes (1897–1961), ecclesiastical historian and dean of Winchester, whom he very greatly admired:

Genial in temper
Quick in mind
Ready in speech
Generous in counsel
To lovers of sound learning.

That was not Gordon Fallows' vocation. He was made and prepared for leadership as a 'Bishop in the Church of God'. His bookshelves were packed with biographies which he devoured and whose lives he penetrated. Episcopal biographies occupied much space and it was to the men beneath the mitres, as much as, if not more than, the episcopates themselves, which arrested his mind. Figures from the Reformation period and beyond were high on his list but, as we have noticed, the alluring period was the nineteenth century. Why? William Temple introduces his life of John Percival (1834–1918), Bishop of Hereford for twenty-two years, and another bishop admired by Fallows, in this way, contrasting two centuries:

The increasing pace of modern life had done much to rob the world of great personalities. The ease of movement and communication has made almost impossible the relative isolation in which marked individuality is shaped. We run to and fro, and knowledge is increased. But the men of our generation have little time to strike deep roots; they are not thrown upon their own resources; they do not fully find themselves. The average and moral and intellectual attainment is probably higher than in former times. But the overcoming of obstacles, which were too great for the many to surmount, was strengthening and stimulating to the few who were successful. The nineteenth century was marked by many great and outstanding figures, who made their own careers, to a great extent developed their own minds, formed and expressed their own judgments, firmly went their own way, lived in a certain detachment from the world about them, and therefore influenced that world as none who more fully shared its life and outlook could ever do. Such a figure was John Percival. One who knew him intimately in old age said of him that in memory he stood out like a sunlit promontory. It is an apt figure. The recollection of him is of one who stood rooted in his own conviction; storms and conflicts of opinion and passion might surge round him; but he still stood firm, and not only firm, but calm, peaceful and bright, because he knew his own mind, and the grounds on which he had made it up, and the God to whom it was utterly devoted.

The historian's pen can afford to be candid and acerbic but when the historian is or becomes a bishop he must be aware that his judgements on other bishops may cause the spotlight to shine on himself with equal candour. Occasionally Fallows is drawn to the men in a way that he distances himself from their traits of personality, to be avoided in himself. He is less fulsome in applauding their virtues. Extracts from three of his reviews reveal something of himself both positively and negatively. The first is favourable but of a bishop far removed from himself: *Arthur Cayley Headlam, Bishop of Gloucester*, by Ronald C.D. Jasper (1960):

> He was a man, at once formidable, brusque to the point of rudeness, and yet without malice and capable of deep affection and loyalty. He invites comparison with his contemporary and friend Hensley Henson. Both were sturdy independents who disagreed much but always respected each other. Henson once compared Headlam to a Brazil nut, 'repulsively hard in the shell and admirable in the kernel.' But unlike Henson, Headlam did not attract public notice; he was never a well-known figure. Headlam's power of diplomacy, administration and foresight served him well in the work of re-constituting King's College and incorporating it in London University. His broad theological sympathies led him to break a long connection with the *Church Quarterly Review* when the editorial policy of that journal was antagonistic to the *Lux Mundi* group. As Regius Professor of Divinity at Oxford Headlam welcomed the advent of Ripon Hall to Oxford saying to the Rev. H.D.A. Major its Principal, 'We have two other kinds of Churchmanship here in Oxford and we shall welcome you: but don't think I agree with you, for I don't.' Headlam was himself a solid, orthodox, middle-of-the-road Church of England man. As a Bishop he was strong and dignified, free from all pretentiousness and fuss. He would never wear a mitre, which he regarded as a rather ridiculous headdress ... His outstanding contribution was in the sphere of inter-church relations ... One of the few outstanding figures in the twentieth century.

The second biography is another from Ronald Jasper: *George Bell, Bishop of Chichester* by Ronald C.D. Jasper (1967):

> George Bell was the one English bishop who was a national, a European and a world figure ... Yet there was a flaw. It was not simply because he lacked popular gifts and because he failed to impress public assemblies where Temple and Garbett, too, were effective. His influence over others tended to suffer from the very persistence with which it was yielded. He was resilient, tireless and tough. But he was sometimes pertinacious to the point of obstinacy, and courageous to the point of indiscretion. He lacked any lightness of touch. Bell seems to have lacked humour and playfulness. Like all successful agitators he took himself seriously, not too seriously as to make himself a fanatic but seriously enough to make himself a little tedious even to those who shared his conviction.

Cyril Forster Garbett, Archbishop of York by Charles Smyth (1959) is the third biography:

> Garbett was a stern, austere, dedicated man; industrious but uninspired. He was a glutton for work and felt depressed and ill at ease when wartime 'blackout' and petrol rationing interfered with his laborious routine. As Vicar of Portsea his large staff had little easy intimacy with their master. There was no feeling of home in the Portsea Clergy House over which he ruled. He was a distant, lonely figure, inspiring respect but little affection. So, too, he was a lonely Bishop of Southwark where, perhaps, he did his best work as a Diocesan Administrator. But he was too formidable to be popular and he lacked geniality. When he was Bishop of Winchester, Wolvesley was not the kind of home where you would ever dare to ask for a second helping, for the Bishop was itching to get back to work. Here too he had periods of acute mental depression, especially when deprived of a domestic chaplain. There was however an attractive side to his character. He had no illusions about himself; he knew his own limitation ... At bottom there was a deep and redeeming humility in the man. He was dignified without a trace of pomposity. He had no side and could not stand fussiness. He generally managed to forget his decorations at banquets. Though he cultivated good relations with the Press, with the business men in the North, and with his colleagues in the House of Lords, he never for one moment courted popularity ... As a pastoral administrator Garbett was well endowed with common sense but there was little of the liberal spirit ... Readers of the biography will love the man who was always trying to make time to visit more the clergy in their homes. What a pity that this austere, lonely, dedicated man, did not feel more at home when he had rung the Vicarage bell.

Fallows was an admirer of Herbert Hensley Henson, Bishop of Durham, the most distinctive bishop of the twentieth century. Fallows imbibed the wisdom contained in his published ordination charges rather than being drawn to his strangely mingled character or the constant adversarial causes and controversies which he caused or joined. Above all others it was Mandell Creighton 1843–1901 who captured Fallows' mind and for whom he was a great man and bishop. His only book *Mandell Creighton and the English Church* (1964) was a gem of a work and widely noticed. Many of Fallows' extended articles on freedom and authority were ideas absorbed from Creighton. This hero of Fallows was the most versatile of English prelates. He had a large-hearted tolerance and was one of the most eminent historians of his time. In numerous ways Fallows attempted to emulate Creighton. Neither of them compromised their claims to the public confidence by a too ardent advocacy of any cause which could be described as partisan. They laboured for peace with unwearied effort. Words of Erasmus, admired by each of them, written in 1532, well express their joint attitude on conflicts of the hour:

> I cannot help hating dissension and loving peace. I see how obscure all human affairs are. I see how much easier it is to stir up confusion than to allay it. I have learned how many are the devices of Satan. I should not dare to trust my own spirit in all things, and I am far from being able to pronounce with certainty on the spirit of another. I would that all might strive together for the triumph of Christ and the peace of the Gospel, and that without violence, but in truth and reason, we might take counsel both for the dignity of the priesthood and for the liberty of the people, whom our Lord Jesus desired to be free. But if anyone desires to throw everything into confusion, he shall not have me either for a leader or a companion.

How was Fallows' character an antidote to what he saw as negative traits? What kind of leadership did he applaud and how far was he an example of it? Mere prominence, which may owe nothing to personal quality or exertion, can hardly deserve the name, though it may usurp the function and even acquire the reputation. Leadership is more than a courtier's compliment or a historian's label. Success is not to be identified with leadership, of which, indeed it may be the negation.

Away from leadership on the grand scale there are attributes which are relevant to a consideration of Gordon Fallows as leader, and readers of this book may decide where and whether he is placed. First, moral qualities are indispensable in leadership. The attempt to separate private behaviour from public action, as if the two had properly no connection, has often been made; and it is indisputable that personal goodness carries no sufficient guarantee of political or religious sagacity. The long reach of history provides examples of great statesmen being knaves and great saints being fools. But the absence of sound personal character, and the lack of a background of domestic felicity, have always been factors which embarrass, enfeeble, and discredit public action.

Secondly, Fallows learned that for a Church of England bishop, leadership is costly. During his episcopate at Pontefract and Sheffield, the Church was increasingly counting for little in the life of the nation. Despite the fuss and flap generated by the reports of commissions and working parties, the 'new' theology and the 'new' morality, a disillusioned temper was spreading throughout the rank and file of clergy, and confidence in the Church's witness, which is the essential of loyal membership, was giving place to a defeatism which went far to ensure the disaster which is evidently to be expected. Broad churchman Fallows was important when the Church was required to undertake the difficult and salutary task of setting forth the Gospel, in right relation to the sum of knowledge, and commend it to the acceptance of informed and considering people. Although Fallows was not theologically timid, he had neither the will nor the temperament to lead in this particular way.

Individual bishops are variously described as Father in God; Brother in God; Mother in God; even Solicitor in God. None of these adequately or wholly is a fitting description of Gordon Fallows. Friend of God is nearer the mark. Is not this another kind of leadership? His friendship was always and everywhere. Its private expression was in spontaneous acts of care. One day he visited a hard-working curate in his home and asked when he last had a day off and then, putting his car keys on the table, said, 'My car is outside, the tank is full of petrol, take your wife and have a good day at Southport'. On another occasion he informed a priest that he would collect him for lunch at a country pub. Bishopscroft was a venue for hospitality and friendship, people in need of a break were summoned at short notice, had good food and wine and left with a cheque. There was leadership of friendship with other Churches. He supported ecumenical ventures in Sheffield, brought Anglican and Nonconformist churches together as a result of his friendship with ministers, not excluding the Roman Catholic Bishop of Leeds, William Gordon Wheeler, a former Anglican priest.

The number of ordinands increased in the diocese. During the eighteen months to July 1978, twenty-one candidates were sent to the Bishops' Selection Conference arranged by ACCM, of whom fourteen were recommended or conditionally recommended. Sheffield was putting more than its quota of six deacons a year. Fallows stressed and ensured the practice of after-care of 'not recommended' candidates, those who felt a call that was contrary to the Bishops' Selectors decision.

No mention has yet been made of another inheritance. That exquisite patron of the arts, Dean Eric Milner-White of York, asked Bishop Leslie Hunter if he would appoint the architect, George Gaze Pace (1915–1975) as surveyor to the Diocese of Sheffield in 1949. This he did, with a further appointment as consultant architect to Sheffield Cathedral from 1953, and a member of the Diocesan Advisory Committee in 1956. George Pace recoiled from the aims of contemporary architects, 'the pursuit of excitement based on sensations, on tone colour, on the dream images of the subconscious, on shock and disturbance and titillation, and novelty.' Even his great restoration of Llandaff Cathedral with Sir Jacob Epstein's controversial *Majestas* does not refute Pace's belief that 'the one great unifying theme of the art of say, Beethoven, Shakespeare or Tolstoy, was that it was above all rooted in obedience to the external moral and natural order, in the perception of those simple, unchanging truths which are at the root of all human wisdom.'

Pace earned his bread and butter in the diocese with fabric repairs, conservation and extensions to churches. He designed everything from crucifixes, windows, pulpits and aumbries to fair linen cloths, gilded angels and bookstands. In the region of one hundred churches in the diocese had examples of Pace's work from the evangelical stronghold of St Thomas, Crookes, to the Anglo-Catholic citadel of St Matthew's, Carver Street, in Sheffield. Pace's industry does not mean that he was a man in a hurry or one who could be pressurised. After Llandaff Cathedral it is reckoned that St Mark's, Broomhill, which took seventeen years from conception to completion (1950–1967) is his best and most remarkable new church building. The original church perished in a fire caused by incendiary bombs on 12 December 1940, but the spire, tower and south porch were repairable and Pace integrated them into the new hexagonal main building. It received much attention at the Royal Academy Summer Exhibition in 1958. He was responsible for two other new churches, All Saints, Intake; and St Leonard and St Jude, both in Doncaster. Fallows enjoyed the new and many of the additions to the old churches of the diocese. Pace had a strong feeling for liturgy and had witnessed the liturgy in action in some new church buildings on the Continent. He produced some magnificent plans for the completion of Sheffield Cathedral (1959–1961). It was a difficult assignment as he inherited the unfinished remains of an early extension scheme built to the designs of Sir Charles Nicholson between 1919 and 1936. There were problems over cost, the final estimate almost doubling the appeal budget. The cathedral authorities procrastinated and required far-reaching changes to plans and ultimately caught that virulent disease of 'mind-changing'. Pace resigned as he could not approve either architecturally or liturgically of the new proposals. A new architect, Arthur Bailey, was responsible for a remarkable transformation in 1966 when the Cathedral of St Peter and St Paul came into its own dignity and spaciousness. Of the three Yorkshire 'parish church cathedrals' of Wakefield, Bradford and Sheffield, the last named was now pre-eminent. And Fallows gloried in his cathedral. People had worshipped God on the site for more than one thousand years. The Norman church was replaced in 1280 only to be destroyed 150 years later. It is the fifteenth-century chancel and sanctuary which were incorporated into the present cathedral. The Provost at the time of Fallows' enthronement was Ivan Delacherois Neill, a chaplain to the Forces from 1939 and Chaplain General until the time of his appointment as Provost. He was succeeded by Wilfrid Frank Curtis in 1974 (until 1988), the Home Secretary of the Church Missionary Society, with whom Fallows' relations were cordial and frequent.

It was a period of liturgical change, A good liturgy is historical and contemporary. It should accurately reflect a New Testament view of the Church and its ministry, not a view belonging to a particular society and a particular moment in history. Fallows saw real merit in the alternative services, for in one way Cranmer was deficient. The Consecration prayer at the Eucharist was atonement-centred. There was little mention of the Resurrection, Ascension or of the outpouring of the Spirit. The sixteenth century was a period of 'guilt' and the liturgy reflected this character of the age. A number of liturgical revisionists argued that the *Book of Common Prayer* was guilt-orientated whereas the new services moved away from too much guilt towards more love. Fallows was anxious that a balance should be struck between the human and the divine, and was watchful lest a quiet sense of mystery and awe in God's presence was diminished. He hesitated:

> Modern language services generally are favoured by those who are not completely sold on the glories of the *Book of Common Prayer*. But these glories cannot be gainsaid and so there is loss as well as gain in the liturgical revision of recent years. Some parts of our liturgical inheritance are in danger of being lost altogether.

Prayers were no longer known by heart and that was loss. Fallows particularly missed the 'General Thanksgiving' and the 'Prayer for all Conditions of Men,' which he used whenever opportunity arose, and occasionally when it didn't! One can almost hear his voice, 'Bless Thee for our creation, preservation, and all the blessings of this life; but above all for Thine inestimable love in the redemption of the world by our Lord Jesus Christ; for the means of grace, and for the hope of glory . . .' And:

> O God, the Creator and Preserver of all mankind, we humbly beseech Thee for all sorts and conditions of men; that Thou wouldest be pleased to make Thy ways known unto them, Thy saving health unto all nations . . . We commend to Thy fatherly goodness all those, who are in any ways afflicted, or distressed, in mind, body, or estate, that it may please Thee to comfort and relieve them, according to their several necessities, giving them patience under their sufferings, and a happy issue out of all their afflictions . . .

How often he may have made these latter words his own. He was looking
forward to attending his second Lambeth Conference in 1978. His September
'Letter' in the *Diocesan News* did not carry a report of the Conference. Instead:

> I went away for the opening of the Lambeth Conference at Canterbury not
> knowing what the immediate future would hold in store for my family and me.
> The opening Eucharist on Sunday July 23 was an impressive event. The
> procession of four hundred bishops with their consultants and observers from
> other Churches was a moving reminder that we belong to a worldwide Anglican
> family in an ecumenical age. The service was the Holy Communion rite of the
> Church in Tanzania, with the Archbishop of Tanzania as Celebrant, and the
> Archbishop of Canterbury preached. I felt specially proud as we sang the Bishop
> of Doncaster's (Stewart Cross) splendid hymn, 'Father Lord of all creation.' The
> Canterbury bells rang out hopefully and joyfully . . . The following day – the
> first working day of the conference – I was summoned home by the death of
> our dear daughter (Angela Mary Orchard). My personal word must now be one
> of profound gratitude, in which my wife joins, for all the heartfelt prayers and
> loving sympathy by which we have been consoled, encouraged and sustained in
> our great sorrow.

Earlier in the year Fallows underwent surgery and in mid-April a post-
operative infection set back the progress he was making. He was not really
sufficiently fit to attend the Lambeth Conference, and afterwards was unable
to operate at full pressure and there were times when he could not function
at all. This fell-walker shuffled in pain. At the beginning of 1979 he was struck
down with a fever with mysterious physical symptoms. It was now known
that in addition to the malignant cancer he was suffering from Parkinson's
Disease. He refused to totally 'give in' or 'give-up'. At a confirmation service
in Balby, near Doncaster (his last), lacking the physical strength to walk into
church, he sat in a chair and was carried to his place, likewise at an Institution
service. In June he made a personal statement:

> For some time now I have been inwardly wrestling with a problem that has
> caused me acute anxiety – namely whether I should continue to hold the
> Bishopric of Sheffield in view of the condition of my health and the nature of
> my illness . . . After very searching consideration I have come to the conclusion
> that as a matter of conscience and Christian duty I ought to make way for a
> younger and healthier man to shoulder the heavy responsibilities of the office of
> diocesan bishop.

It was Fallows' intention that his resignation would become official towards
the end of the year. There was an outpouring of love and of grief. An appeal
was launched for a farewell presentation. Was ever such a sum raised? Fallows
knew he was dying but also knew that the sum had reached £17,000, which

rose to £23,000. Mrs Fallows said he never thought it would be more than £5,000. 'He was upset in a way it could be so much. But you don't know how much you are loved.' The money enabled Mrs Fallows to buy a house in Sheffield.

CHAPTER 16

Weeping o'er the grave, we make our song: Alleluya

WILLIAM GORDON FALLOWS died on 17 August 1979. His coffin was taken into Sheffield Cathedral and rested on a catafalque draped in purple velvet. His personal life and public ministry were movingly marked by both a bouquet of roses which Edna Fallows had picked from their garden and the Bishop's own pastoral staff which had been presented to him when he was consecrated bishop in 1968, being placed on the coffin. When I had visited Gordon Fallows six months earlier he met my train and took me to Bishopscroft. He shuffled and was plainly in pain when he walked to the car, but his mind was clear and bright, our conversation stimulating. One memory has stayed with me. As he said grace before lunch he looked at his wife and they held hands.

The cathedral was full for the funeral service on 24 August. The Earl of Scarborough was present, though it was primarily a Sheffield gathering with luminaries of the city, all of whom knew Fallows personally, all the diocesan clergy, people from the parishes, ecumenical representatives from the Roman Catholic Bishop of South Yorkshire (now the diocese of Hallam) to the South Yorkshire Divisional Commander of the Salvation Army. The Archbishop of York, Stuart Blanch, who gave the blessing, was accompanied by the bishops of Durham, Derby, Bradford, Wakefield, Bristol, Southwell, Sherwood, Pontefract and Doncaster as well as Bishop Gordon Arthur, former Bishop of Gippsland in Australia, who had come to Sheffield and helped in the diocese. The Provost of Sheffield, Frank Curtis, gave the Address. The time-honoured phraseology in legal documents refers to a bishop 'By Divine Permission'. The Provost thought Fallows was brought to Sheffield 'By Divine Guidance'. 'And as I have heard him reflect upon his ministry, not least in these past few weeks when he was made so aware of the love and gratitude, caring and concern of the Diocese, he was in effect saying "William Gordon, by Divine Enabling, Lord Bishop of Sheffield".' There were damp eyes as the Cathedral Songmen sang 'The Contakion of the Departed':

> Give rest, O Christ, to thy servants with thy Saints: where sorrow and pain are
> no more; neither sighing, but life everlasting.

Thou only art immortal, the Creator and Maker of Man: and we are mortal, formed of the earth, and unto earth shall we return: for so Thou didst ordain, when Thou createdst me, saying, Dust thou art, and unto dust shalt thou return.
All we go down to the dust; and, weeping o'er the grave, we make our song: Alleluya, alleluya, alleluya.

Cremation of the body took place at Hutcliffe Wood Crematorium. On 27 September there was a Service of Thanksgiving for the Life and Ministry of Gordon Fallows at the Cathedral, attended by more than a thousand people. The Queen was represented by the Bishop of London, Gerald Ellison, who arrived in top hat, frock coat and gaiters. Ten bishops and a clutch of provosts attended, together with the Lord Lieutenant of South Yorkshire, the County High Sheriff, Members of Parliament, Chief Constable, civic worthies. And people representing a wealth of organisations which Fallows had touched by his presence, including Sheffield University, Sheffield Polytechnic, the National Coal Board, the Sheffield and Rotherham area health authorities, Chambers of Trade and Commerce, Scouts, Council for Voluntary Service.

It was an emotional occasion for Canon F.W. Dillistone. He had preached at Fallows' Consecration and was here to give the Address. His theme was once again that of bridge building:

Through the dramatic picture of the compassionate Samaritan, Jesus Himself built an imaginative bridge between Jew and Samaritan which, in a marvellous way, has stood the test of the centuries as a connecting link between those who are alienated from one another by race, party, tradition, temperament. It was supremely a picture of Jesus Himself, the chief reconciler: it was a model on which Gordon sought, I am confident, to fashion his own ministry. To connect man with man and man with God.

How do we evaluate Gordon Fallows in the transfiguring light of time? 'Good people here are much scandalised at Thirlwall's being made a bishop,' wrote Edward FitzGerald on hearing that his former tutor had been nominated by Lord Melbourne to the See of St David's. (Connop Thirlwall was a historian and broad churchman of the nineteenth century). 'I do not think, however, that I would have made him bishop: I am all for good and not great bishops.'
William Gordon Fallows was a good bishop. He was also a good man.